To mom & Marc
Sherrels family

"THAT ALL
MAY BE
EDIFIED"

Elder Boyd K. Packer

"THAT ALL MAY BE EDIFIED"

TALKS, SERMONS & COMMENTARY BY

BOYD K. PACKER

Illustrations by Hagen G. Haltern

BOOKCRAFT
Salt Lake City, Utah

Library of Congress Catalog Card Number: 82-73311
ISBN 0-88494-473-5

First Printing, 1982

Lithographed in the United States of America
PUBLISHERS PRESS
Salt Lake City, Utah

Acknowledgments

My wife and family are an essential part of the sermons that are presented here. There are many others whose help, encouragement, and prayers have made possible this book. To them I have verbally expressed my deep appreciation.

There must be added one special acknowledgment. It was my privilege to work closely with Sister Lucile C. Tate as she wrote the biography of my beloved friend and fellow Apostle, LeGrand Richards. During that period she became aware of the many requests for a book of my talks and of my reluctance to have them published. She urged me to do so. I invited her assistance which she willingly gave as a service to those who might read the book. Without her encouragement the project would not have been started. Without her help it would not have been finished. To her and her husband, George, himself gifted and able, I owe my deep appreciation.

About the artist and his illustrations:

Hagen Haltern, a convert from Bonn, Germany, now teaches drawing at Brigham Young University. His work reflects the Old World heritage that is familiar to all whose family and cultural roots are found there. As such it is a fitting accompaniment to a book about edifying, a word that was widely used in former times to mean *build* and still holds that connotation.

The first six drawings are not of any given door, room, buttress, etc., but are traditional archetypal forms of these elements. They represent basic structural functions within or without an edifice and, as such, lend a visual dimension to the book's theme.

The seventh drawing is different. It illustrates a particular building—the Brigham City Tabernacle—one of the many buildings of the Restoration which was erected out of labor, love, and sacrifice. The structure is of great significance to Elder Packer. It was here, as a small boy, that he received his first spiritual witness. In a meeting held there, it was made known to him that the man who was speaking was truly an Apostle of the Lord Jesus Christ.

Contents

That All May Be Edified

That All May Be Edified

One of the most profound statements in scripture describes the servants of the Lord as *edifiers* of the Saints. The Apostle Paul wrote to the Ephesians:

> And he gave some, apostles; and some, prophets;...
> For the perfecting of the saints, for the work of the ministry, for the *edifying* of the body of Christ;
> Till we all come in the unity of the faith, and of the knowledge of the Son of God, unto a perfect man, unto the measure of the stature of the fulness of Christ. (Ephesians 4:11-13; italics added.)

The nouns *edifice* and *building* are synonymous and may be used interchangeably. Each has a complementing verb: *to build* and *to edify*. Each of the verbs is commonly used to designate a process other than putting up a material structure. We "build" character, "build" confidence, "build" spirituality. We understand this to mean to increase, to strengthen, to organize, and to set permanently in place. To edify, as the word is used in the scriptures, is to do those very things and more.

The word *edify* has a significant place in both secular and religious writing. Whether used as a verb or as the noun edification, it consistently refers to some aspect of building. The definition that fits our present use is "something built up in a manner analagous to the erection of an architectural structure." In Paul's epistle that "something" is the individual. Each person has the capacity for growth and the potential to reach perfection. It is in this sense that the word *edify* is used throughout this book as a central thought or recurring theme, and you will understand why the illustrations depict some features of buildings or edifices. These are symbolic of the less visible but more permanent results of that construction which takes place in the building of the souls of men.

These lines from an unidentified writer compare the two kinds of buildings:

The Builder

A Builder builded a temple,
He wrought it with grace and skill;

1

That All May Be Edified

Pillars and groins and arches
All fashioned to work his will.
Men said, as they saw its beauty,
"It shall never know decay;
Great is thy skill, O Builder!
Thy fame shall endure for aye."

A Teacher builded a temple
With loving and infinite care,
Planning each arch with patience,
Laying each stone with prayer.
None praised her unceasing efforts,
None knew of her wondrous plan,
For the temple the Teacher builded
Was unseen by the eyes of man.

Gone is the Builder's temple,
Crumpled into the dust;
Low lies each stately pillar,
Food for consuming rust.
But the temple the Teacher builded
Will last while the ages roll,
For that beautiful unseen temple
Was a child's immortal soul.

The foundation of the edifice is instruction.

Instruction

"In the midst of all that is transitory in our age, we may yet discover something permanent, something that will outshine and outlast all the violence and struggle and brutality that is in the daily fare. . . . Not dominion over other lives and lands, but over ourselves through learning. I believe that . . . the art or process of acquiring knowledge, comprehension, understanding, skills, all of which may, with time and effort mature into wisdom, is eternally worthwhile. But quoting Spinoza, 'All things excellent are as difficult as they are rare.'" (From an address given at BYU Summer Commencement Exercises on August 21, 1981.)

3

That All May Be Edified

Thoughts are like water. If you want water to stay in its course, you have to make a place for it to go." These words demonstrate the technique of teaching something intangible by relating it to something about which everyone knows. It is the approach so often used by the ideal teacher—the Master. Who does not recall the Savior's unforgettable lessons—the kingdom of heaven is "likened unto ten virgins" (Matthew 25:1), or faith is likened to a "grain of mustard seed" (Luke 17:6). I readily admit to a desire to teach as the Master taught. Though that may be far beyond my capabilities, He is nevertheless the ideal.

Many years ago, the deep desire to emulate the Master intensified, I read and pondered the scripture:

> Deny not the gifts of God, for they are many; and they come from the same God. And there are different ways that these gifts are administered; . . . .
> For . . . to one is given by the Spirit of God, that he may teach the word of wisdom;
> And to another, that he may teach the word of knowledge by the same Spirit;
> And all these gifts come by the Spirit of Christ; and they come unto every man severally, according as he will. (Moroni 10:8-10, 17.)

I determined that among all the gifts that might make one useful to the Lord the gift to teach by the Spirit would be supreme. I came to feel that if one desired it, asked for it, prayed for it, studied, pondered, and earned it, and believed with sufficient faith that he could possess it, the gift would not be withheld from him.

Accordingly I turned to the New Testament to "associate" with and learn from the Lord, who as a teacher is the ideal. When it came time to submit a subject for a master's thesis, I presented to my committee the proposal that I study the teaching techniques used by Jesus. With some considerable reluctance, they approved the subject. It was a most enlightening experience to "walk" with Jesus and "observe" Him teach. Thereafter, I began with all diligence to pattern my teaching efforts after Him. Through this association I came to know Him—Jesus Christ, the Son of God, the Only Begotten of the Father—and that He lives. I stand in reverence before Him, with deep regard for *what* He taught and deep regard for *how* He taught. It is this knowledge and reverence that can give to us penetrating power. I have tried to develop the gift so deeply desired—the gift to teach by the Spirit.

That All May Be Edified

From my youth I have been acutely interested in and tried to be observant of everything around us—birds, animals, and plant life— their species, forms, colors, characteristics, and habits. I found that we can, as the Savior did, draw lessons from everyday occurrences. We can note the behavior of people in all their individuality and sameness. I developed the desire, as a teacher, to share the things I had observed. I found that by diligent, consistent observation, notetaking, and filing, one can store up a vast reservoir of knowledge, examples, lessons, feelings, experiences, and stories. One can come to know the verity of the scripture "treasure up in your minds continually the words of life, and it shall be given you in the very hour that portion that shall be meted unto every man." (D & C 84:85.) That supply is there whenever one needs to draw from it for teaching or speaking assignments. Whatever else we are in life, we are teachers—as parents, in church service, in all else that we do.

In my effort to study the way the Master taught I noticed that He was always concerned about "the one." I have tried to follow that example in teaching our children, in teaching or supervising in the seminaries of the Church and as a General Authority. I find that I do not do well if I try to speak to an "audience." It is much easier, and I feel much more effective, if I speak to an individual soul in the audience.

The five talks that make up this section I hope are examples of edification by instruction. They demonstrate some of the teaching techniques of the Master, and the content perhaps will be useful to individual Latter-day Saints.

(1) When we study how Jesus taught, we note that He employed one principle of instruction more than any other—that of apperception. If we understand and employ it, it will help us as teachers of religion more than any other thing we could learn of His teaching techniques. Apperception is defined as "the process of understanding something perceived in terms of previous experience." This means that if we have something difficult to teach, such as honesty, reverence, or love, we should begin with the experience of the listener and talk about the things he already knows. Then when we make a transfer or comparison with what we want him to know, he will perceive the meaning. "Prayers and Answers" is an effort to use experience and observation

6

That All May Be Edified

to make clear how one may develop spiritual sensitivity to the still small voice and thus receive daily guidance.

(2) In "Behold Your Little Ones" I was speaking to little children—to each little child, really. I had prayerfully prepared the talk over a very long period of time. Can you imagine how I felt when we entered the Tabernacle that morning to find that 350 Primary children were to sing to us? I was deeply moved to realize that after determining to talk to little children, they would be present to give me additional inspiration. It came as something of a confirmation of the inspiration to choose the subject in the first place. I used a glove, with which all children are familiar, in an effort to teach with total simplicity the concepts of birth, death, and the relationship of body and spirit. This illustration has been very helpful to me in explaining to little children, for instance in a funeral, the death of a family member.

(3) The General Authorities are very seldom given an assigned subject for general conference talks. One of a few times I have been assigned by the First Presidency to talk on a specific subject was in a general priesthood meeting. I was invited to speak to the boys about the Aaronic priesthood. The focus of this talk was to teach each boy his privilege, responsibility, and the power which comes when the Aaronic Priesthood is bestowed by one having authority. An experience of one of our sons with his horse was used to teach the young brethren that the power comes through obedience and worthiness.

(4) "Let Virtue Garnish Thy Thoughts" centers on an analogy designed to teach a lesson in thought control applicable to every individual regardless of age. It answers a specific need at a time when the minds of all people are fair game for every form of evil persuasion.

(5) "Seek Learning Even by Study and Also by Faith" was given to the teachers of religion at Brigham Young University at a time when there had been a change in leadership of the College of Religious Instruction. The thoughts contained in it are useful, perhaps, to other teachers—parents, primary and Sunday School teachers, etc. The address was given at a dinner, in a room not suited for use of a projector. Because an overhead projector would have been useful, I determined to speak as though one were there and ask the audience to visualize what might have been projected.

There are many ways in which individuals are edified. They are instructed, encouraged, comforted, enlightened, warned, exhorted, and

That All May Be Edified

have witness borne to them, or in some cases, borne against them. Whatever the mode or tone, edification is always an upward-reaching process. It is always for the purpose of building up the individual.

The building materials in this "construction work" are *words*, but words charged with power and authority and given by the Lord to His servants. It is through words that the work of the ministry is done. It is an exacting work in which Church members all have a vital charge.

The Apostle Paul told the Saints in his time "to know them which labour among you, and are over you in the Lord, and admonish you; And esteem them very highly in love for the work's sake." (1 Thessalonians 5:12-13.) He pled with the members to "pray for us, that the word of the Lord may have free course, and be glorified." (2 Thessalonians 3:1.) He also indicated the manner in which the Apostles labored. They "exhorted and comforted and charged every one of you, as a father doth his children." (1 Thessalonians 2:11.)

It is with fatherly love that the Lord's servants come and go as they labor among the people in this day. It is in this spirit and with a desire to edify the Saints that this collection of talks and sermons has been prepared. They were assembled in answer to many requests that have come for them. They are arranged for their use as material for building in the edification process, and each is likened to some part of a building.

The foundation of the edifice is *instruction*. Walls of *encouragement* are lifted up. *Comfort* spreads a shelter against despair. Windows of *enlightenment* let in the light of faith. A closed door symbolizes a *warning*, for there are some places that we must not enter if we are to be protected against danger. An *exhortation* is a buttress to correct error and strengthen the structure. Pure *witness* becomes the steeple, the capstone, the pinnacle. It is set at the highest place on the structure, pointing always upward. The humble testimony of the Latter-day Saint becomes the crowning contribution in the building of lives. For he that gives and he that receives are edified together. It is not a new thing to liken virtues to the architectural features of a building, of an edifice. Paul did so when he said:

"Now therefore, ye are...of the household of God; And are built upon the foundation of the apostles and prophets, Jesus Christ himself being the chief corner stone. In whom all the building fitly framed together groweth unto an holy temple in the Lord." (Ephesians 2:19-21.)

1

Prayers and Answers

My brethren and sisters, I pray for inspiration as I speak to young people about prayer and about the things that happen afterwards.

We succeed in the Church, by and large, in teaching our members to pray. Even our little ones are taught to fold their arms and bow their heads, and with whispered coaching from their parents and from brothers and sisters, they soon learn to pray.

There is one part of prayer—the answer part—that perhaps, by comparison, we neglect.

There are some things about answers to prayer that you can learn when you are very young, and they will be a great protection to you.

The Sounds We Recognize

Many years ago John Burroughs, a naturalist, one summer evening was walking through a crowded park. Above the sounds of city life he heard the song of a bird.

He stopped and listened. Those with him had not heard it. He looked around. No one else had noticed it.

It bothered him that everyone should miss something so beautiful.

He took a coin from his pocket and flipped it into the air. It struck the pavement with a ring, no louder than the song of the bird. Everyone turned; they could hear that.

It is difficult to separate from all the sounds of city traffic the song of a bird. But you can hear it. You can hear it plainly if you train yourself to listen for it.

One of our sons has always been interested in radio. When he was a little fellow, his Christmas present was a very elementary radio construction set.

Address given at general conference October 1979.

As he grew, and as we could afford it, and as he could earn it, he received more sophisticated equipment.

There have been many times over the years, some very recently, when I have sat with him as he talked with someone in a distant part of the world.

I could hear static and interference and catch a word or two, or sometimes several voices at once.

Yet he can understand, for he has trained himself to tune out the interference.

It is difficult to separate from the confusion of life that quiet voice of inspiration. Unless you attune yourself, you will miss it.

How Answers Come

Answers to prayers come in a quiet way. The scriptures describe that voice of inspiration as a still small voice.

If you really try, you can learn to respond to that voice.

In the early days of our marriage, our children came at close intervals. As parents of little children will know, in those years it is quite a novelty for them to get an uninterrupted night of sleep.

If you have a new baby and another youngster cutting teeth, or one with a fever, you can be up and down a hundred times a night. (That, of course, is an exaggeration. It's probably only twenty or thirty times.)

We finally divided our children into "his" and "hers" for night tending. She would get up for the new baby, and I would tend the one cutting teeth.

One day we came to realize that each would hear only the one to which we were assigned and would sleep very soundly through the cries of the other.

We have commented on this over the years, convinced that you can train yourself to hear what you want to hear, to see and feel what you desire, but it takes some conditioning.

There are so many of us who go through life and seldom, if ever, hear that voice of inspiration, because "the natural man receiveth not the things of the Spirit of God: for they are foolishness unto him: neither can he know them, because they are spiritually discerned." (1 Corinthians 2:14.)

The scriptures have many lessons on this subject.

Lehi told his sons of a vision, but Laman and Lemuel resisted his teachings:

> For he truly spake many great things unto them, which were hard to be understood, save a man should inquire of the Lord; and they being hard in their hearts, therefore they did not look unto the Lord as they ought. (1 Nephi 15:3.)

They complained to their younger brother Nephi that they could not understand their father, and Nephi asked this question:

> Have ye inquired of the Lord?
> And they said unto [him]: We have not; for the Lord maketh no such thing known unto us. (1 Nephi 15:8-9.)

Later they intended to do Nephi harm and he said to them:

> Ye are swift to do iniquity but slow to remember the Lord your God. Ye have seen an angel, and he spake unto you; yea, ye have heard his voice from time to time; and he hath spoken unto you in a still small voice, but ye were past *feeling,* that ye could not *feel* his words. (1 Nephi 17:45; italics added.)

I have come to know that inspiration comes more as a feeling than as a sound.

Conditions Required for Inspiration

Young people, stay in condition to respond to inspiration.

I have come to know also that a fundamental purpose of the Word of Wisdom has to do with revelation.

From the time you are very little we teach you to avoid tea, coffee, liquor, tobacco, narcotics, and anything else that disturbs your health.

And you know that we get very worried when we find one of you tampering with those things.

If those "under the influence" can hardly listen to plain talk, how can they respond to spiritual promptings that touch their most delicate feelings?

As valuable as the Word of Wisdom is as a law of health, it may be much more valuable to you spiritually than it is physically.

Even if you keep the Word of Wisdom, there are some things that can happen to you physically, but those things don't generally damage you spiritually.

When you become a father or a mother, don't live so that your children go unled because of habits that leave you uninspired.

The Lord has a way of pouring pure intelligence into our minds to prompt us, to guide us, to teach us, to warn us. You can know the things you need to know *instantly.* Learn to receive inspiration.

Even in our youth activities there is something to do with inspiration, for they include service to others. Inspiration comes more quickly when we need it to help others than when we are concerned about ourselves.

Now, I know that some young people resent it a little when we comment upon such things as the wild music that is served up nowadays.

Can you not see that you are not going to get much inspiration while your mind is filled with that?

The right kind of music, on the other hand, can prepare you to receive inspiration.

You should know also that, in addition to static and interference which jam the circuits, there are counterfeit signals.

Some have received revelations and heard voices that are put there deliberately by wicked sources to lead astray. You can learn to recognize those and tune them out if you will.

Judging Good from Evil

Now, how do you tell the difference? How can you know if a prompting is an inspiration or a temptation?

My answer to that must surely expose my great confidence in young people. I believe young people, when properly taught, are basically sensible.

In the Church we are not exempt from common sense. You can know, to begin with, that you will not be prompted from any righteous source to steal, to lie, to cheat, to join anyone in any kind of moral transgression.

You have a conscience even as a little boy and girl. It will prompt you to know the things that are wrong. Don't smother it.

Once again the scriptures tell us something. Read the Book of Mormon—Moroni, chapter 7. I quote only one verse:

> For behold, my brethren, it is given unto you to judge, that ye may know good from evil; and the way to judge is as plain, that ye may know with a perfect knowledge, as the daylight is from the dark night. (Moroni 7:15.)

You read the whole chapter. It tells of a way to judge such things.

If ever you are confused and feel that you are being misled, go for counsel to your parents and to your leaders.

Young people, you are going to be leading this Church tomorrow, or the next day, or the day after that. We are organized to bring you as fully as possible into Church activities and administration.

Already you have been taught to pray. You need to know how to get answers.

Spiritual Things Cannot Be Forced

It is good to learn when you are young that spiritual things cannot be forced.

Sometimes you may struggle with a problem and not get an answer. What could be wrong?

It may be that you are not doing anything wrong. It may be that you have not done the right things long enough. Remember, you cannot force spiritual things.

Sometimes we are confused simply because we won't take no for an answer.

On several occasions when a member has insisted that something be done his way, I have remembered that great lesson from Church history. I have said to myself in my mind:

All right, Joseph, give the manuscript to Martin Harris. Do it your own way and see where you get. Then when you're confounded and confused, come back and we'll get you set on the course that you might have taken earlier if you had been submissive and responsive.

Someone wrote:

> With thoughtless and impatient hands
> We tangle up the plans
> The Lord hath wrought.
> And when we cry in pain, He saith,
> "Be quiet, man, while I untie the knot."
> (Anonymous.)

Put difficult questions in the back of your minds and go about your lives. Ponder and pray quietly and persistently about them.

The answer may not come as a lightning bolt. It may come as a little inspiration here and a little there, "line upon line, precept upon precept." (D & C 98:12.)

That All May Be Edified

Some answers will come from reading the scriptures, some from hearing speakers. And, occasionally, when it is important, some will come by very direct and powerful inspiration. The promptings will be clear and unmistakable.

You can learn now, in your youth, to be led by the Holy Ghost.

As an Apostle I listen now to the same inspiration, coming from the same source, in the same way, I listened to as a boy. The signal is much clearer now.

And on occasions, when it is required for His work, for instance, when we are to call members to high positions in the stakes, we can ask a question in prayer and receive an immediate, direct revelation in return.

No message is repeated more times in scripture than the simple thought: "Ask, and ye shall receive." (D&C 4:7.)

I often ask the Lord for direction from Him. I will not, however, willingly accept promptings from any unworthy source. I refuse them. I do not want them, and I say so.

Young people, carry a prayer in your heart always. Let sleep come every night with your mind centered in prayer.

Keep the Word of Wisdom.

Read the scriptures.

Listen to your parents and to the leaders of the Church.

Stay away from places and things that common sense tells you will interfere with inspiration.

Develop your spiritual capacities.

Learn to tune out the static and the interference.

Avoid the substitutes and the counterfeits.

Learn to be inspired and directed by the Holy Ghost.

Follow the Beam

It has been many years, but I have not forgotten that as pilots in World War II we did not have the electronic equipment that we have today. Our hope in a storm was to follow a radio beam.

A steady signal, and you were on course. If you moved to one side of the steady signal, it would break up to a "dit-da," the Morse code for the letter *A*.

If you strayed to the other side of the signal, the beam would break up into a "da-dit," the Morse code signal for *N*.

Prayers and Answers

In stormy weather there was always static and interference. But the life of many a pilot has depended on his hearing, above the roar of the engines and through all the static and interference, that sometimes weak signal from a distant airfield.

There is a spiritual beam, with a constant signal. If you know how to pray and how to listen, spiritually listen, you may move through life, through clear weather, through storms, through wars, through peace, and be all right.

Prayer can be a very public thing. We teach you often about prayer, about the asking part.

Perhaps we have not taught you enough about the receiving part. This is a very private, a very individual thing, one that you must learn for yourself.

Begin now, and as the years unfold before you, you who are very young, you will be led. That still small voice will come to you, and then you can come to know as many, many of us have come to know, and as I bear witness, that the Lord lives. I know His voice when He speaks.

I know that Jesus is the Christ, that He directs this Church, that He is close to it, that He directs His prophets and His leaders and His people and His children, in the name of Jesus Christ, amen.

2

Behold Your Little Ones

W ho has not been touched by the singing of these innocent children? I think of the account in 3 Nephi, chapter 17, when the Lord commanded that the little ones should be brought. As they brought them they placed them upon the ground. He commanded that the multitude should give way until all the little ones were there. Then He commanded that the multitude should kneel. He knelt among the little children and prayed.

"Behold Your Little Ones"

The account records:

> The eye hath never seen, neither hath the ear heard, before, so great and marvelous things as we saw and heard Jesus speak unto the Father;
> And no tongue can speak, neither can there be written by any man, neither can the hearts of men conceive so great and marvelous things as we both saw and heard Jesus speak. (3 Nephi 17:16-17.)

After the prayer, it is recorded that He wept. And then:

> he took their little children, one by one, and blessed them, and prayed unto the Father for them.
> And when he had done this he wept again;
> And he spake unto the multitude, and said unto them: Behold your little ones. (3 Nephi 17:21-23.)

I confess, I am not ashamed to confess, that little children get inside of me very easily. We have a little fellow at home not quite four. All he has to say to turn lights on in me is one word, *Dad*. I am indebted to him for some of the help with this assignment today.

Talk to Children

Children are an heritage of the Lord (Psalm 127:3), and I desire

---

Address given at general conference April 1973.

Behold Your Little Ones

today to talk to little children. Many of them are here in the choir. Others, a great number of them, are listening in. I think the grown-ups won't mind if I don't talk to them.

There is something very important that I want to say to you children. Something I hope you'll always remember. Something you should learn when you are children and things are easy to remember.

Did you know that you lived before you were born on earth? Before you were born to your father and mother you lived in the spirit world.

That is a very important thing to know. It explains many things that otherwise are very difficult to understand. Many people in the world do not know that, but it is the truth.

When you were born into this life you were not created then. Only your physical body was created. You came from somewhere. You left the presence of your Heavenly Father, for it was your time to live upon the earth.

Reasons for Mortality

There were two reasons you were to come into this life. First, to receive a mortal body. This is a great blessing. Our Heavenly Father arranged things so that through a very sacred expression of love between your father and mother your body was conceived and began to grow. Then at some time, I don't know just when, your spirit entered into your body and you became a living person. But it did not all begin with your birth as a little baby.

Your body becomes an instrument of your mind and the foundation of your character. Through life in a mortal body you can learn to control matter, and that will be very important to you through all eternity.

Pretend, my little friends, that my hand represents your spirit. It is alive. It can move by itself. Suppose that this glove represents your mortal body. It cannot move. When the spirit enters into your mortal body, then it can move and act and live. Now you are a person—a spirit with a body, living on the earth.

Death a Separation

It was not intended that we stay here forever. Just for a lifetime. Little ones, you are just beginning your lifetime. Your grandparents and great-grandparents are nearly finished with theirs. It wasn't long ago that they were little fellows and little girls just like you are now. But one day they will leave this mortal existence and so will you.

Someday, because of old age, or perhaps a disease, or an accident, the spirit and the body will be separated. We then say a person has died. Death is a separation. All of this was acccording to a plan.

Remember, my hand represents your spirit, and the glove represents your body. While you are alive the spirit inside the body can cause it to work and to act and to live.

When I separate them, the glove, which represents your body, is taken away from your spirit; it cannot move anymore. It just falls down and is dead. But your spirit is still alive.

"A spirit born of God is an immortal thing. When the body dies, the spirit does not die." (First Presidency, *Improvement Era,* March 1912, p. 463.)

It is important that you get in your mind what death is. Death is a separation.

The part of you that looks out through your eyes and allows you to think and smile and act and to know and to be, that is your spirit and that is eternal. It cannot die.

Do you remember when someone, perhaps a grandmother, died? Remember your parents explained to you that it was just her body lying in the casket, that grandmother had gone to live with Heavenly Father, and that she would be waiting there. You remember having them say that, don't you?

Death is a separation and is according to the plan. If the plan ended there, it would be too bad, because we came to obtain a body and it would be lost.

God's Plan

When He made it possible for us to come into this world, our Heavenly Father also made it possible for us to return to Him, because He is our Father and He loves us. Do not think that because we are living on this earth, away from Him, and because we can't see Him, He has forgotten us.

Didn't you notice, when your older brother was away on his mission, or your sister was away at school, how your parents did not stop loving them? Sometimes it seemed to you they loved them more than they did you. At least they would talk about them and sometimes worry about them. They sent help and messages to encourage them. Distance can make love grow stronger.

Little children, our Heavenly Father knew that we would need help. So, in the plan, He provided for someone to come into the world and help us.

This was Jesus Christ, the Son of God. He is a spirit child, as all of us are; but also, Jesus was His Only Begotten Son on the earth. I speak very reverently of Him. And He it was, my little friends, who made it possible for us to overcome death and get things put back the way they should be.

You are learning about Him in Primary and in family home evening. It is very important that you remember Him and learn all you can about what He did.

He overcame the mortal death for us. Through the Atonement, He made it possible for our spirit and body to be one again. Because of Him, we will be resurrected. He made it possible for us to be resurrected, for the spirit and the body to be put back together. That is what the Resurrection is. That is a gift from Him. And all men will receive it. That is why He is called our Savior, our Redeemer.

Learning Good from Evil

The second reason you came here was to be tested: something like going away to school to learn good from evil. It is very important for us to be able to know the right from the wrong.

It is important for us to know that there is an evil one who will tempt us to do wrong. Because of this, there is another separation you should know about. Even when you are very young you should know about it. There is another separation that you need to think about—not the separation of the body from the spirit; rather, a separation from our Heavenly Father.

If we remain separated from Him and can't get back to His presence, then it would be as though we were spiritually dead. And that would not be good. This separation is like a second death, a spiritual death.

You are now learning to read, and you can begin to read the scriptures: the Bible, especially the Book of Mormon, the Doctrine and Covenants, and the Pearl of Great Price. From them we know that little children can learn spiritual truths. For the prophet said:

He imparteth his word by angels unto men, yea, not only men but women also. Now this is not all; little children do have words given unto them many times, which confound the wise and the learned. (Alma 32:23.)

Importance of Cleanliness

In the scriptures we learn that our spirits must be clean, in order to return to the presence of our Heavenly Father: "...there cannot any unclean thing enter into the kingdom of God...." (1 Nephi 15:34.)

Two important things must happen to us then. First, somehow we must get our body back after we die—that is, we want to be resurrected; and we must find a way to keep ourselves clean, spiritually clean, so that we will not be separated from our Heavenly Father and may return to where He is when we leave this earth life.

We are sure you will overcome mortal death. You will be resurrected because of what Christ did for us. Whether or not you overcome the spiritual death—that separation from the presence of our Heavenly Father—will depend a great deal upon you.

When Jesus Christ was living on the earth, He taught His gospel and organized His church. If we live the gospel, we will remain spiritually clean. Even when we make mistakes, there is a way to become clean again. That is what repentance is.

Steps to Enter Church

To enter His church we must have faith in the Lord Jesus Christ. We must repent, and we must be baptized.

Baptism is like being buried in the water. When we come out of the water, it is like being born again, and we are clean. We receive a remission of our sins. That means they are taken away. We can retain this remission of our sins if we will.

We are then confirmed members of His church, The Church of Jesus Christ of Latter-day Saints. We may have the gift of the Holy Ghost to guide us. That is like receiving messages from our heavenly home, to show us the way to go.

The Lord called prophets and Apostles to lead His church. He has always revealed His will through His prophets.

An Apostle of the Lord

Let me tell you something I learned when I was about your age. I think I was about six or seven years old. My brother and I (we were about the same age) walked to the stake conference together. I can still go in that building in Brigham City and go back just under the balcony, and say, "I was sitting about there when it happened."

What was it that happened? There was a man speaking at the pulpit, Elder George Albert Smith. He was a member of the Council of the Twelve at that time. I do not remember what he said, whether he was talking about the Word of Wisdom, or about repentance, or about baptism. But somehow while he was speaking it was fixed in my little-boy mind that there stood a servant of the Lord. I have never lost that testimony or that feeling. In my mind I came to know that he was an Apostle of the Lord Jesus Christ.

My little friends, although I sit now in the Council of the Twelve, I have never lost that feeling about these men. Often when we meet in the Council, I look around the circle and know again that these are the Apostles of the Lord Jesus Christ upon the earth. They are special witnesses of Him.

A Time of Testing

Little ones, you will be tested, perhaps more than any other generation that ever lived here. You will meet many people who do not believe in Christ. Some will be agents for the evil one and teach wickedness. Sometimes this will be very tempting. There will be times when you will make mistakes (and all of us make mistakes). There will be times when you will wonder if you can live the way He taught we should live. When you are tested, when you are disappointed, or ashamed, or when you are sad, remember Him and pray to your Heavenly Father in His name.

Some men will say that He did not come to earth. But He did. Some will say that He is not the Son of God. But He is. Some will say that He has no servants upon the face of the earth. But He has. For He lives. I know that He lives. In His church there are many thousands who can bear witness of Him, and I bear witness of Him, and tell you again the things you should remember, things you should learn when you are yet a little one.

Remember that each of you is a child of our Heavenly Father. That is why we call Him our Father.

You lived before you came to this earth. You came to receive a mortal body and to be tested.

21

Redemption of Christ

When your life is over, your spirit and body will be separated. We call that death.

Our Heavenly Father sent His Son, Jesus Christ, to redeem us. Because of what He has done we will be resurrected.

There is another kind of death you should think of. That is the separation from the presence of our Heavenly Father. If we will be baptized and live His gospel, we may be redeemed from this second death.

Our Heavenly Father loves us, and we have a Lord and Savior.

I thank God for a church where you, our little children, are precious above all things. I thank God for our Savior who suffered the little children to come unto Him.

You sang these words, just a few minutes ago:

> I think when I read that sweet story of old,
> When Jesus was here among men,
> How he called little children like lambs to his fold,
> I should like to have been with him then.
> I wish that his hands had been placed on my head,
> That his arms had been thrown around me,
> That I might have seen his kind look when he said,
> "Let the little ones come unto me."

> ("I Think When I Read That Sweet Story of Old,"
> *Sing With Me,* no. B-69.)

My little brothers and sisters, my little children, I know that God lives. I know something of how it feels to have His hand put upon you, to call you to His service. I bear witness and share with you the witness that has been given me, that special witness. He is the Christ! He loves us! I pray for you, our little ones, and plead with Him to behold our little ones and to bless them, in the name of Jesus Christ, amen.

3

The Aaronic Priesthood

I always come to the Tabernacle early for priesthood meeting in order to shake hands with the deacons, teachers, and priests. I have to sift through a lot of elders, seventies, and high priests to find them, but it's well worth it to meet the Aaronic Priesthood. We who hold the higher priesthood salute you, our brethren of the Aaronic Priesthood.

I want to tell you about the unseen power of the Aaronic Priesthood. A boy of twelve is old enough to learn about it. As you mature you should become very familiar with this guiding, protecting power.

Some think that unless a power is visible it cannot be real. I think I can convince you otherwise. Do you remember when you foolishly put your finger in that light socket? While you did not see exactly what happened, surely you felt it!

No one has ever seen electricity, not even a scientist with the finest instruments. Like you, however, they have felt it. And we can see the results of it. We can measure it, control it, and produce light and heat and power. Simply because he cannot see it, no one questions that it is real.

You Can Feel the Power

Although you cannot see the power of the priesthood, you can *feel* it, and you can see the results of it. The priesthood can be a guiding and protecting power in your life. Let me give you an example.

After President Wilford Woodruff joined the Church he desired to serve a mission.

"I was but a Teacher," he wrote, "and it is not a Teacher's office to go abroad and preach. I dared not tell any of the authorities of the Church that I wanted to preach, lest they might think I was seeking for

---

Address given at general conference October 1981.

an office." (*Leaves From My Journal,* Salt Lake City: Juvenile Instructor Office, 1882, p. 8.)

He prayed to the Lord, and without disclosing his desire to any others, he was ordained a priest and sent on a mission. They went to the Arkansas Territory.

He and his companion struggled through a hundred miles of alligator-infested swamps—wet, muddy, and tired. Brother Woodruff developed a sharp pain in his knee and could go no further. His companion left him sitting on a log and went home. Brother Woodruff knelt down in the mud and prayed for help. He was healed and continued his mission alone.

Three days later he arrived in Memphis, Tennessee, weary, hungry, and very muddy. He went to the largest inn and asked for something to eat and for a place to sleep, although he had no money to pay for either.

When the innkeeper found he was a preacher, he laughed and decided to have some fun with him. He offered Brother Woodruff a meal if he would preach to his friends.

A large audience of the rich and fashionable people of Memphis gathered and were quite amused by this mud-stained missionary.

None would sing or pray, so Brother Woodruff did both. He knelt before them and begged the Lord to give him His Spirit and to show him the hearts of the people. And the Spirit came! Brother Woodruff preached with great power. He was able to reveal the secret deeds of those who came to ridicule him.

When he was finished, no one laughed at this humble holder of the Aaronic Priesthood. Thereafter he was treated with kindness. (See *Leaves From My Journal,* pp. 16-18.)

He was under the guiding, protecting power of his Aaronic Priesthood. The same power can be with you as well.

Let me teach you some very basic things about the Aaronic Priesthood.

It "is called the Priesthood of Aaron, because it was conferred upon Aaron and his seed, throughout all their generations." (D & C 107:13.)

The Aaronic Priesthood goes by other names as well. Let me list them and tell you what they mean.

The Lesser Priesthood

First, the Aaronic Priesthood is sometimes called the lesser priesthood.

> Why it is called the lesser priesthood is because it is an appendage to the greater, or the Melchizedek Priesthood, and has power in administering outward ordinances. (D & C 107:14.)

This means that the higher priesthood, the Melchizedek Priesthood, *always* presides over the Aaronic, or the lesser, Priesthood. Aaron was the high priest, or the presiding priest, of the Aaronic Priesthood. But Moses presided over Aaron because Moses held the Melchizedek Priesthood.

The fact that it is called the lesser priesthood does not diminish at all the importance of the Aaronic Priesthood. The Lord said it is necessary to the Melchizedek Priesthood. (See D & C 84:29.) Any holder of the higher priesthood should feel greatly honored to perform the ordinances of the Aaronic Priesthood, for they have great spiritual importance.

I have, as a member of the Quorum of the Twelve Apostles, passed the sacrament. I assure you I have felt honored and humbled beyond expression to do what some might consider a routine task.

The Levitical Priesthood

The Aaronic Priesthood is also called the Levitical Priesthood. The word *Levitical* comes from the name Levi, one of the twelve sons of Israel. Moses and Aaron, who were brothers, were Levites.

When the Aaronic Priesthood was given to Israel, Aaron and his sons received the *presiding* and administrative responsibility. The male members of all other Levite families were put in charge of the ceremonies of the tabernacle, including the Mosaic law of sacrifice.

The law of sacrifice had been observed since the days of Adam. It was symbolic of the redemption that would come with the sacrifice and the atonement of the Messiah. The Mosaic law of sacrifice was fulfilled with the crucifixion of Christ.

Anciently they looked forward to the atonement of Christ through the ceremony of the sacrifice. We look back to that same event through the ordinance of the sacrament.

Both sacrifice before and the sacrament afterward are centered in Christ, the shedding of His blood, and the atonement He made for our sins. Both then and now the authority to perform these ordinances belongs to the Aaronic Priesthood.

This is indeed a sacred responsibility and includes you in a brotherhood with those ancient servants of the Lord. It is no wonder that we feel so humble when we participate in the ordinances assigned to the Aaronic Priesthood.

Can you see that it is correct to call it the Aaronic or the Levitical Priesthood? It is a matter of designating duties; it is all one priesthood.

The Preparatory Priesthood

Finally, the Aaronic Priesthood is referred to as the preparatory priesthood. This, too, is a proper title because the Aaronic Priesthood prepares young men 1) to hold the higher priesthood, 2) for missions, and 3) for temple marriage.

I have thought it very symbolic that John the Baptist, a priest in the Aaronic Priesthood, prepared the way for the coming of the Lord in ancient times. He came also to restore the Aaronic Priesthood to the Prophet Joseph Smith and Oliver Cowdery to prepare for the coming of the higher priesthood. The Lord Himself said that there "hath not risen a greater than John the Baptist." (Matthew 11:11.)

You would do well to watch your fathers and your leaders, to study how the Melchizedek Priesthood works. You are preparing to join the elders, seventies, high priests, and patriarchs and to serve as missionaries, quorum leaders, bishoprics, stake leaders, and fathers of families.

A few of you who now sit there as deacons, teachers, and priests will one day sit here as Apostles and prophets and will preside over the Church. You must be prepared.

It is indeed correct to call the Aaronic Priesthood the preparatory priesthood.

Priesthood Principles

Let me teach you some important principles of the priesthood. When you receive the Aaronic Priesthood, you receive all of it. There are three kinds of authority relating to your priesthood. You should understand them.

26

(1) First, there is the priesthood itself. The ordination you received carries with it the overall authority to perform the ordinances and to possess the power of the Aaronic Priesthood.

(2) Next, there are offices within the priesthood. Each has different privileges. Three of them—deacon, teacher, and priest—may be conferred upon you when you are in your teenage years.

(3) The fourth office, that of bishop, may come to you when you are mature and worthy to become a high priest as well.

The deacon is to watch over the Church as a standing minister. (See D&C 84:111; 20:57-59.) The quorum consists of twelve deacons. (See D&C 107:85.)

The teacher is to "watch over the church always, and be with and strengthen them." (D&C 20:53.) The teachers quorum numbers twenty-four. (See D&C 107:86.)

The priest is to "preach, teach, expound, exhort, and baptize, and administer the sacrament, and visit the house of each member." (D&C 20:46-47.) The priests quorum numbers forty-eight. The bishop is the president of the priests quorum. (See D&C 107:87-88.)

You always hold one of these offices. When you receive the next higher office, you still retain the authority of the first. For instance, when you become a priest, you still have authority to do all that you did as a deacon and teacher. Even when you receive the higher priesthood, you keep all of the authority of, and, with proper authorization, can act in the offices of, the lesser priesthood.

Elder LeGrand Richards, who was Presiding Bishop for fourteen years, has often said, "I'm just a grown-up deacon."

There is no rigid form of wording for your ordination. It includes the conferring of the priesthood, the giving of an office, and also a special blessing.

I once attended a meeting with President Joseph Fielding Smith. Someone asked President Smith about a letter that was then being circulated by an apostate who claimed that the Church had lost the priesthood because certain words had not been used when it was conferred. President Smith said, "Before we talk about his claim, let me tell you a little about the man himself." He then described the character of the man and concluded, "And so you see, that man is a liar pure and simple—well, maybe not so pure."

That All May Be Edified

The offices are a part of the priesthood, but the priesthood is greater than any of the offices within it.

The priesthood is yours forever unless you disqualify yourself through transgression.

When we are active and faithful, we begin to understand the power of the priesthood.

There is one other kind of authority that comes to you if you are set apart as a quorum president. You then are given the keys of authority for that presidency.

You receive the priesthood and the office you hold within the priesthood (deacon, teacher, and priest) by ordination. You receive the keys of presidency by setting apart.

When you become a deacon, your father may, and generally should, ordain you; or another who holds the proper priesthood could do it.

If you are called as president of your quorum, your bishopric would set you apart. You can receive the keys of presidency only from those who have received them.

Unless your father is also your bishop, he would not have those keys.

These keys of presidency are temporary. The priesthood, and the offices within it, are permanent.

One more thing: You can receive the priesthood only from one who has the authority and "it is known to the church that he has authority." (D & C 42:11.)

The priesthood cannot be conferred like a diploma. It cannot be handed to you as a certificate. It cannot be delivered to you as a message or sent to you in a letter. It comes only by proper ordination. An authorized holder of the priesthood has to be there. He must place his hands upon your head and ordain you.

That is one reason why the General Authorities travel so much—to convey the keys of priesthood authority. Every stake president everywhere in the world has received his authority under the hands of one of the presiding brethren of the Church. There has never been one exception.

Remember these things. The priesthood is very, very precious to the Lord. He is very careful about how it is conferred, and by whom. It is never done in secret.

The Aaronic Priesthood

I have told you how the *authority* is given to you. The *power* you receive will depend on what you do with this sacred, unseen gift.

Your authority comes through your ordination; your power comes through obedience and worthiness.

Let me tell you how one of our sons learned obedience. When he was about deacon age, we went to his grandfather's ranch in Wyoming. He wanted to start breaking a horse he had been given. It had been running wild in the hills.

It took nearly all day to get the herd to the corral and to tie his horse up with a heavy halter and rope.

I told him that his horse must stay tied there until it settled down; he could talk to it, carefully touch it, but he must not, under any circumstance, untie it.

We finally went in for our supper. He quickly ate and rushed back out to see his horse. Presently I heard him cry out. I knew what had happened. He had untied his horse. He was going to train it to lead. As the horse pulled away from him he instinctively did something I had told him never, never to do. He looped the rope around his wrist to get a better grip.

As I ran from the house I saw the horse go by. Our boy could not release the rope; he was being pulled with great leaping steps. And then he went down. If the horse had turned to the right, he would have been dragged out the gate and into the hills and would certainly have lost his life. It turned to the left and for a moment was hung up in a fence corner—just long enough for me to loop the rope around a post and to free my son.

Then came a father-to-son chat. "Son, if you are ever going to control that horse, you will have to use something besides your muscles. The horse is bigger than you are, it is stronger than you are, and it always will be. Someday you may ride your horse if you train it to be obedient, a lesson that you must learn yourself first." He had learned a very valuable lesson.

Two summers later we went again to the ranch to look for his horse. It had been running all winter with the wild herd. We found them in a meadow down by the river. I watched from a hillside as he and his sister moved carefully to the edge of the meadow. The horses moved nervously away. Then he whistled. His horse hesitated, then left the herd and trotted up to them.

That All May Be Edified

He had learned that there is great power in things that are not seen, such unseen things as obedience.

Just as obedience to principle gave him power to train his horse, obedience to the priesthood has taught him to control himself.

Throughout your life you will belong to a quorum of the priesthood; your brethren will be a strength and a support to you.

More than that—you will have the privilege of being a support to them.

Much of what I have told you about the Aaronic Priesthood applies to the Melchizedek Priesthood as well. The names of the offices change, more authority is given, but the principles remain the same.

Power in the priesthood comes from doing your duty in ordinary things: attending meetings, accepting assignments, reading the scriptures, keeping the Word of Wisdom.

President Woodruff said: "I traveled thousands of miles and preached the Gospel as a Priest, and, as I have said to congregations before, the Lord sustained me and made manifest His power in the defense of my life as much while I held that office as He has done while I have held the office of an Apostle. The Lord sustains any man that holds a portion of the Priesthood, whether he is a Priest, an Elder, a Seventy, or an Apostle, if he magnifies his calling and does his duty." (*Millennial Star,* September 28, 1905, p. 610.)

John the Baptist restored the Aaronic Priesthood with these words:

> Upon you my fellow servants, in the name of Messiah I confer the Priesthood of Aaron, which holds the keys of the ministering of angels, and of the gospel of repentance, and of baptism by immersion for the remission of sins. (D & C 13.)

You—our deacons, teachers, and priests—have been given sacred authority. May the angels minister unto you. May the power of the priesthood be upon you, our beloved young brethren, and upon your sons throughout the generations ahead. I bear witness that the gospel is true, that the priesthood holds great power, a guiding, protecting power for those who hold the Aaronic Priesthood. In the name of Jesus Christ, amen.

4

Let Virtue
Garnish Thy Thoughts

I am particularly grateful to be here at the first devotional at the opening of the school year. The opening of school, somehow, brings with it a keen longing to those who have been teachers, but are no longer privileged to teach. There is a joy that a teacher knows—not talked about or shared, but it is experienced as school begins, this compelling spirit of anticipation—a touch of pure joy.

Students, if your teachers have lost that, *you* have lost much. Teachers, if you have lost that, *you* have lost almost everything.

I talked with Dr. Ward Lowe, a physicist at MIT, about an illustration I intend to use. In the conversation, with a very difficult subject in mind, I quoted Agnes's law. I don't know whether you are acquainted with Agnes's law, but it reads: "Some things are a lot harder to get out of than to get into." It is a very provable law; it fits *everything* from Volkswagons to trouble, and includes subjects for sermons.

Now, in turn, Brother Lowe quoted Murphy's law—I can see where it would appeal to the scientific mind. It reads: "If anything *can* go wrong, it *will*." I think he told me that to encourage me.

I do take courage from the certainty that there are higher laws and from a confidence in you, college students, who are old enough to understand and yet young enough to profit from knowledge.

In 1945, as World War II was drawing to a close, Sir Winston Churchill, speaking to Lord Morran, said: "The next war will be an ideological one." (*Diaries of Lord Morran* [Boston: Houghton Mifflin Co., 1966], p. 241.) This giant of a man, whose prophetic assessment of world affairs is a matter of record, was right. The war which he foresaw has begun.

Address given at Brigham Young University September 1967.

That All May Be Edified

A new and frightening invasion threatens mankind. It has spread like a pestilence among our college-age youth. Silently it moves, fixing itself to any whose resistance is at a low ebb. More pernicious than leukemia, it ignores the corpuscles of the blood and the organs of the body and attaches itself to our thoughts. Our thoughts become diseased, distorted and changed, servile to some malignant influence.

Heretofore, the intrusions into men's minds have been merely persuasions. But now evil agents, clamoring for the attention of our college-age youth, want more than that. In a way not before known, they seek to possess men's minds: first, to enlist them for wicked purposes; or, failing in that, to render them useless to resistance, complacent, and impotent to righteousness.

It is not accidental that the common name of a thought-conditioner, LSD, circulated by the carriers of this disease, is so close in approximation to the abbreviation for Latter-day Saint.

Because you may be susceptible to the plague and knowing that healthy, clean thoughts are resistant, even immune to it, I venture to talk with you about your thoughts, and to point out the danger of the undisciplined mind. Each of us must learn self-control of his thoughts. We *must* learn to control our thoughts, or someone or something else *will* control them. Untrained, unemployed thoughts are soon enslaved.

In school, particularly in this school, you can find worthwhile, productive employment for your mind. Success in life depends upon the management of your thoughts. Your very salvation depends upon it.

The Book of Mormon has a surprising number of references on the subject. I will read but a few. From Alma:

> For our words will condemn us, yea, all our works will condemn us; we shall not be found spotless; and our *thoughts* will also condemn us. (Alma 12:14; italics added.)

And from 2 Nephi comes instruction, repeated not only in the Book of Mormon, but also in biblical scripture:

> Remember, to be carnally-*minded* is death, and to be spiritually-*minded* is life eternal. (2 Nephi 9:39; italics added.)

We don't have to press upon you college intellects, do we, the generally accepted and accurate assessment that "The idle mind is the devil's workshop," or that "As [a man] thinketh in his heart, so is he"? (Proverbs 27:3.)

How many times have we heard it, over and over again? "Guard your thoughts; keep your mind in the right place."

And yet it occurred to me that, with all of the urging I had been given on this subject, never had anyone told me *how*. Never did I receive any specific instruction on how to do what I had been urged to do—control my thoughts. So I, too, wondered, *Does this control of one's thoughts have to be an individual discovery for every soul? Or can self-control of thoughts be taught? Are there things one can do, exercises that one can perform, or procedures that one can learn to help him?* I have often lamented not having learned or been taught in my early college years more mastery of thoughts.

It is to this subject, self-control of thoughts, that we turn.

Thought Controls Action

There are, if we control them, things we ought to know about thoughts. First, that they sponsor all action. Our thoughts are the switchboard, the control panel governing our actions. While some acts may seem so impulsive, and our reactions to things so automatic that they seem to be done without thinking, nonetheless, thought controls action.

Recently I read of a fire in a large gasoline storage tank. The fire was spreading through the pipelines and threatening the entire refinery. The firemen were battling the blazes as they erupted in various places. Then one of the fire chiefs, in a wise and heroic move, donned some protective clothing. Disregarding his own safety, he went in and turned off the valve. The fire was then contained in the single tank. It had been cut off at its source. It could not spread through the pipelines.

Our minds can do that. Our thoughts can turn on or turn off our actions.

Thoughts Are Powerful

Do you realize how important our thoughts are, how necessary it is to keep them healthy? Do you sense how powerful they are? Quoting again from Sir Winston Churchill:

33

That All May Be Edified

You see these dictators on their pedestals, surrounded by bayonets of their soldiers, the truncheons of their police. On all sides they are guarded by masses of armed men, cannons, aeroplanes, fortifications, and the like—they boast and vaunt themselves before the world, yet in their hearts there is an unspoken fear. They are afraid of words and thoughts: words spoken abroad, thoughts stirring at home—all the more powerful because forbidden—terrify them. A little mouse of thought appears in the room and even the mightiest potentates are thrown into a panic. (*In His Own Words;* from an address to the people of the United States given in 1938.)

Let me read that again. I like that sentence: "A little mouse of thought appears in the room and even the mightiest potentates are thrown into a panic."

Thoughts Cannot Be Hidden

"Thought," someone said, "is a conversation we hold with ourselves." While it is a very silent conversation, that we hold it with ourselves alone I very much doubt. Thoughts cannot be hidden.

In the Book of Mormon, again there is considerable information on the subject. Let me read just a few of the references. There are many more; these are just selected. From Alma:

And it came to pass that Ammon, *being filled with the Spirit of God,* therefore *he perceived the thoughts* of the king. (Alma 18:16; italics added.)

From Jacob:

But behold, hearken ye unto me, and know that *by the help of the all-powerful Creator* of heaven and earth I can *tell you concerning your thoughts.* (Jacob 2:5; italics added.)

From 3 Nephi:

And he said unto them: Behold I know your thoughts. (3 Nephi 28:6.)

And again from Alma:

Now when the king had heard these words, he marveled again, for he beheld that Ammon *could discern his thoughts.* (Alma 18:18; italics added.)

This power of discernment is a very real spiritual gift. It is often conferred as a blessing upon men ordained as bishops, stake presidents, and so forth. Many can bear witness to the fact that they do not have to hear or to see all that they know, that they can discern thoughts when the purpose of their office is served.

34

I have often thought, as members of the Church come to us as General Authorities for counsel, that they are not aware that sometimes their words are in one avenue and their thoughts are in another, and yet it is important that we learn that we cannot hide our thoughts. You can't hide them. Sooner or later, they will be known; they will express themselves in actions. "As [a man] thinketh in his heart, so is he." (Proverbs 23:7.) As a man thinketh in his heart, so he does.

One Thought at a Time

The next thing I mention about thoughts is of signal importance. You may disagree, but I suggest you consider it *very* carefully before you decide.

Did you know that you can only think of one thing at a time? Did you know that every time you think a good thought, there is no room for a bad one?

To know this is of significant worth. Our minds may switch from one thought to another very quickly; nevertheless, there is only a single circuit—only one thought is processed at a time.

The matter I discussed with Dr. Lowe related to time-sharing on computers. Many organizations that could profitably use a computer cannot afford one. Therefore, there are agencies which sell time on computers. From a business office one can feed information by dataphone to the computer and receive back, at the end of its calculation, the processed data.

Several may want to use the computer at exactly the same time. Inasmuch as the computer has a one-track mind, a priority-interrupt system is employed.

If you can pay for the highest priority, no matter what the computer is doing when you send the signal in, it will stop. It can store that operation in its auxiliary memory bank, complete your work, return it to you, and then resume what it was doing. If you have a lower priority, your work has to wait.

Our thoughts are like that—one operation at a time, but shifting back and forth, paying attention to priority items. It is important that we know this because then we can give priority to significant and important thoughts.

That All May Be Edified

Thoughts Can Be Influenced

Thoughts are subject to influence. Students, occasionally, hopefully, your thoughts are even influenced by college teachers. Our thoughts are subject to influence from other sources—good and evil, both from without, from the physical and the environmental world, and from sources within.

Our thoughts control the behavior of the physical body. If our thoughts are lazy and undisciplined, this process may be (and unfortunately very often is) reversed—with the physical body controlling the thoughts—a bondage, as it were, to clay.

Our thoughts are subject to spiritual influence. Inspiration can and does come from God. He is real, and it is real.

Temptation, another kind of inspiration, can assert itself from the adversary; it is equally real. (My secretary, in typing the foregoing sentence, misspelled a word and inadvertently invented a very usable one—"sinspiration".) So we are subject to inspiration and sinspiration. But, regardless of the influence and regardless of the source, the most important consideration is that *we may choose.* We are free to choose. The Lord said to Adam:

> Nevertheless, thou mayest *choose* for thyself, for it is given unto thee. (Moses 3:17; italics added.)

In a similar way, the opportunity to choose is given to us. Herein lies the agency of man. There is no more ennobling or exalted concept than to know that men are free, if they will, to think what they will.

> All the water in the world, however hard it tried,
>   Could never sink the smallest ship, unless it gets inside.
> All the evil in the world, the blackest kind of sin,
>   Can never hurt you one least bit, unless you let it in.
>
> (Author unidentified.)

It is important to know that we have our agency. The Book of Mormon confirms that "men are instructed sufficiently that they know good from evil." (2 Nephi 2:5.)

We *are accountable* for what we think; we *are responsible* for what we think. We *can* tell good from evil *if we will.* Therefore, I repeat again those things that we should know about our thoughts:

— That they are the control center for all action;

— That they are powerful;

— That they are individual, meaning that we can think of only one thing at a time;

— That they are subject to influence—both from the physical and from the environmental world, and from the realm of the spiritual—both good and bad;

— That we are free to choose.

Channel Your Thoughts

When I was about ten years old, we lived in a home surrounded by an orchard. There never seemed to be enough water for the trees. The ditches were always fresh-plowed in the spring, but after the first few irrigating turns, the weeds would spring up in the ditch bottoms and soon they were choked with water grass, June grass, and redroot. One day, in charge of the irrigating turn, I found myself in trouble. As the water moved down the rows choked with weeds, it carried enough leaves and grass and debris to lodge against the weed stocks and flood the water from the ditch. I raced through the puddles, trying to build the banks up a little higher, to keep the water in the channel. As soon as I had one break patched up there would be another one flooding over in another spot.

About that time an older brother came through the lot with a friend of his who was majoring in agriculture. He watched me for a moment, then with a few vigorous strokes of the shovel he cleared the weeds from the dampened ditch bottom and allowed the water to course through the channel he had dug.

"You will waste the whole irrigating turn patching up the banks," he said. "If you want the water to stay on its course, you have to make a place for it to go."

I have learned that thoughts, like water, will follow the course if we *make* a place for them to go. Otherwise, we may spend all our time frantically patching up the banks and may find that our "turn" is over and that we have wasted the day of our probation.

Now, for a moment, could I leave off being a *speaker* and be a *teacher?* I have great reverence for the title "teacher." I want to tell you of one way you can control your thoughts. It is simple. It may seem so elementary that you will think it unimportant. But, if you will, it may help you.

37

That All May Be Edified

The Mind Is a Stage

The mind is like a stage. Except when we are asleep, the curtain is always up. Always there is some act being performed on that stage. It may be a laughing comedy or an aggrieved and tragic drama. It may be interesting or dull. It may be clear or it may be confused. It may be strenuous or perhaps relaxing. But *always,* except when we are asleep, *always* there is some act playing on that stage of the mind.

Have you noticed that, without any real intent on your part and almost in the midst of any performance, a shady little thought may creep in from the wings and endeavor to attract your attention? These delinquent little thoughts, these unsavory characters, will try to upstage everybody. If you permit them to go on, all other thoughts, of any virtue, will leave the stage. You will be left, because you consented to it, to the influence of unworthy thoughts.

If you pay attention to them, if you yield to them, they will enact for you on this stage of the mind, anything to the limit of your toleration. It may be vulgar, immoral, depraved, ugly. Their theme may be of bitterness, jealousy, excessive grief, even hatred. When they have the stage, if you let them, they will devise the cleverest persuasions to hold your attention. They can make it interesting, all right, even apparently innocent—for they are but thoughts.

What do you do at a time like this, when the stage of your mind is commandeered by these imps of unclean thinking? Whether they be the gray ones that look almost white; or the dustier ones, more questionable yet; or the filthy ones, which leave no room for doubt, what do you do?

This, then, is what I would teach you: Let me suggest that you choose from among the sacred music of the Church one favorite hymn. I have reason for suggesting that it be a Latter-day Saint hymn, one with lyrics that are uplifting and the music reverent. Select one that, when it is properly rendered, makes you feel something akin to inspiration.

Now, go over it in your mind very thoughtfully a few times. Memorize the words and the music. Even though you have had no musical training, even though you do not play an instrument, and even though your voice may leave something to be desired, you can think through a hymn. I suspect you already have a favorite. I have stressed

38

Let Virtue Garnish Thy Thoughts

how important it is to know that you can only think of *one* thing at a time. Use this hymn as your emergency channel. Use this as the place for your thoughts to go. Anytime you find that these shady actors have slipped in from the sideline of your thinking onto the stage of your mind, think through this hymn. "Put the record on," as it were, and then you will begin to know something about controlling your thoughts. "Music is one of the most forceful instruments for governing the mind and spirit of man." (William F. Gladstone.) It will change the whole mood on the stage of your mind. Because it is clean and uplifting and reverent, the baser thoughts will leave.

While virtue, by choice, *will not* endure the presence of filth, that which is debased and unclean *cannot* endure the light.

Virtue *will not* associate with filth, while evil *cannot* tolerate the presence of good.

Something of this is also explained in the Book of Mormon, when we are told:

> Ye would be more miserable to dwell with a holy and just God, under a consciousness of your filthiness before him, than ye would to dwell with the damned souls in hell. (Mormon 9:4.)

That is all I have come here to say. At first this simple little procedure may seem to you so trivial as to be unimportant and ineffective. With a little experimenting, you will learn that it is not easy, but it is *powerfully* effective.

No Good Thought Is Ever Lost

One final declaration: No good thought is ever lost. No turn of the mind, however brief or transitory or illusive, if it is good, is ever wasted. No thought of sympathy, nor of forgiveness, no reflection on generosity or of courage or of purity, no meditation on humility or gratitude or reverence, is ever lost. The frequency with which they are experienced is the measure of you. The more constant they become, the more you are worth, or, in scriptural terms, the more you are worthy. Every clean thought *becomes* you. Every clean thought becomes *you.*

I pay tribute to the faculty, the teachers at this great university—inspired men and women working with dedication. You who are students have the great privilege of spending with them your waking

That All May Be Edified

hours; your minds are productively employed under the tutelage of inspired teachers:

> That you may be instructed more perfectly in theory, in principle, in doctrine, in the law of the gospel, in all things that pertain unto the kingdom of God, that are expedient for you to understand;
>
> Of things both in heaven and in the earth, and under the earth; things which have been, things which are, things which must shortly come to pass; things which are at home, things which are abroad; the wars and the perplexities of the nations, and the judgments which are on the land; and a knowledge also of countries and of kingdoms—
>
> That ye may be prepared in all things. (D & C 88:78-80.)

We come to bear witness that the gospel of Jesus Christ is true, that The Church of Jesus Christ of Latter-day Saints is His Church, that this is His school. And as you study here we admonish you:

> Let virtue garnish thy thoughts unceasingly; then shall thy confidence wax strong in the presence of God; and the doctrine of the priesthood shall distill upon thy soul as the dews from heaven.
>
> The Holy Ghost shall be thy constant companion, and thy scepter an unchanging scepter of righteousness and truth; and thy dominion shall be an everlasting dominion, and without compulsory means it shall flow unto thee forever and ever. (D & C 121:45-46.)

In the name of Jesus Christ, amen.

5

Seek Learning Even by Study and Also by Faith

I have regarded the assignment to speak to you much as I regard an assignment to speak in general conference. This is a much smaller audience than we face at general conference, but I do not see just a group of faculty members and their partners assembled here. I see through you to the classes assembled before you. My vision does not stop there: I see through them to their families; I see classes and congregations and conferences led by those you teach.

Students Vary

Your students vary in preparation. Some, with hardly a flicker of a testimony, are acquainted with only the mere rudiments of gospel learning. They need to be taught more, enlarged more, before a permanent testimony can find a place with them. With these be wise. Feed them milk before they receive meat. Others come eager, converted, yet unlearned, seeking to enlarge their knowledge of the gospel and strengthen their testimonies. With these be careful.

I see, also, missionaries in goodly numbers: home from the service with the maturity of veterans. Some of them do not quite understand all they know about the gospel, although they desire to appear otherwise. This constitutes a challenge to you—and an unequaled opportunity.

I see others, sharp, cynical, skeptical, in the know-it-all arrogance of blossoming young manhood and womanhood. They have inquisitive minds. They are easily taught—and easily led astray. Teach these with extra care.

I see a few others, also, whose lives are tainted already. Transgressors, yet groping and reaching. Let them know there is a way for

---

Address given to the instructors of religion at Brigham Young University April 1974.

them to bathe in the refreshing, cleansing waters of repentance and to become clean again. Guide them to the branch president.

They come in all different combinations of these types. You are to teach them the gospel.

Through an Overhead Projector

Most of you have used an overhead projector. You therefore know what a transparency is and what an overlay is. One can project a map or a plan and then, with a transparent overlay, emphasize some detail that otherwise may be overlooked. What I shall attempt to do is to pinpoint a feature or two against the background history of religious education at Brigham Young University and in the Church. You should already be familiar with that history, and we can give it little attention, save to spotlight a place or two where we may have stubbed our toe, where we have tripped and almost stumbled. If we are wise we will step over such places in the future.

Long before the University was organized, Brigham Young stated:

> We want every branch of science taught in this place that is taught in the world. But our favorite study is that branch which particularly belongs to the Elders of Israel—namely, theology. Every Elder should become a profound theologian—should understand this branch better than all the world. (*Journal of Discourses* 6:317.)

And we are all familiar with President Young's classic instruction to Brother Maeser: "I want you to remember that you ought not to teach even the alphabet or the multiplication tables without the spirit of God." (*Karl G. Maeser: A Biography by His Son,* p. 79.) And so the University was established.

Softening Early Unpopularity

The Church was *most* unpopular in those days. For instance, there appeared in a national magazine a series of three articles entitled "The Viper on the Hearth." The pages were bordered with drawings of rattlesnakes. The President of the Church was cartooned as an octopus. It was declared to be an authentic treatment of the Church, for the author had not written from a distance: He had come to Salt Lake City himself. He stayed in a leading hotel and engaged a cabby who seemed very knowledgeable on the goings-on in the city. The cabby became the "reliable source." Nevertheless, much of what was printed then, as now, was believed by the world. We were *very* unpopular.

We wanted—and not without good reason—to be more accepted than we were. We wanted to say to the world somehow, "We are decent folks. We are interested in the things that decent people are interested in. We have a university, and it shall be a good one. We will not merely meet your standard; we shall surpass it."

From the very beginning, courses in theology were basic at the University. Evidently we wanted very much to grow in the eyes of the world, for in reaching for a standard of gospel scholarship we even looked outside of the Church.

As early as 1922, Dr. Charles Edward Rugh came to the campus to teach at the Summer School. "Religious Education" and "How to Teach the Bible" were his subjects. Later came Dr. Coe from the Teacher's College of Columbia. Doctors Graham, McNeil, and Bower followed. And no less than Dr. Edgar J. Goodspeed, eminent New Testament translator and authority, and Dr. William J. Allbright, archaeologist and biblical scholar, were invited to the campus to instruct our teachers of religion.

And so the process began. They learned that we were decent folks, and we learned from them. But there was a limit to what they could contribute; for although they were gentlemen and scholars indeed, they were without the priesthood and were therefore essentially uninspired.

Institute of Religion

At about that time (1926), the institutes of religion were established; and soon there was encouragement, both for the men in the institute program and for the teachers of religion at Brigham Young University, to go away and get advanced degrees. "Go study under the great religious scholars of the world," was the encouragement, "for we will set an academic standard in theology."

And a number of them went. Some who went never returned. And some of them who returned never came back. They had followed, they supposed, the scriptural injunction: "Seek learning, even by study and also by faith." (D & C 88:118.) But somehow the mix had been wrong. For they had sought learning out of the best books, even by study, but with too little faith. They found themselves in conflict with the simple things of the gospel. One by one they found their way outside the field of teaching religion, outside Church activity, and a few of them outside the Church itself. And with each went a following of his students—a

43

That All May Be Edified

terrible price to pay. I could name a number of these men, as could many of you. Somehow the mix had been wrong: too much "by study," too little "by faith."

Happily, though, some of those who went away to study returned magnified by their experience and armed with advanced degrees. They returned firm in their knowledge that a man can be in the world but not of the world. They had mastered their subjects without, as President John Taylor had warned,

> Imbibing, at the same time, the spirit of infidelity concerning our great creator and his attitudes and the plan of salvation which he has revealed. (Letter to Presidents of Stakes and Bishops of Wards. *The Inquirer,* June 10, 1887.)

This pulling at the moorings by some of our teachers of religion did not go unnoticed in the councils of the Church. Dr. John A. Widtsoe and Dr. Joseph F. Merrill of the Council of the Twelve (I refer to them by their academic titles instead of by *Elder* for a purpose) were directed by the First Presidency to conduct courses for the teachers of religion to anchor them again to the moorings.

Checking the Moorings

Such efforts were repeated from time to time. In 1938 all seminary and institute personnel were assembled for Summer School in Aspen Grove. They were not a large group by present standards. President J. Reuben Clark, Jr., speaking for the First Presidency of the Church, presented instruction entitled "The Charted Course of the Church in Education."

We have, I am sure, all read this document. But some of us have not read it enough. President Clark was a prophet, seer, and revelator. There is not the slightest question but that exceptional inspiration attended the preparation of his message. There is a clarity and power in his words, unusual even for him. I know you have read it before, some of you many times, but I assign you to read it again. Read it carefully and ponder it. For by applying the definition the Lord Himself gave, this instruction may comfortably be referred to as scripture.

I leave out much that might be said of these most interesting years. This, I remind you, is but an overlay, a transparent page over a well-known background, with a few markings here and there to emphasize this feature or that. The dichotomy between learning "by study" and learning "by faith" was receiving attention when I was hired as a seminary teacher twenty-five years ago. The Brethren had more confidence in the teachers of religion at Brigham Young University then, than in those in the institute program.

At about that time there was a change in the leadership of Church education. It was time once again to check the moorings. So, in 1954, all the seminary and institute teachers (by this time a goodly number) were assembled for the first time in many years for a Summer School of intensive instruction. The Brethren sent a teacher, Elder Harold B. Lee, of the Council of the Twelve Apostles. We met two hours each day, five days a week, for five weeks. Frequently he would invite other members of the Council of the Twelve and members of the First Presidency of the Church to instruct us in class or in special evening sessions.

There was good reason to check the moorings. For there had grown up among many teachers the feeling that the teaching of basic principles of the gospel might somehow be left perhaps to the Sunday School. These few teachers felt there were more interesting things to do in their classes. They could explore some of the side roads, those that had not received attention in Sunday School or from the Brethren.

They seemed to feel that a testimony would come automatically to their students. Perhaps by accretion the environment would satisfy that need, and they would add the unusual things that they had discovered in their academic wandering. Some took their students with them on these academic excursions, and many of them were lost.

Follow the Brethren

I recall that day nearly twenty years ago when I was appointed as supervisor of seminaries. In those days President Berrett, Brother Tuttle, and I spent no small part of our time trying to satisfy the inquiries of General Authorities who had been to conferences throughout the Church and had received complaints that some students, while studying religion at Church schools, had lost their testimonies.

On one significant occasion, Brother Tuttle and I set aside our appointments for the day. We spent the day wrestling with the problems of our seminary and institute teachers. No small amount of time was spent on our knees appealing to the Almighty for guidance. We did not think then—nor do I think now—that we or you should work without inspiration in our assignments. The exertions of that day brought us three simple words: Follow the Brethren. This became our motto. With the encouragement of William E. Berrett, this we would teach, and this we would live.

As we moved about the Church, meeting with the seminary and institute men, all, save a few, rallied—most with rejoicing, for they had not been comfortable about the drifting.

"Division of Religion"

At about that time I had my first close association with the teachers of religion at Brigham Young University. In those days they labored under a designation that unfortunately was only too descriptive, the "Division of Religion."

They were not only divided among themselves, but from the faculties of the other disciplines at the University. They were divided from their brethren in the seminaries and institutes of religion, compatriots who, like themselves, had chosen to devote themselves to the occupation of teaching the gospel of Jesus Christ in the classroom. Some of them were divided in lengthy philosophical contests, for the most part over what mix there would be in the learning "by study" and also "by faith."

It is not uncommon when men square off in such debates for them to back up after each swing, to get a little more throwing room. They find themselves increasingly further apart, backing in disagreement until they find themselves defending ground that neither would have claimed at the beginning of the contest. How difficult a thing it is and how humbling it is to come all the way back to middle ground, close enough to touch again, to shake hands, and to work shoulder to shoulder thereafter!

Those were difficult days. They are long since gone, and, oh, how little the grief at their passing!

In the Division of Religion, the brethren wanted, and naturally so, a place in the sun. They wanted more attention for their work and perhaps for themselves. The Division of Religion, which in the beginning had five faculty members (not all of whom taught courses in religion exclusively), had grown in 1958 to twenty-eight members. They petitioned the Board of Education for college status. I quote from a paragraph from Brother Cowan's "History of the College of Religious

46

Instruction" and will emphasize—perhaps exaggerate—a word or two from that petition to make a point:

> The faculty believed there were definite reasons for granting college status to the Division of Religion. The Division, for example, now offered graduate degrees, while some "colleges" granted undergraduate degrees only. The title, "director," furthermore, did not have the same prestige as "dean." In a memorandum the faculty declared that "The recommended change would do much for the *prestige* of the *academic* religion program of the University." They added: "We believe that these proposals will help to elevate religion *in fact* to the high level of academic respectability which we are sure the President of the University and his Associates and the General Authorities of the Church wanted to have on this campus." (Pp. 27-28; emphasis added.)

College of Religious Instruction

In January of 1959, the College of Religious Instruction was organized.

On the day following the Board action, President Ernest L. Wilkinson met with the First Presidency of the Church. He reported in a memo to Earl Crockett, Academic Vice-President, that President McKay had cautioned him that "We must always remember at BYU that religion is to be taught in any and all subjects and not confined to the College of Religion."

With the establishment of the College of Religious Instruction came the responsibility to offer doctorates in several areas: Church history and doctrine, religious education, and ancient scripture. A great deal of work was done by worthy and dedicated brethren to establish the college. An adequate faculty was assembled; and, in line with the desire to achieve excellence, the college was subjected to continual academic refinement. In 1966 it became fully accredited. The question of whether or not graduate degrees in religion should be granted, however, continued to be a subject of discussion. And somewhere in the middle of those discussions was always the basic question of learning out of the best books "even by study" and "also by faith."

There were practical problems to face, for when a man had earned his degree, there was, after all was said and done, but a single marketplace for the sale of his services. That was the Church Educational System. If he did not prove to be an able teacher, he had no other place

47

to turn for employment. This problem was not lightly considered by the faculty, by the Board of Education, or by the individuals themselves. I had to wrestle with this problem myself. I was determined to pursue a doctorate and after much reflection and prayer and after seeking counsel, turned to the College of Education.

The breadth and depth of this problem in Church education can hardly be touched here. I remind you that this is but an overlay, highlighting a point here and there.

On May 3, 1972, the Board of Education decided that no doctor's degrees would be awarded by the College of Religious Instruction and that courses of study leading to the master's degree in religion were to be discouraged.

This decision could not help producing, in the minds and feelings of many faculty members, several serious questions. The way the decision was accepted by the faculty of the college is indeed a remarkable thing in the history of education and in the history of the Church.

You, my brethren, are something special. I salute you. Where else on this earth could we find such a collection of men to trust? You are independent in your feelings and in your thinking. You hold the highest degrees offered by institutions of higher learning. And yet, you were not only obedient to the decision, but participated in making it. It is, indeed, a remarkable thing and will not go unnoticed when each is individually called up on that day for further examination of a spiritual kind.

The college continued. And you continued to be regarded as ordinary faculty members of a college at the University. The expression "Publish or perish," understood by all of you, was thought to apply to you as it might to others.

It is, of course, the hope that faculty members in the other colleges will lead the world in their disciplines. And ideal it would be to have the highest authority in these fields at our own University.

It is not to a university, however, that the world must turn for ultimate authority in the field of religion. In your field something else obtains. By direction of Him whose Church this is, that authority is held by a group of ordinary men called from many walks of life, including yours, who are ordained as Apostles, sustained as prophets, seers, and revelators, and presided over by one authorized to exercise all the keys of spiritual authority existing upon the earth. And so, the next step, the logical one and the right one, was not long in coming.

New Vision of Religious Instruction

The College of Religious Instruction was dissolved. Your work is not to be isolated as the other disciplines may well be. It was announced that hereafter religious education would not be limited to one college. It will be an influence contributing to, and drawing from, every segment of the University. This decision could not help but cause some anxiety and raise questions with many of you. Among the questions: "Did the administration intend to eliminate the position of teaching religion full time?" In no meeting of the Board or of the Executive Committee was that matter even discussed. Those who were concerned about it experienced what one little boy described as "a waste of worry."

Once again, the acceptance of the decision was a remarkable thing. It could not have been achieved with an assembly of brethren less than you are. I hope you can understand how this decision is a significant vote of confidence in you. Perhaps we needed the experience of having a college of religion. Certainly that experience will serve us for generations to come.

And so now, with the retirement of Brother Doxey as the Dean of the College of Religious Instruction, we reach a milestone in the history of the Church. After these many years of preparation, our efforts and exertions have brought us at last to the place where we belong.

The title Division of Religion is gone, and its uncomplimentary meaning has faded. The College of Religious Instruction has now been dissolved; for that too, by the very title, tended to isolate you from the other faculties, who sometimes assumed that they had little responsibility for the spiritual development of their students. Now they all become eligible to join you in the teaching of religion classes. And though they are specialists in other fields, they should be adequate in the teaching of these classes.

Now, will our men who are to teach religion full time go away for their advanced degrees? Yes, many will, but there is a big difference now as compared with earlier years. Now there is an institute of

49

religion there, where they may refuel their faith as they seek learning out of the best books by study.

Your work has now moved from *a* college to *the* University. And it goes beyond that: Because the fences between you and your companions in the seminaries and institutes have largely been taken down, your influence will extend more easily across the Church.

Jeffrey Roy Holland

A new leader has now been appointed: Brother Jeffrey Roy Holland (I refer to him by the title *Brother* rather than by his academic title for a purpose), dean of Religious Instruction. The appointment of Brother Holland, I am sure, has raised in the minds of many of you, three questions. First, Who is he? Next, How was he chosen? And finally, Why was he chosen?

The first question: Who is he? Well, at this point he is just somebody. He served as a missionary in Great Britain. He graduated from Brigham Young University. And while working on his master's, he taught undergraduate courses in your field. He has had some considerable success as a scholar, and he received his doctorate in American studies at Yale University. He has taught in the institutes of religion at Yale, at Seattle, and at the University of Utah.

He has served as a bishop and as a member of a stake presidency. Recently he has been serving as executive secretary of the Melchizedek Priesthood Mutual Improvement Association of the Church and as a member of the General Board of that organization. This has brought him into close association with the General Authorities and has given him insights on how the Church is administered.

The second question: How was he chosen? Well, how would you want the dean of religious education to be chosen? Like the dean of engineering or of physical education? Would you appoint a search committee, have them survey the field, request dossiers, advertise for applicants, interview every member of the faculty for a possible candidate?

Well, of course, there was much of that. But mostly it was done in the way a bishop is chosen, or a stake president, or a General Authority. That is the way the President of this University was chosen. Doing it that way means that some very eligible candidates may not receive much attention. But the right one was not missed. Invariably he is found. Ordinarily he is found hanging back a little, wanting to stand just halfway behind someone else: sensing, perhaps, what is coming and not anxious to meet it.

When Brother Holland began to emerge as the choice, I was asked, as a member of the Executive Committee of the Board, to take a look at him. I invited him to attend a stake quarterly conference at some distance from Church headquarters, in order that we could have many hours of travel time together. I examined him against every measurement with which I am conversant. My recommendation was firm and affirmative.

The third question that might be asked is, Why was he chosen? Let me tell you of an experience I had as president of a mission. I needed a new assistant and had prayed much about the matter. I then called zone conferences, where I met and interviewed every missionary, always with the thought in my mind, "Is this the man?" The answer finally came: "This is the man." He was appointed. He had been permitted to come on a mission only after some considerable shaping up to become eligible.

After the announcement one of the zone leaders came to see me privately. He came from the same community in the West as did the new assistant. He was obviously disturbed. His first question was, "Do you really know the elder you have appointed as your assistant?"

"Yes, Elder. I know all that you know about him, and a good deal more," was my answer.

"Why, then, was *he* appointed your assistant?"

I pondered for a moment and then said, "Elder, why don't you ask the question that you came to ask?"

"What do you mean?"

"Ask the question that is really on your mind," I encouraged.

"But I did," he said.

"No," I said. "There is another question. The thing that is on your mind is not 'Why did you appoint him as your assistant'; it is 'Why did you not appoint me?'"

Now please understand. I thought his unexpressed question to be a very logical and sensible one. For it included this thought: *Here I am. I have worked as hard as I know how to work. All my life I have been a straight arrow. I have not rebelled nor been disobedient. I have prepared myself for a mission in every way I knew how to prepare. I have been*

51

That All May Be Edified

trained, and I have studied. I have respected my parents and my bishop, and I have presided over my quorums. And here I am a missionary.

Now another, whose path has been crooked, who has skipped meetings and dabbled in mischief, who winked at restriction and snickered at obedience, has been elevated above me. I had sympathy for this young man and admired him greatly for his courage to speak.

"If you should ask why you were not chosen," I said, "I would have to answer, 'I do not know, Elder.' I only know that he was chosen. Perhaps he may fail. But at least I know he is the one with the combination of talents and ability and qualities best calculated to get done what the office needs at the moment.

"This is no reflection upon you. You may yet preside over him and many above him. You may be his bishop or his stake president. You may preside over the Church. I do not know. But his call is no reflection upon you. Do not be injured by it.

"Go back to work and serve the Lord. Sustain him," I counseled. "Your contest is not with him but with yourself."

And then I gently added, "You may have a bit of repenting to do."

Some weeks later I saw him again. This time he said with simple assurance, "I know one reason why he was appointed your assistant. So that I could learn the greatest lesson that I have ever learned in my life."

And now, to give Brother Holland perspective, I quote from a letter I received when I was appointed supervisor of seminaries. It came from Brother Wilford W. Richards, Director of the Institute of Religion at Utah State University. He had been my teacher and was my friend. After a sentence of congratulation, he said, "You are just the man for the job. Now all you have to do is prove it."

On Course

So, here we are. We find ourselves on course. We are in the right place, and we are on schedule. Your influence will be extended. If faculty members from other disciplines make disparaging remarks about you—as some might—because you do not fit *anywhere,* be wise enough to accept the remark as a compliment and know that you fit *everywhere.* In so doing, they are, for the most part, trying to reassure themselves that what they do is worthwhile. And it is. Very much worthwhile.

On the other hand, be careful lest you be condescending toward your brethren in the seminaries and institutes of the Church. If you are critical of them, as some have been, it may be an effort to reassure yourself that what you do is as important as what they do. And it is. But how could it be any more important?

I remind you again that these thoughts have been but a few pin-points on a transparent overlay. Behind them is the background of history, deserving more attention than we could possibly give it here, or than it could receive in a single book.

May I counsel you as to where you might stumble. First, avoid the tendency to feed meat when milk would suffice. Surely that reference needs no explanation to you.

Next, there may be the tendency for you to teach without talent and inspiration because you have a captive audience. Every student at the University is obliged to take religion courses during every semester that he is in residence. No student will be penalized by this rule unless you take advantage of it and become lazy.

Next, many of you are specialists, and you ought to continue to specialize. But please know that however specialized you become in one thing, you must remain expert in several others. For instance, if you are a specialist in the archaeology of the Old Testament, there is not the slightest excuse for you to be deficient as a teacher of the Book of Mormon or of the Doctrine and Covenants or of the New Testament. If you are assigned to teach these areas to undergraduates and feel that you are being misused because you are a specialist, you need to repent. If you have a tendency to set aside these things, you are drifting from what it is all about.

The adulation of the young can easily be misunderstood and mis-used. If you are a talented teacher, you may have the tendency to be as foolish as the missionary who draws a convert, not to the gospel and the Church, but to himself. I caution you vigorously about that.

I add the tendency to be diverted from your teachings to do research and writing. Now, that may sound strange to you, but it seems to me that writing and research are, in true perspective, subsidiary to teaching. Both can make teaching more effective. Each has a proper place. I do not say ignore them; I say do not be diverted by them.

May I mention something about writing? Some of you are very interested in writing and in compiling (there is a very big difference). It is easy to become a good deal more interested in what writing or compiling the work of others will draw from the marketplace than in what it might yield to a student.

Finally, I speak of pedagogical hobbies. A teacher may see something to which others may not be paying adequate attention. He may appoint himself to see that it is not neglected, and then overdo it. Almost anything can be overemphasized, as well as neglected. We have examples of that in religious education as it relates to economics or politics, to patterns of Church government, even to the priesthood. I advise you to be careful and remember this Book of Mormon definition:

> Priestcrafts are that men preach and set themselves up for a light unto the world, that they may get gain and praise of the world; but they seek not the welfare of Zion. (2 Nephi 26:29.)

In the words of President J. Reuben Clark:

> You teachers have a great mission. As teachers you stand upon the highest peak in education, for what teaching can compare in priceless value and in far-reaching effect with that which deals with man as he was in the eternity of yesterday, as he is in the mortality of today, and as he will be in the forever of tomorrow. Not only time but eternity is your field. Salvation of yourself not only, but of those who come within the purlieus of your temple, is the blessing you seek, and which, doing your duty, you will gain. How brilliant will be your crown of glory, with each soul saved an encrusted jewel thereon.
>
> But to get this blessing and to be so crowned, you must, I say once more, you must teach the gospel. You have no other function and no other reason for your presence in a Church school system....
>
> So I say I pay my tribute to your industry, your loyalty, your sacrifice, your willing eagerness for service in the cause of truth, your faith in God and in His work, and your earnest desire to do the things that our ordained leader and Prophet would have you do. And I entreat you not to make the mistake of thrusting aside your leader's counsel, or of failing to carry out his wish, or of refusing to follow his direction. David of old, privily cutting off only the skirt of Saul's robe, uttered the cry of a smitten heart: "The Lord forbid that I should do this thing unto my master, the Lord's anointed, to stretch forth mine hand against him, seeing he is the anointed of the Lord."
>
> May God bless you always in all your righteous endeavors, may he quicken your understanding, increase your wisdom, enlighten you by experience, bestow upon you patience, charity, and, as among your most precious gifts, endow you with the discernment of spirits that you may certainly know the spirit of righteousness and its opposite as they come to you; may he give you entrance to the hearts of those you teach and then

_____

Seek Learning Even by Study and Also by Faith

make you know that as you enter there you stand in holy places, that must be neither polluted nor defiled, either by false or corrupting doctrine or by sinful misdeed; may he enrich your knowledge with the skill and power to teach righteousness; may your faith and your testimonies increase, and your ability to encourage and foster them in others grow greater every day—all that the youth of Zion may be taught, built up, encouraged, heartened, that they may not fall by the wayside, but go on to eternal life, that these blessings coming to them, you through them may be blessed also. (*The Charted Course of the Church in Education,* pp. 9-11.)

Again I commend you, our brethren. I bear testimony that the gospel of Jesus Christ is true, that the Church is precisely what the Lord defined it to be, the only true and living church upon the face of the whole earth. These major decisions that have been made with reference to your work have been righteous decisions. You have accepted them well. They have been made by the servants of the Lord. I bear testimony that they are correct. For the Lord has said:

What I the Lord have spoken, I have spoken, and I excuse not myself; and though the heavens and the earth pass away, my word shall not pass away, but shall all be fulfilled, whether by mine own voice or by the voice of my servants, it is the same.

For behold, and lo, the Lord is God, and the Spirit beareth record, and the record is true, and the truth abideth forever and ever. (D&C 1:38-39.)

In the name of Jesus Christ, amen.

Walls of encouragement *are lifted up.*

Encouragement

"Right now I may not know who you really are or where you have been or what you have done. Most of that... will not matter. I take you just as you are and stamp you 'A-Grade, Number 1.' You can prove yourself to be less than that, but you will have to work at it. I will be very reluctant to believe it. If there is something about yourself that you do not like, now is the time to change it. If there is something in your past that has been disabling, spiritually or otherwise, now is the time to rise above it." (From Boyd K. Packer, *Teach Ye Diligently.* Salt Lake City: Deseret Book Co., 1975, p. 78.)

That All May Be Edified

The young man approached me, his seminary teacher, and hesitantly said, "Brother Packer, I think you have made a mistake. You have given me someone else's grade." I examined the *B* on his report card. (All his other grades were *C, D,* or *F.*)

"Yes, that is what I intended to write down," I told him. "If there has been a mistake, it has been a mistake in timing. Perhaps I have given it to you a little before you have earned it, but I think it is not a mistake."

The motivational principle of treating a person "as if" is one which I firmly believe. My observation and experience have led me to know that, with very few exceptions, people want to rise above themselves. This attitude of confidence and trust has a stabilizing effect in all of our relationships. This attitude was not always mine. Because I had once been badly used by someone I trusted, I tended to be suspicious of those I met and was reluctant to trust them.

Serious and sincere introspection revealed that this was a weakness that I must overcome if I were to progress spiritually. And so, with effort (as all change requires) I cultivated an attitude of trust. If someone proves unworthy of trust, it is *his* responsibility to show it—not mine to find it out. People, including our own children, I believe, will rise to our high expectation of them. I have found few exceptions. They do not trouble me. If one exception is the price of extending trust to everyone, I am glad to pay it. It may be painful when trust or confidence is not honored. That kind of pain is bearable for it is only pain. It is not agony; but I have known agony when I have discovered that inadvertently I have misused someone.

Experience has made me sensitive and aware of human frailty (including my own). Coupled with this trust of people, a faith in their ultimate potential makes it possible to effectively encourage them toward it.

Basic to our ability in this area is the knowledge that we all had a pre-mortal state and that we share a parent-child relationship to God the Father. This truth means that some spiritual ideals that would be difficult to teach may be *caught* as well as *taught* and are found as a natural possession of even little children.

With this in-depth spiritual knowledge, we are able to "show" a person his divine potential in such a way that he, too, can catch the vision of it. Beyond that, skilled teachers have the gift of encouraging by example and practical suggestion the sincere, seeking, willing candidate to expend the necessary soul energy to make the desired change toward the goal of perfection.

The talks in this section were prepared for a variety of audiences and they span a sixteen-year period.

(6) "The Balm of Gilead" recognizes a common debilitating malady—hurt and bitterness—which always robs us of joy and hampers or stops our spiritual growth. This chapter is aimed at "making the wounded whole." Years ago we had a stake president who later became our patriarch. He had served three times as a mission president. When he was older, his eyesight would not permit him to drive at night. He would reluctantly ask if I would drive him to Salt Lake City to the mission reunion. My wife always encouraged me to go, to learn all I could from this wonderful spiritual man. It was on one of those occasions that he opened his heart to me and told me the experience of his early married life which now, by the telling of it in general conference, has helped so many people. The week following conference, I received two telephone calls reporting that lawsuits had been dropped or had been settled by those who had finally realized the value of leaving some things alone. The lesson it contains has as many counterparts as there are people who suffer from the affliction. The true cure is prescribed for those who have the courage and the desire to take it.

(7) "To Help a Miracle" is specifically addressed to sisters whose husbands are not yet members or who are not active in the Church. It is an example of treating the individual "as if" he had already attained his desired level of performance. This talk was first given at the Relief Society session of the area general conference in Manchester, England. Soon letters began to come from sisters who had changed their approach in dealing with an inactive or nonmember husband. By request it was repeated in a Relief Society conference in the Tabernacle. Over the years letters come now and then from sisters who have found the talk, followed the principles it outlines, and, to my great joy, end with such expressions as, "We are going to the temple with our family to be sealed for time and eternity."

(8) Although it was given four years later, "An Appeal to Prospective Elders" follows in natural sequence "To Help a Miracle." The title

indicates to whom it is addressed. The illustration of the "forgotten" language—Japanese—analogous to the forgotten language of the premortal existence—our former home—somehow seems to encourage those who are not yet on the right path. Their redemption is so valuable to the work of the Lord.

(9) Much is written and spoken by Church leaders about welfare storage. "Solving Emotional Problems in the Lord's Own Way" was first given to the students at Brigham Young University and later, by request of the First Presidency, repeated in the welfare session of general conference. It contains the suggestion that a disease of epidemic proportions has infected the Saints. It is "counselitis." As a preventative, it is recommended that members of the Church should store a sufficient supply of emotional and spiritual stability at home rather than at the bishop's office.

(10) This talk is from the early (1962) years of my calling as a General Authority. Although I was speaking to the seminary and institute faculty at Brigham Young University, the message could be useful for all who now teach or desire to teach. I served for several years as a Supervisor of Seminaries and Institutes of Religion and had the opportunity to observe many teachers. I tried to pinpoint superior traits and characteristics from many of them and encourage excellence in teaching by "creating" a compound image of "The Ideal Teacher."

6

The Balm of Gilead

My message is an appeal to those who are worried or restless or anxious, a plea to those who are not at peace. If your life is touched with disappointment, grief, or bitterness; if you struggle constantly with worry, frustration, with shame or anxiety, I speak to you.

The Bible records that in ancient times there came from Gilead, beyond the Jordan, a substance used to heal and soothe. It came, perhaps, from a tree or shrub, and was a major commodity of trade in the ancient world. It was known as the Balm of Gilead. That name became symbolic for the power to soothe and heal.

The lyrics of a song record:

> There is a Balm in Gilead,
> To make the wounded whole.
> There is a Balm in Gilead,
> To heal the sin sick soul.

("There Is a Balm in Gilead," *Recreational Songs,* The Church of Jesus Christ of Latter-day Saints, 1949, p. 130.)

I recently asked a doctor of family medicine how much of his time was devoted purely to correcting physical disorders. He has a large practice, and after thoughtfully considering, he answered, "Not more than 20 percent. The rest of the time I seem to be working on problems that very much affect the physical well-being of my patients but do not originate in the body.

"These physical disorders," the doctor concluded, "are merely symptoms of some other kind of trouble."

In recent generations one after another of the major diseases has yielded to control or cure. Some very major ones still remain, but we now seem able to do something about most of them.

Address given at general conference October 1977.

That All May Be Edified

Man's Spiritual Side

There is another part of us, not so tangible, but quite as real as our physical body. This intangible part of us is described as mind, emotion, intellect, temperament, and many other things. Very seldom is it described as spiritual.

But there is a *spirit* in man; to ignore it is to ignore reality. There are spiritual disorders, too, and spiritual diseases that can cause intense suffering.

The body and the spirit of man are bound together. Often, very often, when there are disorders, it is very difficult to tell which is which.

There are basic rules of physical health that have to do with rest, nourishment, exercise, and with abstaining from those things which damage the body. Those who violate the rules one day pay for their foolishness.

Rules of Spiritual Health

There are also rules of spiritual health, simple rules that cannot be ignored; for if they are, we will reap sorrow by and by.

All of us experience some temporary physical sickness. All of us now and again may be spiritually ill as well. Too many of us, however, are chronically spiritually sick.

We don't need to stay that way. We can learn to avoid spiritual infections and maintain good spiritual health. Even though we have a serious physical ailment, we can be spiritually healthy.

If you suffer from worry, from grief or shame, from jealousy, disappointment, or envy, I have something to tell you.

Somewhere near your home there is a vacant corner lot. Although adjoining yards may be well tended, a vacant corner lot somehow is always full of weeds.

There is a footpath across it, a bicycle trail, and ordinarily it is a collecting place for junk. First someone threw a few lawn clippings there. They would not hurt anything. Someone added a few sticks and limbs from a nearby yard. Then came a few papers and a plastic bag, and finally some tin cans and old bottles were included.

And there it was—a junkyard.

64

The neighbors did not intend it to be that. But little contributions from here and there made it so.

This corner lot is like, so very much like, the minds of many of us. We leave our minds vacant and empty and open to trespass by anyone. Whatever is dumped there we keep.

We would not consciously permit anyone to dump junk into our minds, not old cans and bottles. But after lawn clippings and papers, the other things just don't seem all that much worse.

Our minds can become veritable junk heaps with dirty cast-off ideas that accumulate there little by little.

No Dumping Allowed

Years ago I put up some signs in my mind. They are very clearly printed and simply read: No Trespassing, No Dumping Allowed. On occasions it has been necessary to show them very plainly to others.

I do not want anything coming into my mind that does not have some useful purpose or some value that makes it worth keeping. I have enough trouble keeping the weeds down that sprout there on their own without permitting someone else to clutter my mind with things that do not edify.

I've hauled a few of these away in my lifetime. Occasionally I've tossed these thoughts back over the fence where they came from, when it could be done in a friendly manner.

I've had to evict some thoughts a hundred times before they would stay out. I have never been successful until I have put something edifying in their place.

I do not want my mind to be a dumping place for shabby ideas or thoughts, for disappointments, bitterness, envy, shame, hatred, worry, grief, or jealousy.

If you are fretting over such things, it's time to clean the yard. Get rid of all that junk! Get rid of it!

Put up a No Trespassing sign, a No Dumping sign, and take control of yourself. Don't keep anything that will not edify you.

The first thing a doctor does with a wound is to clean it out. He gets rid of all foreign matter and drains off infection—however much it hurts.

Once you do that spiritually, you will have a different perspective.

You will have much less to worry about. It is easy to get all mixed up about worry.

Somewhere there is a message in the protest of a man who said: "You can't tell me worry doesn't help. The things I worry about never happen."

"I Was Taught a Lesson"

Many years ago I was taught a lesson by a man I admired very much. He was as saintly a man as I have ever known. He was steady and serene, with a deep spiritual strength that many drew upon.

He knew just how to minister to others who were suffering. On a number of occasions I was present when he gave blessings to those who were sick or otherwise afflicted.

His life had been a life of service, both in the Church and in the community.

He had presided over one of the missions of the Church and looked forward to the annual missionary reunion. When he was older he was not able to drive at night, and I offered to take him to the reunions.

This modest gesture was repaid a thousandfold.

On one occasion when we were alone and the spirit was right, he gave me a lesson for my life from an experience in his. Although I thought I had known him, he told me things I would not have supposed.

He grew up in a little community. Somehow in his youth he had a desire to make something of himself and struggled successfully to get an education.

He married a lovely young woman, and presently everything in his life was just right. He was well employed, with a bright future. They were deeply in love, and she was expecting their first child.

The night the baby was to be born there were complications. The only doctor was somewhere in the countryside tending to the sick. They were not able to find him. After many hours of labor the condition of the mother-to-be became desperate.

Finally the doctor arrived. He sensed the emergency, acted quickly, and soon had things in order. The baby was born and the crisis, it appeared, was over.

Some days later the young mother died from the very infection that the doctor had been treating at the other home that night.

My friend's world was shattered. Everything was not right now; everything was all wrong. He had lost his wife, his sweetheart. He had no way to take care of a tiny baby and at once tend to his work.

Grief Turns to Bitterness

As the weeks wore on his grief festered. "That doctor should not be allowed to practice," he would say. "He brought that infection to my wife; if he had been careful she would be alive today." He thought of little else, and in his bitterness he became threatening.

Then one night a knock came at his door. A little youngster said, simply, "Daddy wants you to come over. He wants to talk to you."

"Daddy" was the stake president. A grieving, heartbroken young man went to see his spiritual leader. This spiritual shepherd had been watching his flock and had something to say to him.

The counsel from this wise servant was simply: "John, leave it alone. Nothing you do about it will bring her back. Anything you do will make it worse. John, leave it alone."

My friend told me then that this had been his trial, his Gethsemane.

How could he leave it alone? Right was right! A terrible wrong had been committed, and somebody must pay for it.

He struggled in agony to get hold of himself. It did not happen at once. Finally he determined that whatever else the issues were, he should be obedient.

Obedience is a powerful spiritual medicine. It comes close to being a cure-all.

He determined to follow the counsel of that wise spiritual leader. He would leave it alone.

Then he told me, "I was an old man before I finally understood. It was not until I was an old man that I could finally see a poor country doctor—overworked, underpaid, run ragged from patient to patient, with little proper medicine, no hospital, few instruments. He struggled to save lives, and succeeded for the most part.

"He had come in a moment of crisis when two lives hung in the balance and had acted without delay.

"I was an old man," he repeated, "before finally I understood. I would have ruined my life," he said, "and the lives of others."

Many times he had thanked the Lord on his knees for a wise spiritual leader who counseled simply, "John, leave it alone."

"John, Mary, Leave It Alone!"

And that is my counsel to you. If you have festering sores, a grudge, some bitterness, disappointment, or jealousy, get hold of yourself. You may not be able to control things out there with others, but you can control things here, inside of you.

I say, therefore: John, leave it alone. Mary, leave it alone.

You may need a transfusion of spiritual strength to be able to do this. Then just ask for it. We call that prayer. Prayer is powerful spiritual medicine. The instructions for its use are found in the scriptures.

One of our sacred hymns carries this message:

> Ere you left your room this morning,
> Did you think to pray?...
> When your soul was full of sorrow,
> Balm of Gilead did you borrow
> At the gates of day?
> O how praying rests the weary!
> Prayer will change the night to day;
> So when life gets dark and dreary,
> Don't forget to pray.
>
> ("Ere You Left Your Room This Morning," *Hymns,* no. 31.)

All of us carry excess baggage around from time to time, but the wisest ones among us don't carry it for very long. They get rid of it.

Some of it you have to get rid of without really solving the problem. Some things that ought to be put in order are not put in order because you can't control them.

Often, however, the things we carry are petty, even stupid. If you are still upset after all these years because Aunt Clara didn't come to your wedding reception, why don't you grow up? Forget it.

If you brood constantly over some past mistake, settle it—look ahead.

If the bishop didn't call you right—or release you right—forget it.

If you resent someone for something he has done, or failed to do—forget it.

We call that forgiveness. It is powerful spiritual medicine. The instructions for its use are found in the scriptures.

I repeat: John, leave it alone. Mary, leave it alone. Purge and cleanse and soothe your soul and your heart and your mind.

It will then be as though a cloudy, dirty film has been erased from the world around you; and though the problem may remain, the sun will come out. The beam will have been lifted from your eyes. There will come a peace that surpasseth understanding.

A great significant message of the gospel of Jesus Christ is exemplified by the title given to Him: the Prince of Peace. If we follow Him, we can have that individually and collectively.

He has said: "Peace I leave with you, my peace I give unto you: not as the world giveth, give I unto you. Let not your heart be troubled, neither let it be afraid." (John 14:27.)

If you, my brother or sister, are troubled, there is at hand, not just in Gilead, a soothing, healing balm.

Consider this:

> If ye shall ask any thing in my name, I will do it.
> If ye love me, keep my commandments.
> And I will pray the Father, and he shall give you another Comforter, that he may abide with you for ever;
> Even the Spirit of truth; whom the world cannot receive, because it seeth him not, neither knoweth him; but ye know him; for he dwelleth with you, and shall be in you.
> I will not leave you comfortless: I will come to you. (John 14:14-18.)

I bear witness of Him who is the Great Comforter and as one authorized to bear that witness testify that He lives. In the name of Jesus Christ, amen.

7

To Help a Miracle

W hen I see this large congregation and recognize the weather we have, I am convinced that if we have fair-weather Saints in the Church they are not in the Relief Society. A few lines of verse I recall:

> These skies of June, and flowers of June
> And clouds of June together,
> Cannot rival for one hour
> October's bright blue weather.

I quote that as an act of faith.

My invitation is to represent the fathers in the priesthood. I address my remarks to the Relief Society sisters whose husbands are not at present active in the Church, or who are not yet members of the Church. In so doing I realize I speak to a very large audience. To those of you fortunate enough to have husbands who are active, I would speak through you to the sisters who need some help. You'll notice I didn't say anything about nonmembers. I just said, to those of you whose husbands are not yet members.

Each weekend we meet one or two stake leaders who joined the Church after many years, through the encouragement of a patient, not infrequently a long-suffering wife.

I have often said that a man cannot resist that step if his wife *really* wants him to. And if she knows how to give him encouragement.

You Can't Ever Give Up

Frequently we give up on this matter. Now, you can't ever give up. You can't ever give up, not in this life or in the next. You can never give up.

Some have joined the Church after finding it at a very late hour in their life, or after lingering (you almost could use the word *malingering*)

Address given at Relief Society conference October 1978.

for many years before taking that step. Then comes the regret over the wasted years, and the question, "Why couldn't I have realized earlier? It is too late for me to learn the gospel, or to progress in it."

I think we should take great comfort in the parable of the householder who hired laborers and set them to work at the first hour at an agreed price. Then, and I quote, he

> ...found others standing idle, and saith unto them, Why stand ye here all the day idle?
> They say unto him, Because no man hath hired us. He saith unto them, Go ye also into the vineyard; and whatsoever is right, that shall ye receive. (Matthew 20:6-7.)

And so it was, even to the eleventh hour, that he hired others and set them to work. And when the day was over he gave the same pay to every one of them. Those who had come early murmured,

> Saying, These last have wrought but one hour, and thou hast made them equal unto us, which have borne the burden and the heat of the day. (Matthew 20:12.)

And the Lord said to them,

> Friend, I do thee no wrong: Didst not thou agree with me for a penny?
> Take that thine is, and go thy way: I will give unto this last, even as unto thee.
> Is it not lawful for me to do what I will with mine own? (Matthew 20:13-15.)

He wasn't talking about money.

President Lee reminded us of that day when there were probably many eyebrows raised, that day when Paul was called to the Council of the Twelve.

The gates of the celestial kingdom will open to those who come early or late. Sisters, you must never give up. If you have faith enough and desire enough, you will yet have at the head of your home a father and a husband who is active and faithful in the Church.

Why Not a Miracle?

Some who have long since lost hope have said bitterly, "It would take a miracle." And so I say, "Why not?" Why not a miracle! Is there a purpose more worthy than that?

71

At the conference in England I spoke to the sisters along this line and encouraged them to regard their husbands as though they were active members of the Church, to do this with a gesture of faith, that it might bring about the very thing they desired.

A few days ago I received a long letter from a sister who had attended that meeting. I can only quote several sentences.

"In my patriarchal blessing," she said, "I was told that by gentle persuasion and guidance, teaching love and understanding, my husband would mellow toward the Church and given the opportunity, he would accept the gospel. He would find it difficult, but if he opened his heart and let the Lord and the Holy Spirit work within him, then he would recognize the gospel and follow its course.

"I worried," she said, "because I was not always gentle, loving and understanding, but more angry with him at times, and yet I knew this was wrong. I prayed to the Lord to help me and this help was spoken by you, when you said that we were to treat our husbands as though they were members of the Church.

"This I have done these past few days and it has helped me tremendously, for if my husband held the holy priesthood of God, then I would be a more obedient wife and honor the priesthood.

"We have become closer and I realize that unless I become gentle, loving, and understanding now, I am unworthy to be honored with the priesthood in my home."

And then this lovely sister said with hope:

"That my husband and I and our six lovely children may be sealed in the holy temple and serve the Lord as a family united in Christ."

What Is a Man?

In order to help with a miracle like this I would like to talk about what a man is, and make suggestions as to how you might approach this challenge.

First, virtually every man knows that he should be giving righteous spiritual leadership in the home. The scriptures say very clearly that

Men are instructed sufficiently that they know good from evil. (2 Nephi 2:5.)

Often when a woman joins the Church before her husband, or if she is a member of the Church when they marry, she readily becomes the spiritual leader in the family. The father then, doesn't quite know how to step to her side, even though he may see this as his proper place. He somehow feels that he might be replacing her. Often a man will feel uncomfortable, hold back, resist, not knowing quite how to wrest that spiritual leadership from his wife.

Now, sisters, there are some very delicate feelings related to this matter that have to do with the male ego and touch the very center of the nature of manhood.

And I must say in all candor that not infrequently a woman can become so determined to lead her husband to activity in the Church that she fails to realize that she could *let him* lead her there very quickly.

Remember, dear sisters, that the home and the family is a unit of the Church. Once you recognize that, you come to know, in a very real sense, when you are at home you are at Church, or at least you should be.

Somehow we get set in our minds that a man is not active unless he is attending meetings regularly at the chapel. I recall President Lee saying once that someone close to him, if judged by that term, was inactive, and yet he knew him to be a saintly man. The mere act of leaving home and going to the other building is somehow a symbol of his activity in the Church.

Helping a Miracle

This then, becomes the first thing we try to do, to get him to attend meetings at the chapel, when generally this is not the beginning at all. This happens later. Now let me make this suggestion.

It is difficult to get a man to go to Church when he doesn't feel at home. It may be new and different to him, or perhaps there are habits he has not yet overcome and he may feel self-conscious and just not feel at home at Church. There is another solution, you know, that of making him feel like Church while at home.

We often don't properly credit what he does at home. It's that going to the chapel that gets fixed in our minds as the symbol of Church activity. In many ways it can be the things that he does at home that are more important as a beginning.

And so the suggestion, why don't you begin where you are, right at home. And I repeat, if your husband doesn't feel at home going to Church, then do everything you can to make him feel at Church while he's at home.

73

That All May Be Edified

How can you do this? The Relief Society can answer that. To me the greatest challenge before Relief Society in our day is to assist these lovely women to provoke their husbands to good works.

In a study which involved families with inactive or nonmember fathers, these fathers agreed, after some persuasion, to institute the family home evening program in their homes. Gradually the fathers were drawn into participation. It had an appeal because it was in their own comfortable environment and they could do it about as they wished. The family home evening program is just that adaptable.

There was an interesting result. When they felt comfortable with the Church at home then they began to go with their families to Church.

Bring Heaven into the Home

To bring some of the things of heaven into the home is to insure that family members will graduate to Church participation. The family home evening is, of course, ready-made for this—a meeting at home that can be organized to fit every need, and it's just as much a Church meeting, or can be, as those held at the chapel.

So again I say, Sisters, if your husband doesn't feel comfortable or at home in the Church, why not, as a beginning, make him feel at Church while he's at home.

It may take a miracle for your husband to be active or to join the Church. Some of us think a miracle is a miracle only if it happens instantly, but miracles can grow slowly. And patience and faith can compel things to happen that otherwise never would have come to pass. It took a sister of mine seventeen years of patience, but it was well worth it. I know a bishop who took thirty years to become active. He said he didn't believe in rushing into things.

Begin Where You Are

Sisters, begin where you are, in the home, and have patience if it takes a little while, or a long while, or if it takes nearly an eternity. There is a meaningful scripture in the book of Ether: "Dispute not because ye see not, for ye receive no witness until *after* the trial of your faith." (Ether 12:6; italics added.)

74

To Help a Miracle

Building a heaven in your home will do much to make these miracles.

One family in this experiment, when visited after a few months of having family home evening, was asked the question, "Did you have family home evening every week?"

The wife replied, "We don't know. There was one week when we don't know if we had family home evening or not."

The question was asked, "What did you do?"

With tears in her eyes she said, "That's the night our family went to the temple to be sealed together."

The husband, who was now a Melchizedek Priesthood holder, sat straight in his chair and was filled with joy as he related how family home evening had caused them to sense the true importance of family life and the need for spirituality.

The wife explained, "The night we went to the temple was my birthday. I didn't get a present because now that we are paying tithing we don't have any extra money." Then she looked at her husband and said, "The greatest present I ever received from you was the night you took us all to the temple."

Another woman said of her husband, "The best family home evenings we had were when my husband taught."

As the husband heard this he said, "Oh, I didn't do so good."

She said, "Oh, but you did. I was really proud of you."

Then he said, and isn't this like a man, "I guess I did do pretty good. You know, I've always been a black sheep, but when I taught my own family" (remember, a Church at home), "I got a feeling that I had never had before, and everything seemed to make sense."

And now this man comes over to the chapel and is active there. It all started at Church at home.

Now if your husband does not, in the beginning, hold up his end of making miracles, and he probably won't, then you do your part all the better. Make the gospel seem so worthwhile to him that he can't resist it.

Some years ago Brother Tuttle and I called to see a local leader of the Church in the early evening before going on to another city. He had not arrived home from work and his wife was busy in the kitchen. She invited us to sit at the kitchen table and visit while she continued her work.

The Gospel and Cherry Pies

Box lunches were set on the counter. She explained that there was a box supper at the branch that night and she'd spent the whole day preparing the finest lunches she could.

About the time that he arrived she took from the oven some hot cherry pies. Being a hospitable woman she insisted that we be served hot cherry pie smothered in ice cream. Of course, we did not resist.

She then glanced at her husband and I could tell what she was thinking: *He'd like a piece of pie too, but it will dull his appetite for the box supper later. But it isn't kind to have him sit and watch them eat. But if he eats, he won't enjoy the meal that I've worked so hard to prepare.*

This silent argument in her mind was soon ended, and she cut another piece of pie—noticeably bigger than the ones we had, with just a little bit more ice cream. She set it on the table before him and slipped her hands down under his chin, squeezed him just a little and said, "Honey, it kind of makes the gospel seem worthwhile, doesn't it."

Later, when I teased her a little about spoiling him that way, she said, "He'll never leave me. I know how to treat a man."

I repeat—the greatest challenge facing Relief Society in our day is to assist these lovely wives of these hundreds of thousands of men to encourage their husbands, to make a heaven in their homes. Sisters, make the gospel seem worthwhile to him and then let him know that that is your purpose.

Most women expect men to perceive those things, and get irritated and sometimes upset when they don't. But men just aren't that sensitive. A man can be thick-skulled, dull-witted, and unconscious sometimes when it comes to things like this. When you say to yourself, or to another, "Well, he ought to know what it is I want the most," perhaps he ought to know, but he probably doesn't and he needs to be told.

Why Don't You Tell Him?

I was told of a home teacher trying to encourage the father to pray in the home. The father resisted and sat down on the couch. Finally he knelt but wouldn't pray. His wife was then invited to pray and through her tears she poured out her heart to the Lord, pleading with Him for what she wanted most.

When the prayer was over, this husband, a startled man, and I think in many ways an innocent man, said "I didn't know that. I didn't know that was what you wanted. You're going to see some changes in me."

You've heard the lyrics of that song of yesterday, "I've told every little star... Why haven't I told you?" Why don't you tell him, sisters.

He needs to know, he needs to be told that you care about the gospel as deeply as you do and that you care about him infinitely more because of the gospel and what it means to you.

Let him know that your goodness as a wife and as a mother, as a sweetheart and as a companion in love, grows from your testimony of the gospel.

You Who Are Alone

I want to say a brief word or two to you lovely sisters who are left alone. Now, that's not right, I should rephrase that I think, for no one of you is left alone. I refer to those of you who have not had the privilege of marriage or who have lost your husbands through the tragedy of divorce or perhaps through the inevitable call of death.

Some of you are struggling alone to raise little families, often on meager budgets and often with hours of loneliness. I know there is a great power of compensation. I know that there is a spirit that can give you power to be both father and mother if necessary.

There stands in our small circle of General Authorities more than one man who was raised in the home of an attentive, lovely widowed mother. I heard one of them bear testimony in conference that in his boyhood days they had all the things that money couldn't buy.

The Priesthood Shelter

There is a priesthood shelter, sisters, under which you come. There is the bishop who stands as the father of the ward. Let him help, and the others he may delegate. Let your home teachers assist, particularly when you need the influence of manhood in the raising of boys.

Remember, you are not alone. There is a Lord who loves you and He watches over you, and there is the power of the Spirit that can compensate.

And so, to you also I say, you must never give up. Never, neither in this world nor in the next. For there comes a time when the judgments

77

are rendered and as the Lord said in that parable, "Whatsoever is right, that shall ye receive."

As we close, I say again, in my mind the greatest challenge facing the Relief Society in our day is the responsibility of bringing into Church activity that great army of fathers and husbands who are not yet members of the Church or who are presently inactive.

By Small and Simple Things

There is an interesting scripture in Alma, "Behold I say unto you, that by small and simple things are great things brought to pass; and small means in many instances doth confound the wise." (Alma 37:6.)

So here is a Relief Society sister, a lovely mother, with a spoon and a bowl, with an apron and a broom, with a pie tin and a mixer, and a cookie cutter and a skillet, with a motherly gesture, with patience, with long-suffering, with affection, with a needle and thread, with a word of encouragement, with that bit of faith and determination to build an ideal home. With all of these small things you and the Relief Society can win for yourselves and for The Church of Jesus Christ of Latter-day Saints and for the Lord, the strength and power of a family knit together, sealed together for time and for all eternity; a great army of men, some willing and worthy, some not yet worthy, but who must serve in the ministry of our Lord. Men who now stand by the side-lines—husbands and fathers—not quite knowing, some not quite willing, yet all to be strengthened by a handmaiden of the Lord who really cares.

May God bless you sisters. May He bless you who are the widows and the others who are raising families alone everywhere. May He bless you hundreds of thousands of wives and mothers who through the agency of the Relief Society now can be strengthened to the end that your dreams might be realized.

He is the Christ. He lives. This is His Church. The day of miracles has not ceased. And these are the miracles that count with Him. Of this I bear witness in the name of Jesus Christ, amen.

8

An Appeal
to Prospective Elders

I am conscious, my brethren and sisters, that concluding this meeting will be President Kimball. Prior to the meeting I told him that I had three talks of varying length prepared. During the singing I received a note from him asking that I use the longest version.

I was reminded of an experience we had in Colorado when we were reorganizing a stake. The meeting was nearly over, there were about ten minutes left, and neither of us had spoken. The stake president announced me. President Kimball leaned over and said, "Please, you take all of the time."

I bore a one-minute testimony and returned to my seat. As the stake president was announcing President Kimball, I noticed him writing a note. As he stood, he handed it to me. On it were five words, "Obedience is better than sacrifice." And so, obediently, I proceed.

As we come now to the close of another great conference, my brethren and sisters, our hearts have been touched by the sermons, the virtue within us has been stirred, and constantly my thoughts have gone out to those who do not have in their lives a substantial spiritual influence.

Among them is a large body of men in the Church who have missed some of the spiritual advancements that are so important in their lives and who are designated as prospective elders.

The office of an elder is a calling of dignity and honor, spiritual authority, and of power. The designation "prospective" implies hope and optimism and possibility. Now I speak to them today, knowing there are perhaps many others to whom this message will apply.

Am I right to say that occasionally, deep within, you yearn to be a part of the Church? You don't quite know how to get started, and

Address given at general conference April 1975.

perhaps in moments of deep thought you say, "If I just hadn't got off the track."

"If I just had a chance when I was younger."

"I've missed too much."

"It's too late for me."

"There is just too much water under the bridge."

You want to draw close, but you pass over with the feeling and the thought *Well, it's just too hard, and I just don't have anything to begin with.*

I had an experience from which I learned a very important lesson that I should have learned earlier.

During World War II, I was a pilot in the Air Force. After service in the Pacific Islands, I spent a year in Japan with the occupational forces. It was, of course, advisable to learn a few words of Japanese. We needed at least to be able to ask directions, ask for something to eat.

I learned the common greetings and a few of the numbers and salutations, and like many other members of the Church, I spent all my off-duty hours in missionary work among the Japanese people; and I learned from them those few words of what I thought was a very difficult language.

In July of 1946 the first baptisms took place in Osaka. Brother and Sister Tatsui Sato were baptized. And while they had been taught for the most part by others, I was privileged to baptize Sister Sato.

Though we were not unhappy in Japan, there was really only one thing on our minds, and that was home. I had been away for nearly four years. The war was over, and I wanted to go home.

When that day finally arrived, I supposed never to return to Japan, and I just closed that chapter.

The next years saw me busy getting an education, raising a family. I was not around Japanese people and had no occasion to use those few words that I had learned. They were left in the dim and very distant past, erased by twenty-six years of forgetting—gone, as I thought, forever. Then came an assignment to Japan.

The morning after my arrival in Tokyo, I was leaving the mission home with President Abo when a Japanese elder spoke to him in Japanese. President Abo said that the matter was urgent and apologized for the delay.

He went through some papers with the elder, discussing them in Japanese. Then he held up one of the letters and, pointing to a sentence, he said, "*Korewa...*"

And before he could complete the sentence I had completed it in my mind. *Korewa nan desuka.* I knew what he was saying. I knew what he was asking the elder. *Korewa nan desuka* means "What is this?" After twenty-six years, having been back in Japan but overnight, a sentence had come back into my mind—*Korewa nan desuka,* "What is this?"

I had not used those words in twenty-six years. I had thought that I should never use them again. But they were not lost.

I spent ten days in Japan and concluded my tour in Fukuoka. The morning I was to leave, we drove to the airport with Brother and Sister Watanabe. I was in the backseat with their children practicing my long-lost words of Japanese on them. They, in delight, were teaching me some new ones.

And then I recalled a little song that I had learned those twenty-six years before, and I sang it to those children:

> *Momotaro-san, Momotaro-san*
> *Okoshi ni tsuketa kibi dango*
> *Hitotsu watashi ni kudasai na*

I think that may make Brother Ottley restless.

Sister Watanabe said, "I know that song." And so we sang it together to the little children, and then she told me the meaning of it, and as she did so, I remembered that also.

It is the story of a Japanese couple who were childless, and they had prayed for a son. One day, in the stone of a large peach, they found a little boy and they named him Momotaro. The song recounts his heroism in saving his people from a terrible enemy.

Nothing Good Is Ever Lost

I had known that song for twenty-six years, but I didn't know that I knew it. I had never sung the song to my own children. I had never told them the story of it. It had been smothered under twenty-six years of attention to other things.

I have thought that a most important experience and realized finally that nothing good is ever lost. Once I got back among the people who

81

That All May Be Edified

spoke the language, all that I possessed came back and it came back very quickly. And I found it easier then to add a few more words to my vocabulary.

I, of course, do not suggest that this experience was the result of an alert mind or of a sharp memory. It was just a demonstration of a principle of life that applies to all of us. It applies to you, my brethren of the prospective elders, and to others in like situations.

If you will return to the environment where spiritual truths are spoken, there will flood back into your minds the things that you thought were lost. Things smothered under many years of disuse and inactivity will emerge. Your ability to understand them will be quickened.

That word *quickened* is much used in the scriptures, you know.

Make Your Pilgrimage

If you will make your pilgrimage back among the Saints, soon you will be understanding once again the language of inspiration. And more quickly than you know, it will seem that you have never been away. Oh, how important it is for you to realize that if you will return, it can be made as though you have never been away!

When I was presiding over the New England Mission, I attended a zone conference; and as we entered the room where the young elders were waiting, I saw, sitting in the back row, a tall and elderly man.

"I was baptized a few days ago," he said to me. "I'm seventy-four years old, and I found the gospel only now in my life."

In a pleading voice he asked if he might attend the meeting. "I just want to be here to learn," he said. "I'll sit on the back row. I won't interrupt."

Then, almost in tears, he poured out his regret. "Why did I not find it until now? My life is over. My children are all raised and gone, and it is just too late for me to learn the gospel."

What a joy it was to explain to him one of the great miracles that occurs over and over again is the transformation of those who join the Church! (Or I might say of those who rejoin the Church.) They are in the world and they are of the world, and then the missionaries find them. Though they are in the world thereafter, they are not of the world. Very quickly in their thinking and in their feelings and in their actions, it is as though they had been members of the Church all of their lives.

The Law of Compensation

This is one of the great miracles of this work. The Lord has a way of compensating and blessing. He is not confined to the tedious processes of communication and He is not limited to Japanese or English.

There is a sacred process by which pure intelligence may be conveyed into our minds and we can come to know instantly things that otherwise would take a long period of time to acquire. He can speak inspiration into our minds, especially when we are humble and seeking.

As we travel about the Church and meet with stake presidents and other Church leaders, we admire them for their thorough grasp of the gospel and their knowledge of the procedures and principles of the Church. Often we are surprised to learn that there have been periods of inactivity in their lives—sometimes very long periods—or to learn that they have only recently joined the Church.

Those years of the past, that we often think to be wasted, are often rich in many lessons, some of them very hard-earned lessons, which have meaning when the light of inspiration shines upon them.

You may never have read the parable of the laborers in the vineyard, and I would like to quote it for you.

> For the kingdom of heaven is like unto a man that is an householder, which went out early in the morning to hire labourers into his vineyard.
> And when he had agreed with the labourers for a penny a day, he sent them into his vineyard.
> And he went out about the third hour, and saw others standing idle in the marketplace.
> And said unto them; Go ye also into the vineyard, and whatsoever is right I will give you. And they went their way.
> Again he went out about the sixth and ninth hour, and did likewise.
> And about the eleventh hour he went out, and found others standing idle, and saith unto them. Why stand ye here all the day idle?
> They say unto him, Because no man hath hired us. He saith unto them, Go ye also into the vineyard; and whatsoever is right, that shall ye receive.
> So when even was come, the lord of the vineyard saith unto his steward, Call the labourers, and give them their hire, beginning from the last unto the first.

And when they came that were hired about the eleventh hour, they received every man a penny. (Matthew 20:1-9.)

There is enough pay—a penny, as it were—for everyone: those who start early and, I thank the Lord, those who are latecomers. There is no shortage of room in the celestial kingdom. There is room for all.

In this life we are constantly confronted with a spirit of competition. Teams contest one against another in an adversary relationship in order that one will be chosen a winner. We come to believe that wherever there is a winner there must also be a loser. To believe that is to be mislead.

Everyone a Winner

In the eyes of the Lord, everyone may be a winner. Now it is true that we must earn it; but if there is competition in His work, it is not with another soul—it's with our own former selves.

I do not say that it is easy. I am not talking about appearing to change. I am talking about *changing*. I do not say it is easy. I say it is possible and quickly possible.

I did not read all of that parable. There is more to it. The latter part of it, I think, is directed to those of us who are active in the Church. Let me repeat a verse or two and then continue.

> So when even was come, the Lord of the vineyard saith unto his steward, Call the labourers, and give them their hire, beginning from the last unto the first.
>
> And when they came that were hired about the eleventh hour, they received every man a penny.
>
> But when the first came, they supposed that they should have received more; and they likewise received every man a penny.
>
> And when they had received it, they murmured against the goodman of the house,
>
> Saying, These last have wrought but one hour, and thou hast made them equal unto us, which have borne the burden and heat of the day.
>
> But he answered one of them, and said, Friend, I do thee no wrong: didst not thou agree with me for a penny?
>
> Take that thine is, and go thy way: I will give unto this last, even as unto thee.
>
> Is it not lawful for me to do what I will with mine own? Is thine eye evil, because I am good?
>
> So the last shall be first, and the first last: for many be called, but few chosen. (Matthew 20:8-16.)

84

I wish you brethren of the prospective elders knew how hard we are working for your redemption. How anxiously we pray that you can return to the Church and kingdom of God and speak once again the language of inspiration—after two years or twenty-six years or a life-time. And I repeat, it can soon be much as though you had never been away.

Whispered Inspiration

There is something else in your past that you will begin likewise to recall. We know from the revelations that we lived before we came into mortality. We have experience to draw upon from before our mortal earth.

We are the children of God. We lived with Him before we were born. We have come out of His presence to receive a mortal body and to be tested.

Some of us have strayed far from His influence and we think that we have forgotten Him. We sometimes think, also, that He has forgotten us.

But just as those few words of Japanese could be recalled after twenty-six years, so the principles of righteousness that you learned as a child will be with you.

And some you have learned in His presence will return as moments of whispered inspiration, when you will find, then feel, that you are learning familiar things.

This awkward newness of making such a change in your lives will soon fade, and soon you will feel complete and adequate in His church and in His kingdom. Then you will know how much you are needed here and how powerful your voice of experience can be in redeeming others.

I bear witness to you, my brethren, you of the prospective elders and you in like situations, that the gospel of Jesus Christ is true. We love you, and the thousands of voices—the voices of the priesthood home teachers, the Relief Society sisters, the bishops, the stake presidents, the quorum leaders—all speaking through inspiration of Him—the voices of those who are called as leaders in the Church, are calling to you as David called to his wayward son, Absalom, "Come back, my son."

That All May Be Edified

God grant that you who are fathers, who are without that inspiration in your home and in your family, can return and speak once again, after your sojourn in the wilderness with the language of inspiration. You likewise can bear witness that you know, as I know, that He lives. In the name of Jesus Christ, amen.

9

Solving Emotional Problems in the Lord's Own Way

O ur bishops face increasing calls to counsel members with problems that have more to do with emotional needs than with the need for food or clothing or shelter.

My message, therefore, is to the subject: solving emotional problems in the Lord's own way.

Fortunately, the principles of temporal welfare apply to emotional problems as well.

The Church was two years old when the Lord revealed that "the idler shall not have place in the church, except he repent and mend his ways." (D & C 75:29.)

The Welfare handbook instructs:

> [We must] earnestly teach and urge Church members to be self-sustaining to the full extent of their powers. No true Latter-day Saint will...voluntarily shift from himself the burden of his own support. So long as he can, under the inspiration of the Almighty and with his own labors, he will supply himself with the necessities of life. (1952, p. 2.)

Caring for Material Needs

We have succeeded fairly well in teaching Latter-day Saints that they should take care of their own material needs and then contribute to the welfare of those who cannot provide for themselves.

If a member is unable to sustain himself, then he is to call upon his own family, and then upon the Church, in that order, and not upon the government at all.

We have counseled bishops and stake presidents to be very careful to avoid abuses in the welfare program.

When people are *able* but *unwilling* to take care of themselves, we

---

Address given at general conference October 1978.

are responsible to employ the dictum of the Lord that the idler shall not eat the bread of the laborer. (See D & C 42:42.)

The simple rule has been to take care of one's self. This couplet of truth has been something of a model: "Eat it up, wear it out, make it do, or do without."

When the Church welfare program was first announced in 1936, the First Presidency said:

> Our primary purpose was to set up, in so far as it might be possible, a system under which the curse of idleness would be done away with, the evils of a dole abolished, and independence, industry, thrift and self respect be once more established amongst our people. *The aim of the Church is to help people help themselves.* (*Conference Report,* October 1936, p. 3; italics added.)

Occasionally someone is attracted to the Church because of our welfare program. They see material security.

Our answer to them is: "Yes, join the Church for that reason. We can use all of the help we can get. You will be called upon continually to bless and assist others."

Interesting how enthusiasm for baptism often fades away.

A Self-help System

It is a self-help system, not a quick handout system. It requires a careful inventory of all personal and family resources, all of which must be committed before anything is added from the outside.

It is not an unkind or an unfeeling bishop who requires a member to work to the fullest extent he can for what he receives from Church welfare.

There should not be the slightest embarrassment for any member to be assisted by the Church. *Provided,* that is, that he has contributed all that he can.

President Romney has emphasized,

> To care for people on any other basis is to do them more harm than good.
> The purpose of Church welfare is *not* to relieve [a Church member] from taking care of himself. (*Conference Report,* October 1974, p. 166; italics added.)

The principle of self-reliance or personal independence is fundamental to the happy life. In too many places, in too many ways, we are getting away from it.

Spiritual and Emotional Self-Reliance

The substance of what I want to say is this: The same principle—self-reliance—has application to the spiritual and to the emotional.

We have been taught to store a year's supply of food, clothing, and, if possible, fuel—*at home*. There has been no attempt to set up storerooms in every chapel. We know that in the crunch our members may not be able to get to the chapel for supplies.

Can we not see that the same principle applies to inspiration and revelation, the solving of problems, to counsel, and to guidance?

We need to have a source of it *stored in every home,* not just in the bishop's office.

If we do not do that, we are quite as threatened spiritually as we should be were we to assume that the Church should supply all material needs.

Unless we use care, we are on the verge of doing to ourselves emotionally (and, therefore, spiritually) what we have been working so hard for generations to avoid materially.

The "Counselitis" Epidemic

We seem to be developing an epidemic of *counselitis* which drains spiritual strength from the Church, much like the common cold drains more strength out of humanity than any other disease.

That, some may assume, is not serious. It is very serious!

On one hand, we counsel bishops to avoid abuses in welfare help. On the other hand, some bishops dole out counsel and advice without considering that the member should solve the problem himself.

There are many chronic cases—individuals who endlessly seek counsel but do not follow the counsel that is given.

I have, on occasions, included in an interview this question: "You have come to me for advice. After we have carefully considered your problem, is it your intention to follow the counsel that I will give you?"

This comes as a considerable surprise to them. They had never thought of that. Usually they then commit themselves to follow counsel.

The Greatest Therapy

It is easier then to show them how to help themselves, and more than that, how to help others. That is the greatest therapy.

Speaking figuratively, many a bishop keeps on the corner of his desk a large stack of order forms for emotional relief.

When someone comes with a problem, the bishop, unfortunately, without a question, passes them out, without stopping to think what he is doing to his people.

We have become very anxious over the amount of counseling that we seem to need in the Church. Our members are becoming dependent.

We must not set up a network of counseling services without at the same time emphasizing the principle of emotional self-reliance and individual independence.

If we lose our emotional and spiritual independence, our self-reliance, we can be weakened quite as much, perhaps even more, than when we become dependent materially.

If we are not careful, we can lose the power of individual revelation. What the Lord said to Oliver Cowdery has meaning for all of us.

> Behold, you have not understood; you have supposed that I would give it unto you, when you took no thought save it was to ask me.
>
> But, behold, I say unto you, that you must study it out in your mind, then you must ask me if it be right, and if it is right I will cause that your bosom shall burn within you; therefore, you shall feel that it is right.
>
> But if it be not right you shall have no such feelings, but you shall have a stupor of thought that shall cause you to forget the thing which is wrong. (D & C 9:7-9.)

Spiritual independence and self-reliance is a sustaining power in the Church. If we rob the members of that how can they get revelation for themselves? How will they know there is a prophet of God? How can they get answers to prayers? How can they know for *sure* for themselves?

It is not an unfeeling bishop who requires those coming to him for counsel to exhaust every personal and family resource before helping them.

Bishops, be careful with your "emotional order forms." Do not pass them out without having analyzed carefully the individual resources.

90

Follow Proper Channels

Teach our members to follow proper channels in solving problems.

It is not unusual for some to "shop around" to get advice from friends and neighbors, from every direction, and then choose what they think is the best of it. That is a mistake.

Some want to start with psychologists, with professional counselors, or to go directly to the General Authorities to begin with.

The problems may need that kind of attention but only after every personal, and family, and every local resource has been exhausted.

We mentioned that when a member has used all of his own resources there should be no embarrassment in receiving welfare assistance.

That principle holds true with emotional assistance as well.

There may be a time when deep-seated emotional problems need more help than can be given by the family, the bishop, or the stake president.

In order to help with the very difficult problems, the Church has established some counseling services in areas where our membership is large. (Only for those that come through proper channels.)

The first category includes those services that ordinarily require a license from the local, state, or national government. The licensed services include: adoptions; the care of unwed mothers; the foster care of children; and, the Indian Placement Program.

In July of 1977 the First Presidency issued a letter giving some instruction and caution to priesthood leaders, with reference to licensed services.

Our purpose here will be to review principles that apply to the services offered under the heading clinical.

Clinical services are offered (again, through proper channels only) in three successive steps:

First: *consultation*, wherein a priesthood leader consults with an LDS Social Services representative about a member with serious problems. Only the priesthood leader meets with the member.

The next step is *evaluation*, wherein a priesthood leader and the member meet together with an LDS Social Services practitioner to evaluate the problem. Ordinarily this is one meeting only. Thereafter, the priesthood leader continues to help the member.

In difficult and persistent cases, there is *therapy*. The member (and, when possible, the bishop) meets with an LDS Social Services practitioner for counseling. The bishop gives continuing help after termination of these sessions.

Bishops and stake presidents can exemplify self-reliance by resolving these problems locally. Ultimately it is the member who must solve them.

Bishops, you must not abdicate your responsibility to anyone—not to professionals, even to those employed by Church Social Services. They would be the first to tell you so.

You have a power to soothe and to sanctify and to heal that others are not given.

The Key of Forgiveness

Sometimes what a member needs is forgiveness—you have a key to that.

If you find a case where professional help is justified, be very careful.

There are some spiritually destructive techniques used in the field of counseling. When you entrust your members to others, do not let them be subject to these things. Solve problems in the Lord's way.

Some counselors want to delve deeper than is emotionally or spiritually healthy. They sometimes want to draw out and analyze and take apart and dissect.

While a certain amount of catharsis may be healthy, overmuch of it can be degenerating. It is seldom as easy to put something back together as it is to take it apart.

By probing too deeply, or talking endlessly about some problems, we can foolishly cause the very thing we are trying to prevent.

You probably know about the parents who said, "Now, children, while we are gone, whatever you do, don't take the stool and go into the pantry and climb up to the second shelf and move the cracker box and get that sack of beans and put one up your nose, will you?"

There is a lesson there.

Now, a bishop may ask, justifiably, "How in the world can I ever accomplish my job as bishop and still counsel those who really need it?"

One stake president said to me: "Bishops don't have enough time to counsel. With the load we're putting on them, we're killing our bishops off."

While there's some truth in that, I sometimes think it's a case of suicide.

The Role of a Bishop

Our study of the role of the bishop indicates that most bishops spend time ineffectively as program administrators.

The influence of a bishop on a ward is more positive when he functions as a presiding officer, rather than getting so heavily involved in all of the program details.

It is usually in program administration, with all of the meetings, training activities, etc., that the bishop spends too much time.

Bishops, leave that to your counselors and the priesthood leaders and auxiliary leaders. Problems, for instance, that involve need for employment can be solved by the home teacher and the quorum leaders.

Trust them. Let go of it. And you will then be free to do the things that will make the most difference, counseling those who really need it—in the Lord's own way.

Two letters have gone to the field. The one was a two-thirds reduction in the number of personal priesthood interviews required on all levels.

The other was a shifting of major administrative meetings from weekly and monthly to monthly and quarterly.

We have every hope that other relief will be filtering down through channels.

In the meantime, bishop, you are in charge. Get the administrative and training part of your work in such efficient operation that you will have time to counsel your people.

Bishops, keep constantly in mind that fathers are responsible to preside over their families.

Sometimes, with all good intentions, we require so much of both the children and the father that he is not able to do so.

If my boy needs counseling, bishop, it should be my responsibility first, and yours second.

If my boy needs recreation, bishop, I should provide it first, and you second.

If my boy needs correction, that should be my responsibility first, and yours second.

If I am failing as a father, help me first, and my children second.

Do not be too quick to take over from me the job of raising my children.

Do not be too quick to counsel them and solve all of the problems. Get me involved. It is my ministry.

The Philosophy of Instant Gratification

We live in a day when the adversary stresses on every hand the philosophy of instant gratification. We seem to demand *instant* everything, including instant solutions to our problems.

We are indoctrinated that somehow we should always be instantly emotionally comfortable. When that is not so, some become anxious— and all too frequently seek relief from counseling, from analysis, and even from medication.

It was meant to be that life would be a challenge. To suffer some anxiety, some depression, some disappointment, even some failure is normal.

Teach our members that if they have a good, miserable day once in a while, or several in a row, to stand steady and face them. Things will straighten out.

There is great purpose in our struggle in life.

There is great meaning in these words entitled "The Lesson."

> Yes, my fretting,
> Frowning child,
> I could cross
> The room to you
> More easily.
> But I've already
> Learned to walk,
> So I make you
> Come to me.
>
> Let go now—
> There!
> You see?

94

Solving Emotional Problems in the Lord's Own Way

Oh, remember
This simple lesson,
Child,
And when
In later years
You cry out
With tight fists
And tears—
"Oh, help me,
God—please."
Just listen
And you'll hear
A silent voice:

"I would, child,
I would.
But it's you,
Not I,
Who needs to try
Godhood."

(Carol Lynn Pearson, "The Lesson," *Beginnings,* New York: Doubleday and Co., 1975, p. 18.)

Bishop, those who come to you are children of God. Counsel them in the Lord's own way. Teach them to ponder it in their minds, then to pray over their problems.

The Therapy of Reading the Scriptures

Remember that soothing, calming effect of reading the scriptures. Next time you are where they are read, notice how things settle down. Sense the feeling of peace and security that comes.

Now, from the Book of Mormon, this closing thought: The prophet Alma faced a weightier problem than you, bishop, will likely see in your ministry. Like you, he felt uncertain; and he went to Mosiah.

Mosiah wisely turned the problem back to him, saying:

Behold, I judge them not; therefore I deliver them into thy hands to be judged.

And now the spirit of Alma was again troubled; and he went and inquired of the Lord what he should do concerning this matter, for he feared that he should do wrong in the sight of God.

And it came to pass that after he had poured out his whole soul to God, the voice of the Lord came to him. (Mosiah 26:12-14.)

That voice will speak to you, bishop. That is your privilege. I bear witness of that, for I know that He lives.

May God bless you, bishop, the inspired judge in Israel, and those who come to you, as you counsel them in the Lord's own way.

In the name of Jesus Christ, amen.

10

The Ideal Teacher

When I was in a supervisory and an administrative position, it was my responsibility to make appraisals and sometimes render judgments of your contributions as teachers. Sometimes we were heard to say to one another in rendering these appraisals, "He's too strict with his discipline," or, "He places too much emphasis on written work," or, perhaps, "He pays too little attention to the students themselves," or, "He is not systematic enough," or, "He makes too little preparation." Now, in the very saying of "there is too much" or "too little," or "he is too something" or "not enough of something," there is the implication that somewhere there is just enough—that somewhere there is just the right amount of whatever we are talking about. And so the teacher I would like to discuss with you is that teacher we carry in our minds—against whom all of you are measured by those of us who have the responsibility of appraising you. This teacher, of course, is the ideal teacher. The ideal!

The Ideal Teacher

I will admit to being an idealist, not in the strict educational-philosophical definition of the word, because I have little patience—*little* patience—when we want to equate ourselves with or to define ourselves in the terminology of that field. We are not idealists, we are not pragmatists, or existentialists, or naturalists, or realists; and we are not idealistic realists or realistic idealists. We are Christians; we are Latter-day Saints; we are Mormons; and we should fight in context. Let them explain us in their terms, if they will but let us hold and explain ourselves in our own terms. And, philosophically, we are Christians—Latter-day Saints.

Address given to seminary and institute teachers June 1962.

That All May Be Edified

Now, I would like to bring to your attention some of the things I learned about this teacher. No one of us, I am sure, is quite like him. Sometimes I felt I knew him intimately, and other times I was forcefully reminded how very casual my acquaintance was with this teacher. These are some observations regarding him that I would like to present for your consideration. These are things I noticed about him during the twelve years that it was my privilege, with you, to be a companion with him.

Loyalty

I found first that this teacher has a deep sense of loyalty—a naive, simple, childlike loyalty. It is not insincere, and I say that such a loyalty cannot be counterfeited; there is no fabricating it. This loyalty cost him something. If it had not, then he would not have earned it. It cost him viewpoints, it cost him philosophical positions, it cost him that which it takes to humble himself and to commit himself. I never noticed any attempt on his part to search for angles; he is not looking for the angles. I saw very little "I" trouble in him. That "I" trouble is not the kind of eye trouble you see on the physical examination form. It is the other kind. You know the kind. It becomes apparent in an interview with a prospective seminary teacher when one asks, "Why do you want to teach seminary?" Often the answer will be: "*I* think *I* would enjoy it; *I* will get a great deal of good out of it; It will do *me* a great deal of good; *I* have always liked..." And then there is the rare exception who says: "There is service to be rendered; my qualifications are not so much, but I am willing to try." I noticed very little "I" trouble in this teacher.

This "ideal" teacher seems to be comfortable with his coordinators and supervisors. He is not afraid to call on them, *especially* when he is in trouble. He knows that their value to him is most important when he is having difficulty. He does not have a "parade" lesson in his desk drawer which he can bring forth the minute some stranger walks in the room. He has not prearranged with students a signal to be given when someone comes in, in order that the finest demonstration can be observed of what he (the teacher) is supposed to be doing.

And then this—he is willing to accept the decision of any one of the administration as though it were the judgment of all of them. He does not try to play one of them against the other. Because of this, he is unusually easy to work with, and we find ourselves depending upon him.

Earnest Preparation

He is earnest about his preparation and the improvement of his qualifications academically and his capabilities otherwise. Although he is in the routine best described, I suppose, by saying that he is killing himself by "degrees," he does not "aspire." He is not a climber. You know of the bishop who died in Santa Clara in the early days, and it was some time before the brethren came around to reorganize. One of the converts, an immigrant, got up in sacrament meeting once and said, "Bredren und sistern, vat ve need in dis vard iss a bishop. Und da kind off man ve need for bishop iss a man who doesn't vant to be bishop. Bredren und sistern, I am here to tell you I doesn't vant to be bishop."

This teacher of whom I speak is content to do with excellence the job which is assigned him. There are very infrequent glances up, if ever at all. And I often wondered, as I watched him work, if he realized that by so doing, by employing himself intensively at the thing he is assigned, he has almost no chance of staying there. The likelihood that he will stay in that assignment is very remote. When you do exceptionally well that which you are assigned, there is only one way to move, and that is up. And, I suppose, such moving up is somewhat conditioned upon your not aspiring to do so.

He is efficient enough in his details. He answers correspondence promptly. One of the things which sets him apart from most of the teachers is that he never bargains over his salary. When hired he forgot to ask what the salary was to be, so preoccupied was he with the job he would be doing, the service he could render, and the opportunity to be had. He may be discontented, but he never shows it, and he has never once agitated among his fellow teachers, nor does he concern himself with what their salaries are.

Dedication

His dedication is total. He does not sell insurance on the side; he does not have any other job. This teacher somehow has faith enough that if he will commit himself totally to that which is most important, that somewhere (without an assurance from the beginning) things will equalize themselves and finances will resolve themselves. He is content with the middle class—maybe lower middle class—financial economic status with no complaints, because he can serve.

My observation of this teacher indicated he has the general respect of his colleagues. Some one or two of them are critical of him, but an honest judgment, I think, will find him guiltless of any disservice to them. Perhaps there are some misunderstandings, most probably built on the lack of knowledge. In one or two cases some regard him with outright jealousy.

Positive Attitudes

He is positive in his attitudes, and he seems to know—and this is important and I emphasize this—he seems to know that the assignment of the teacher is not analysis; it is synthesis. It is not taking apart, analyzing, and looking for the flaws, the aberrations, the difficulties, the problems. It is synthesis: the putting together, the organizing, the giving of meaning, the working toward wholeness. He is positive, looking for that which is right and, in consequence of his search, finding it—obtaining, just as the Lord has outlined for us in the Book of Mormon, the fruits of his labors and being rewarded according to that which he desires. Every man will be granted according to the desires of his own heart. Those who desire virtue and beauty and truth and salvation shall have it, and those who fail in that desire, or who unfortunately direct their desires in the opposite direction, shall have their agency respected.

Respect

I do not think I ever heard him use a nickname or speak a word of ridicule concerning his colleagues or concerning those who were called to administer his program. He never baits or tempts either his students or his colleagues. And I noticed this—that his colleagues make mistakes. So do those who are assigned to direct his work. And he has had reason to snipe, to heckle, to pick, but this he does not do. I recall when I was in high school, a friend of mine, who was, I think, a sopho-more, was working for the telephone company. In the evenings he swept up the building. One night he found on the basement floor in the dust in back of the furnace, a five-dollar bill—an old bill, dusty and dirty. He picked it up and looked at it. After wrestling with his conscience during the night, he returned to work the next day and gave the five-dollar bill to his employer. His employer said, "Well, thank you. I put it there yesterday. I was testing you." I recall that this young man thoroughly resented the action of his employer, and then he made this observation, "I thought it was Satan who had the job of tempting."

Not Perfect but on the Way

My observation of this teacher convinces me that while he is ideal, he is certainly not perfect. I learned that once or twice, even with the best of intentions, he lost his temper, he broke a promise or two, and on a number of occasions he just plain did not do his best. Then he confided in me that he was not free from moral temptations. As a matter of fact, not infrequently unclean thoughts enter his mind. He has learned, however, that the stage of the human mind is seldom bare. The only time the curtains go down is at night in sleep. If on that stage there is not a production that is wholesome, educational, developmental—or a light, purposeful, and entertaining presentation—if the stage is left bare, suddenly from the wings steal thoughts of ugliness, darkness, and sin to hold the stage and dance and tempt. But he is ideal in the sense that he has developed the ability to combat this. He has chosen a fine hymn or two, and when these thoughts come he will hum one of these songs. This changes his attitude and his mind. He has learned to change his train of thought—to busy himself. Then if these urges to submit and to indulge are persistent, he has learned to skip a meal or two because he has found that the human body, if it is subdued, becomes obedient. Thereby he practices virtue and purity.

Now everything is not always rosy for this teacher. There are moments of disappointment. In fact, there are moments of dispair. But his mistakes, his depressions, his disappointments, and his problems seem to be a source of growth. He finds that they are not merely tolerable, but they are actually necessary. For there must needs be opposition in all things; and after much tribulation cometh the blessings; and whom the Lord loveth, he chasteneth.

This teacher is a manly man, and although his work keeps him as kind of a hothouse plant—indoors all the time—he is not afraid of a rainstorm, a snowflake, a breath of fresh air, or manual labor. He is careful, this teacher with whom we are acquainted, about his appearance, and he dresses appropriately, with shoes polished and a necktie. He wears a coat. There is a certain dignity about that. (I noticed that if it were in Arizona and it was hot, that it was a very light coat.) There is nothing fancy about his clothing. Once in a while the end of his shirt-sleeve, the sleeve on his white shirt, is rather unobtrusively trimmed with his fingernail clipper, but he is neat.

Sensible About Health

He is sensible about his health. As a teacher and our colleague he has to work strenuously; the work is not the type to keep him trim. When he begins to put on weight and starts to get paunchy, he has the simple willpower—the simple willpower that is most appropriate for one in his station or anyone else—to control his passions and his appetites. And this is rather remarkable about him; it shows fortitude and courage.

Respected

Then I observed that this teacher has a certain presence about him. When I visited the classroom in Idaho or in Arizona, I found it the same. The students refer to him in terms of respect. They call him *brother* and not *mister*. He has noticed that students do not need a friend—they have plenty of those. If they want advice from a friend, there are numbers of them around. They need a teacher, a counselor, an advisor. Now this distance that was between him and the students is always there. It is crossed frequently from him to them, but this distance, sometimes called dignity, insures him—both his office and his character and his kindness—against trespass by his students.

A Sense of Humor

I was always grateful, when I met him, to notice that he has a very keen and alert sense of humor. It is just sort of there all the time. Now, it is human enough, and it is plain enough, but it does not depend on the vulgar or the commonplace for its funniness. And never is it the object of his humor to debase or degrade that most sacred and most personal of all human relationships that is so often in the world the centerpoint for all that is presumed to be funny.

Compassion

I noticed that he has a sincere compassion for his students, that he knows them and loves them, and he cannot help himself. And the less they deserve his love, the more of it there seems to be sponsored within him. He has learned that young people need a lot of love, particularly when they do not deserve it. He just has this characteristic about him. I have come to know, after having watched him operate in the classroom in Idaho, Arizona, California, or Wyoming, that this feeling of love was akin to and has a close relationship with discernment—an appropriate power he uses in his work which few other teachers display.

Reverence

Once or twice, when I worked with him outside the classroom, I recognized a reverence for life, something you see, for instance, in Albert Schweitzer. Once a boat, coming into the camp, was overturned by a hippopotamus. A native was drowned, and the tribesmen immediately went for guns to search for the animal and kill it. Albert Schweitzer prayed that they would not find it. David O. McKay was once informed by his farmhand that he had killed a porcupine over on the edge of the grove. "But did you kill it?" asked President McKay. "Oh, yes," replied the farmhand, "I dispatched it with a stick." And David O. McKay, Apostle, climbed over the fence, walked across the field, and found the animal critically and painfully injured but not dead. He mercifully killed it. That interest, that compassion, that reverence for life, is characteristic of the teacher I describe.

Family Life

To a great extent this teacher is what he is because he married "her." She is not so concerned with status symbols. The youngsters have patches on their Levi's, and their shoes are half-soled; they are not always new. Her home is modest, but she keeps it clean. She encourages him, sometimes provokes him, to righteousness. She is in the home. I emphasize again, she is in the home! She has not joined him on the breadwinning line. She is there to comfort, bless, and love him, and to give him that tenderness and compassionate regard that only a wife can give a husband and which inspires him to do that which otherwise he would be incapable of doing.

That All May Be Edified

Now, he noticed children. I was at quarterly conference in Preston, Idaho, with Elder LeGrand Richards. We were late to go into the meeting—about five minutes. The congregation was waiting as we went across the foyer. As he was about to open the door to go into the chapel and to the stand, the door across the foyer opened and in came a little group of homespun youngsters, five or six of them in one family, dressed in the best they had, less fancy than most. Brother Richards, with his cane, held up the meeting, walked back to the door, bent over, and shook hands with each one of those little youngsters, blessed them in his own way, ignored—almost—their parents, and then went in to start the meeting.

I was once on a plane with Elder Harold B. Lee going to Washington State. We got off at Boise. These was a woman sitting on the right side of the aisle in the last seat nearest the exit holding a little boy about a year old. The other passengers waited for just a moment as Brother Lee fussed over the "little fellow," as he called him. The mother was proud as he blessed the boy in passing.

I have had dinner in this teacher's home at Rexburg. He is the head of his household. His wife is a lovely unassuming woman, and he is in charge. The priesthood has the final vote.

Takes Time Now

Part of the genius of this teacher, I noted, is that he lives each particular day. However much he is searching for tomorrow, he takes time. You know, we often say that if we can just get this done, then we will be free for a few weeks—if we can just get this project over with, if we can just get this thesis out of the way, if we can just get this pageant taken care of, if graduation were just out of the way, then we can relax. Have you not learned yet that *it* never will be over? that *it* never will be done? that unless you take time now, *it* is forever gone, forever forfeited? This teacher, with no slackening of his effort, reminds you, as you drive along, that the sunset is beautiful and that he sees the deer almost obscured by the foilage. He takes time to look at his children and be glad he has them, to love them, to hug them, to build a playhouse. He lives as he goes along. That is the genius of this teacher.

The Ideal Teacher Found in Many Places

Where did I see him, this teacher of whom I speak? One morning I saw him down at Beaver, all covered with smudge, giving a lesson on the First Vision. He was kneeling on the floor in front of the classroom as he demonstrated the First Vision—something I would never recommend to any other teacher. But with him it was supernal. I chanced upon him one Saturday morning scrubbing the floors in the Arimo Seminary. The building was finished and in use, but a janitor had not been appointed, so there he was, in some leftover army khaki coveralls, with a bucket of suds and a scrubbing brush. I watched him lead the singing at Reno, bringing out the untalented students' backward, faltering voices and blending them together to complement weakness with strength to produce harmony and spirituality. I hunted deer with him up Manti Canyon and saw the depth of his soul, the vibrance of his humor, the sincerity of the spirit within him.

I have seen him with his arms around an Indian child in Arizona, oblivious to the fact that this was a child of a different race, unbathed, sorrowful, unkempt, but the object of his love. I watched with reverence up at the Ogden State Industrial School as he gave the gift of gentleness to those students, and I saw in him a heart that was larger than the gigantic body which contained it. I heard him give a lesson over at Dragerton in a garage. It was below freezing. There was no door on the garage, but they had a canvas over it, and they had a little gas heater there. After I had been there for a few moments, I did not know but what we were in the finest classroom in the system. And do you know, he had such blindness that he did not know it either? I saw him in the Pocatello Seminary. The windows were clear glass. Across the street a machine was demolishing a building. Suddenly I noticed that I was the only one who was conscious of what was going on across the street; that every student was conscious of what was happening at the head of the classroom.

I saw him giving guidance to a teenage couple—fretful, out of harmony, in difficulty—in Preston, Idaho. I saw him, the mantle of bishop still upon him, and with the depth of his inspiration always apparent. I have ridden in his Chevrolet with him (not without cost). I saw him with his arm around a wayward boy up in Oakley, Idaho, bearing testimony, assuring this lad that if nobody else loved him, he did. I have knelt in prayer with him at 380 Maeser Building, over in the Smoot Administration Building, in the head office of this department, and I felt his spirit. It has been a choice, rewarding association. You see, he sits here with you, next to you, behind me here on the stand, this teacher of whom I speak.

Hidden Qualities

Now, as I met this teacher from time to time, I have sensed that there are some things about him, some depths to him that one from the outside can never probe and that he himself will never reveal. He, alone, knows the sincerity of his prayers, the honesty of his repentance, the reality and actuality of his love for other people, the sheer drudgery he has endured, and the struggle it has been to overcome and to improve. Only he knows the disappointments and the joys that are all a part of this truly great soul. Line upon line, precept upon precept, here a little and there a little, he works with you and me and improves others.

Paid for in Advance

A quotation from Ralph Waldo Emerson's essay "Spiritual Laws" suggests to me this teacher:

> There is no teaching until the pupil is brought into the same state or principle in which you are; a transfusion takes place; he is you and you are he; then there is teaching, and by no unfriendly chance or bad company can he ever quite lose the benefit.

And because I believe that—that a transfusion does take place and that he is you and you are he, that there is teaching—I also believe that the image each of us presents should be most like this ideal teacher.

I said at the beginning that no one of us is quite like him, but I find much of him in many of you. We may ask these questions: What makes him ideal? Can we find whatever this is? If we can find it, can we isolate it, can we get hold of it? I suggest that there is the simplest and most basic of all explanations for it—and that is *faith.* He has it. I repeat, he has it! You see he is willing, without any assurance of any promotion or financial improvement or any assurance of betterment of his circumstances, to go ahead with faith and do that which he is assigned to do.

106

He orders his life first. If I were to tell you one of the most important laws of life that I have learned, I should say this: The good things—that which is desirable, that which tends to elevate, glorify, and exalt—must be paid for in advance. (The opposite items can be paid for afterwards.) Good must be earned.

The Image of the Master Teacher

The attributes which it has been my choice privilege to recognize in you brethren and sisters over these twelve years are no more nor less than the image of the Master Teacher showing through. I believe that to the degree you perform, according to the challenge and charge which you have, the image of Christ does become engraved upon your countenances, and for all practical purposes, in that classroom, at that time and in that expression and with that inspiration, you are he and he is you. And the transfusion takes place. By no unfriendly chance o. bad company can you ever quite lose the benefit of it.

Faith, the Transfusion

How do we achieve this transfusion? First, we ask for it. We pray that we might be ideal. We seek. Now I differentiate between saying prayers and praying. I would like to draw an example which some of you have heard. It is so commonplace. We have a cow. (We live on a little farm just a few miles north of here.) I had not been home in daylight hours for three weeks. One day before catching a later plane, I went out to see the cow. She was in trouble. I called the vet, and he looked at her, tested her, and said, "She has swallowed a wire and it has punctured her heart. She will be dead before the day is over." The next day the calf was to come, and the cow is important to our economy. Also, she kind of "belongs"; you know how that gets to be. I asked him if he could do anything, and he said he could, but it would likely be useless, money down the drain. I said, "Well, what will it cost me?" He told me. (And it did.) I told him to go ahead. The next morning the calf was there, but the cow was lying down gasping. I called the vet again, thinking the calf might need some attention. He looked the cow over, and said she would be dead within an hour or so. I went in to the telephone directory, copied down the number of the animal by-products company, put it on the nail by the phone, and told my wife to call them to come and get the cow later in the day.

107

That All May Be Edified

We had our family prayer before I left to go to Salt Lake to catch the plane out to the Gridley Stake. Our little boy was praying. It was to be his calf, you see, and in the middle of *saying his prayers*—after he said all that he usually says, "bless daddy that he won't get hurt in his travels, bless us at school," and so on—he started to *pray*. There is a difference, and this is the point I should like to make. He then said: "Heavenly Father, please bless Bossy so that she will get to be all right." He said "please," you see. While I was in California I remembered that story, and when we were talking about prayer, I told of the incident, saying, "I am glad he prayed that way because he will learn something. He will mature, and he will learn that you do not get everything you pray for just that easy. There is a lesson to be learned." And truly there was—but it was I who learned it, not my son; because when I got home Sunday night, Bossy had "got to be all right."

Now, pray for this transfusion to take place; work for it. Work that you become worthy of it—morally and spiritually worthy.

I leave my blessings with you, my brethren and sisters, and tell you of the love I have for you. You mean much to me. I tell you how much the Master Teacher among you has influenced me. Now that my companionship with Him has become more intimate, more certain, I bear witness that He lives, that He is all that we know Him to be, and that the work in which we are engaged is at His instance and has His approval. This witness I bear in the name of Jesus Christ, amen.

Comfort *spreads a shelter against despair.*

Comfort

"What need was fulfilled when our forebears were persecuted and driven? What need was fulfilled when they suffered deprivation and want, hunger and cold? Whatever the Lord has in mind for us, our heritage was not established on the granting of every whim, seeing to every comfort, and fulfilling every supposed need of every member.

"That level of expectation can debilitate, even destroy them and the Church.

"I quote from Joseph Smith, 'There is a need for decisions of character aside from sympathy.' " (From an unpublished talk.)

That All May Be Edified

To young people at MIA Conference (1962), I said, "Your parents will be wise (after you have entered the temple, recited the marriage covenants, and become a separate family in the records of the Church) to let you stand as a separate family. They may see you in trouble and have courage enough, *because they love you,* just to leave you there to find your own way out."

This statement is indicative of a basic certainty—that spiritual growth comes not from having every pain, difficulty, and need immediately and artificially relieved, solved, or supplied, but rather by the growing, refining, purifying process of self-effort coupled with faith and determination. Thus, hunger, thirst, longing, labor, struggle, suffering, and sometimes even the ultimate sacrifice are the raw ingredients in the crucible out of which great lives emerge.

On a divine level our Lord became the great High Priest by reason of the things He suffered. Only in that way can He succor true needs. His was the supreme example of this principle. He wrought the Atonement under incomprehensible duress: illegal trials, ignominies, stripes, burdens, wounds, Gethsemane, and the final yielding up of His obedient spirit to His Father. That Father, because He loved not only the Son, but His other children as well, staid His hand from administering to the urgent and terrible needs He saw in order that a higher, eternal purpose might be fulfilled.

In our lives, profound compassion must be paradoxically set against divine restraint and guide us in all areas of our jurisdiction. This restraint makes possible wise and effective succoring and comforting of those in need. Whether as parent to child, teacher to student, or Church leader to member or nonmember, we may deeply, acutely long to help. But we must recognize the necessity of sometimes witholding (out of love) immediate relief or supply so that child, student, member, or other may have unfettered opportunity to grow by helping themselves.

Another characteristic of wise parents or leaders is that they must be both practically and spiritually attuned to the rhythm of life's divinely appointed seasons. A child must learn responsibility, values, and skills commensurate with his age. A couple must wait to consummate their love until marriage sanctions it. A man and his wife should be devoted to one another. They must labor and save to establish a home, however humble, in which they will nurture their little

That All May Be Edified

ones, steady their teenagers, and lead their young adults safely to eternal marriage. They will hunger and hope for conveniences and beautiful things, but will not desert basics to obtain them. Rather, they will, with painstaking effort fashion them from whatever materials are available. While they are home centered, they extend love and service to others as they go. This is made more meaningful because they will have known sickness, deprivation, disaster, even death. They reach maturity blessed with strong family bonds and spiritual riches. For those temporarily denied some fundamental blessings of life, such as a marriage, a home and family, assurance is given that it is only a matter of timing. All of these things will be theirs if they desire them and live for them.

The recurring theme in the following talks, then, is soul growth through obedience, suffering, and sacrifice, counterbalanced with that of compassion, succor, and comfort. The selection is made from a wide variety of both unpublished and published works as well as those of previously limited distribution.

(11) In "A Worthy, Faithful Handmaiden of the Lord," the funeral sermon for Belle S. Spafford, my expression of admiration, love, and appreciation for a long-time friend and associate constituted a tribute which seemed to give solice to her family and to all who knew her. In it I relate, for the first time, a sacred experience I shared with this dear friend. I explained in the telling of it why we do not and should not lightly talk of such experiences and why an exception was made in this case. I felt an unusual spirit of inspiration and consolation on that occasion and felt Sister Spafford was aware of what was done.

(12) President Harold B. Lee died suddenly (1973) after only a year and a half in office. A month to the day after the solemn assembly at which the First Presidency of the Church was reorganized, by assignment I addressed the Coordinating Council of the Church about the change in command. This was the council that President Lee had led for so many years beginning when he was a member of the Twelve. It would not be the same without him. I knew that the foremost thought on the minds of those present would be, *How can we go on without our beloved leader?* So I put together a home-styled parable to verbally put a hand on the collective shoulder of the large body of listeners, steady them, and give them logical rationale for the loss of our leader, and to

112

give assurance that it was the Lord who had called him home and selected another to serve in his stead. After soul-labor, prayer, and pondering, I could speak with great conviction as to the preparation, humility, and superb spiritual qualification which brought Spencer W. Kimball to his sacred call. A few weeks later, Sister Lee called me. She had been given a copy of the talk "A Change in Command," by someone who had been present. In a touching conversation she told of a special peace that had come to her from reading it.

(13) In 1964 I was in Cuzco, Peru, with President A. Theodore Tuttle of the First Quorum of Seventy. We held a meeting and had an unusual experience with a little street urchin. When I returned, I told the incident to Elder Spencer W. Kimball of the Council of the Twelve. Shortly after we arrived in Cambridge, Massachusetts, where I was to preside over the mission, I received a letter from Brother Kimball. He asked if he could use the incident in Cuzco in his general conference talk. In this letter he outlined it as he intended to use it. I was amazed at the accuracy of the detail as he had written it and remembered that he took no notes as I had told him the incident. Twice more, after he became president of the Church he told of the experience in talks to the regional representatives. And then on one occasion as we were on a plane to the East for an area conference he asked if I would relate the experience to some of the party who accompanied us. Then he said to me very seriously, "That was a great experience, and it is more important than you have yet come to realize."

At the dedication of the Brazil Temple in "We Are Going to Find Him," I expressed my deep longing to meet an ancient, present, and eternal need for a total people. The vehicle of this expression is poignantly centered in my experience with and compassion for a small Lamanite street urchin.

(14) This is addressed to those parents whose children have not followed good counsel or whose offspring have rebelled. In "Families and Fences" it is, however, not comfort without pain, for it requires the "comforted" one to search within, to face basic truths concerning his own part in the alienation. That done, the concerned and suffering parent can, with hope, build bridges and never, never give up.

(15) "A Tribute to the Rank and File of the Church" gives to the humble, devoted, high-performing member of the Church the assurance that his efforts do not go unnoticed. Individually he is both

recognized and appreciated; collectively he forms the steady, abiding, core of power upon which conversion, Church growth, and continuance depend. Within the talk is the moving and profound story of Joseph Millet, a little-known missionary of an earlier day.

11

A Worthy, Faithful Handmaiden of the Lord

I should add my testimony of tribute to Belle Smith Spafford beginning where Elder Ashton left off. When all of the tomorrows have passed, Belle Smith Spafford will stand as one of the greatest women of this dispensation.

It was apparent to those of us who knew her well that she had no secret formula for life. Her greatness grew from establishing in her life the principles of the gospel of Jesus Christ. Sister Spafford is a product of the restoration of the gospel. To try to explain her achievement in any other terms is to create a mystery where there is none. I have known her for more than twenty years. For a number of years I was an advisor to the Relief Society and we served together on the Board of Education and as trustees of Brigham Young University.

Some time ago Sister Packer and I were returning from Europe. In New York City we went wearily to the waiting room. There we found Sister Spafford. She had arrived several hours earlier on a flight from Johannesburg, South Africa. She was then in her late seventies. We had hours to wait and we were then, as we had been on many occasions, students of this wise, experienced, inspired woman. Today I will share very briefly only three lessons—three words—which characterize her greatness. Obedience, service, and inspiration.

Her Obedience

Sister Spafford was great because she was obedient. Let me illustrate. When she graduated with her husband from Brigham Young University, they moved with their two children to Salt Lake City where he had found employment. They were, of course, active in the Church,

---

Address given at the funeral of Belle S. Spafford February 5, 1982.

115

and they moved into the Belvedere Ward. The first week there Bishop Bowles called them in. They were building a new chapel and needed all the help they could get. He asked where they would like to serve. Now that's a little unusual but Sister Spafford was happy to have a choice. She loved to teach, had done some professional teaching, so she asked to be assigned to either the Sunday School or the Young Women's organization. So the following Sunday she was sustained as second counselor in the ward Relief Society presidency. She protested. She used the word *shocked* and told Bishop Bowles, "That organization is for my mother, not for me." She said something about old women, claimed she didn't have the right experience, and was bold enough to add, "And I have no desire to learn." But Bishop Bowles prevailed, and she accepted the call. Her husband, Earl, was little comfort. He reminded her that they had made covenants and that they would keep them. This was a very trying time for her.

Because of construction and remodeling they held Relief Society in the basement of the chapel. It was in the furnace room. When the furnace was on it was terrible; when it was off it was intolerable. Her children caught cold. On at least two occasions against the counsel of her husband she asked to be released. On both occasions the bishop said he would think about it. Finally there was an accident in which she was very seriously injured. After a period of treatment she was recovering in her home, but there were complications. And I remind you that fifty years ago we didn't have the medications we do now. A terrible laceration on her face had become infected. The doctor was called, and he said ominously, "We can't touch this surgically. It's too close to the nerve that controls your tongue. You could lose your ability to speak." As the doctor was leaving, Bishop Bowles stopped by. "I'm just on my way home from meeting and saw the lights on. Is there anything I can do for you?" Sister Spafford in agony and tears said, "Yes, Bishop. Now, will you release me from Relief Society?" He said he would pray about it. When the answer came back it was, "Sister Spafford, I still don't get the feeling that you should be released from Relief Society." And she was not released.

Sister Spafford is great because she was obedient. And I remind you that the test of her obedience was not before the prophets and presidents and the Apostles. Her test was before an ordinary bishop, in an ordinary ward, an ordinary young woman had learned an extraordinary lesson.

Her Service

The second word that characterized this great soul is service. Sister Spafford was great because of her reverence for duty. Can't you just hear her say, "Why it's our duty. It's our duty." When the National Council of Women was organized in the 1870s, the Relief Society was a charter member. When Sister Spafford joined the general board she became our delegate to their conventions in New York City. She was a very anonymous delegate, for we received no recognition at all. Shortly after she became president of the Relief Society, however, she was invited to make a presentation on compassionate service. Oh, how she prayed and worked over her assignment! The reputation of the Church, she felt, was hanging in the balance.

After her presentation which she felt went very well, she went to the luncheon in a large ballroom. Prominent women from all over the country were seated at round tables. Because of her presentation she was recognized for the first time as a Mormon woman, as a Latter-day Saint. She went from table to table to find a place to sit. As she would approach a table the chairs would be turned up against the table and she would be pointedly told, "This place is taken." When most of the women were seated, she stood by the door—alone, puzzled, angry, and deeply offended. The national president arrived, complimented her on her presentation, and then sensing her emotion asked, "Is something wrong?" Trying to hold back her tears, Sister Spafford said simply, "Tell me, please, where is it that you would like me to sit?" This gracious woman looked about the room, saw the chairs, and said, "I understand perfectly. I'd like you to sit with me at the head table today." And so she did.

But Sister Spafford was not placated. Soon after her return she went to see President George Albert Smith and recommended that the Relief Society withdraw its membership from the National Council of Women. She explained to the president that it was expensive in both time and money. But most of all she said, "We don't get anything out of it."

117

President Smith, who was known first for his gentle love, became surprisingly stern. He repeated her words, "We should withdraw from the National Council of Women."

"Yes," Sister Spafford recommended.

"We should withdraw because we are not getting anything out of it?"

"That is right," she said.

Then President Smith inquired sternly, "Tell me, please, Sister Spafford, what is it that you are putting into it?"

She left his office that day a different woman. She had been reminded by a prophet of duty and of service, and she would be obedient. The day came when she was president both of the Relief Society, the largest and most important woman's organization in the world, and of the National Council of Women, and for many years she was a delegate and an officer in the International Councils as well.

It was but a year ago that the National Council of Women reluctantly accepted a resignation that had been refused on several previous occasions. I quote from a letter to her from the president of that council, speaking, I think, for all of us. "Your post will never be filled. Your inimitable style will never be duplicated. Your personal standards will never be surpassed. I dread the sorrow that will pervade that gathering when I read your farewell letter."

Her Inspiration

Finally, Sister Spafford was great because she was inspired. Her faith was unshakable, her reverence deep, her spirituality a compelling influence to all around her. She endured searing disappointment and deep sorrow. She bore them with regal silence.

When the Relief Society was organized the Prophet Joseph Smith said that if this society listens to the counsel of the Almighty through the heads of the Church, they shall have power to command queens in their midst. In one way she herself fulfills something of that prophecy. The scriptures speak of a chosen generation and a royal priesthood. That royalty is not confined to the brethren. No one I have known, whether man or woman, listened more closely nor showed more loyalty to the priesthood than Belle Smith Spafford. This was her outstanding trait. I have been in the presence of the queen of more than one nation

118

and have judged them to be no more regal than our own Belle Spafford. I know that the Lord loves Sister Spafford.

We are naturally reluctant to speak of our own spiritual experiences. Nevertheless, I close with an experience that Sister Spafford and I shared. Under ordinary circumstances I should not relate it. Neither of us had spoken of it publicly until a year ago. One morning she called me deeply concerned and wanted to "confess" as she put it. The previous night she had spoken to a large gathering. Without having intended to do so, she was prompted to relate the experience in which I also had a small part. I felt that she had been prompted to do so. And since she has spoken of it then, I will speak of it now.

A Sacred Experience

On Sunday morning September 19, 1977, I awakened in the early hours of the morning greatly troubled over a dream that concerned Sister Spafford. My wife also awakened and asked why I was so restless. "Sister Spafford is in trouble," I told her. "She needs a blessing." When morning came I called her. She was deeply troubled indeed. I told her I had a blessing for her. She wept and said it came as an answer to her fervent prayer the night long. She had not been well. There had been tests. The day before the doctor told her the results. They were frightening—ominous indeed. There was a tumor and other complications. Steven Johnson, an attentive young neighbor, assisted me in the blessing. It was most unusual. Her life was not over. Her days were to be prolonged for a most important purpose. Promises, special promises were given, among them that her mind would be sharp and alert as long as she lived. There would be no diminution of her mental capabilities, and other promises not to be mentioned here, were given. All of them now have been fulfilled, and she has accomplished those things so dear to her. When further tests were made that next week, the tumor was not there.

We have seen the course of nature miraculously suspended before. President Kimball is an example of this. And I tell this incident to assure the sisters that the Lord is equally interested in His daughters. When I talked to her one week ago today her memory was sharp, her mind was clear, and we talked as we had on previous occasions about the day of parting which now has come to her.

I close with a few lines written by a friend of Sister Spafford's and of mine and of yours—President Joseph Fielding Smith. The last two verses of his hymn, "Does the Journey Seem Long?"

> Let your heart be not faint
> Now the journey's begun;
> There is One who still beckons to you.
> Look upward in gladness
> And take hold of his hand,
> He will lead you to heights that are new.
>
> A land holy and pure
> Where all trouble doth end,
> And your life shall be free from all sin,
> Where no tears shall be shed
> For no sorrows remain;
> Take his hand and with him enter in.
>
> (*Hymns,* no. 245.)

Our beloved Sister Spafford has now entered in there—obedient, dutiful, inspired. She is now home to a glorious reunion. God bless her memory. I testify to the reality of the Resurrection. Occasionally we may see beyond the veil—see a glimpse of that which the Father has prepared for those who are faithful to Him. I know that He lives, that Jesus is the Christ. The life of Sister Spafford is the life of a worthy, faithful, handmaiden of the Lord. May God bless all of us as we journey home through the years to that reunion, I humbly pray in the name of Jesus Christ, amen.

12

A Change In Command

Just one month ago today the Council of the Twelve Apostles assembled in the temple in solemn assembly and effected the reorganization of the First Presidency of the Church.

We, likewise, have had the new year—New Year's Day—and I think all of us take time on New Year's to review and evaluate. We look back over our shoulder briefly and then plot the course ahead to see where it is that we are going.

I have, as you have, had some very deep feelings over the events that have transpired. I thought it may not be untoward to expose some of those feelings. I think *feeling* is a more descriptive word than *thought*—relating to what we've witnessed in these last few weeks.

The Architect of Priesthood Correlation

Harold B. Lee—prophet, seer, and revelator. All of us have been close to him and worked closely with him over the last few years. He, of course, could properly be titled the "architect of Priesthood Correlation." Under assignment from President David O. McKay he served as chairman of the Correlation Committee for many years. As a counselor to President Joseph Fielding Smith, and as President of the Church, he directed what is known as Priesthood Correlation. We have visited with him, sometimes in intimate conversations, in travel, or in his office, or in meetings such as this. We've looked back with him to his junior years as a member of the Council of the Twelve.

He saw some drifting and felt some anxiety, and he carried that concern with him for years. There is no question but that he saw today, for he was a seer; or that he understood and saw what was out in the world. He saw the narrow places that we must navigate as a Church.

Address given to the Church Coordinating Council January 30, 1974.

And, over the years, as he grew in stature, there came, as he often expressed, ideas that met their day. You've heard him say that there are ideas that have come up against their day.

We've been workers in this vineyard of correlation, all of us. Many of us, most of us I suppose, were here for the seed planting, when the first changes were made, the first speculations on where we were going, the first analysis of the Church. Then we've seen the correlation program grow and blossom and now come to something of a fruition.

Now, all of this is not without precedent in the Church. In the early days there was what was called the *retrenchment*. If you've read Church history, you know that it was not a program nor an organization. It was a retrenchment—what could be described, I think, as an almost evangelical call across the Church to return to the basic principles; it was a sweeping thing across the Church that had great influence. It was fostered by the Brethren.

"What Does It Mean?"—A Parable

Now, as we were jolted by the death of President Lee and sat up and took note of what happened, all of us, I think, asked ourselves the question and asked one another, "Well, what does it mean? Harold B. Lee has gone. What does that mean?"

I think I could expose my feelings best by resorting to something of a parable—a homemade parable, if you will.

Imagine a group of people who are going on a journey through a territory that is dangerous and unplotted. They have a large bus for transportation, and they are making preparations. They find among them a master mechanic. He is appointed to get their vehicle ready, with all of us to help. He insists that it be stripped down completely, every part taken from the other part and inspected carefully, cleaned, renewed, repaired, and some of them replaced.

Some of the gears are not efficient. They are not producing the power they should for the amount of fuel they use. And so they are replaced. This means a change in linkage, a change in the pattern of connections and delivering the power. So they go to work, with this master mechanic directing the retooling and refitting of this vehicle.

There are steep inclines that must be made and there has to be sufficient power. There will be curves and switchbacks, there will be

122

places where control will have to be perfect, where the braking will have to be perfect.

So, painstakingly and deliberately, without undue pressure, the bus is disassembled and ultimately put together again.

Then comes the time when there has to be a shakedown, a test run, if you will. The signal comes that this master mechanic will also be appointed the driver. He will head the journey.

So the test is run. It is not a very long one, but there are some very difficult obstacles in it so that it is a full test. All of us, as we stand by, are delighted with the result. It is roadworthy. Now we know that it will make every hill and it will go over and, if necessary, through any obstacle in its way.

We see the master mechanic, pleased with his work, step down, and say that it's ready. He dusts a little dust off the radiator cap.

Then comes the signal that another will drive. And the protest comes: "Oh, but not another! We need him to drive. There's never been anyone who has seen so much and knows so much about the vehicle we are going to use. No man in all history has so completely gone through this vehicle and no one knows as much as he knows. No one is so thoroughly familiar with it."

But the command is definite. Another will drive. Some protest that the new driver isn't so much a mechanic. "What if there is trouble along the way?" And the answer comes back, "Perhaps that's all to the good that he may not be a mechanic. It may well be, for should there be a little grinding of the gears he won't be quite so inclined to strip it down, take out all the gears, and start to overhaul it again. He'll try first a little lubrication perhaps, a little grease here and there, and that will be all it needs."

Another Must Drive

We must now move forward and move out. The signal comes to all of us who are on the crew. "Climb aboard. Another's been appointed to drive." We obediently and with acceptance move out into that journey.

The death of a prophet is never accidental. A prophet cannot be taken, save his ministry is complete. Those of us who were present in that first meeting that first morning after that night of shock came to know that *He* is in charge. This is His work and He will do as He will do. We of the Twelve were reminded in those meetings as the reorganization was effected that "...my thoughts are not your thoughts, neither are your ways my ways." (Isaiah 55:8.)

The work of President Harold B. Lee will have effect just as long as this Church endures; until the Lord Himself says, "It is finished," until His work is done. Never through all generations can it be minimized or mitigated.

Never will the Church be the same, always it will run with more precision, more power. So that as we are on the hills, we will make the grade. When we are on the switchbacks, we will have the control. The brakes are intact so that they can be applied if we move too quickly or stray too closely to the edge of safe travel.

And so the question then: What about those of us of the crew? What's ahead then? What's our signal?

I would like to give some feelings on that and remind you that he told us that also if we were listening. Several times in the last few months he said in our meetings, and I am sure in your hearing, "Brethren, we must begin to gear down. We must begin to reduce the pattern of changes. We must now turn from restructuring, remodeling, and overhauling, and dedicate ourselves and employ ourselves to maintenance and to operation."

I remind you that Brother McConkie said that essentially in his talk. I remind you that Brother Monson concluded his talk with the same thought. "We'll move into the house now and live in it. We've moved the walls enough. We've shifted the doors enough and rearranged the windows enough."

A Respite from Change

I say this with deep conviction, that *no change now, no improvement now, is anywhere near so vital as a respite from change* and that *no weakness in our programs can be quite so damaging or so dangerous as a continual restructuring to avoid or erase that weakness.*

So, I would think it's time now to put the major construction tools in the back of the shop. They'll be there if we need them. Bring out the tune-up equipment and the tools for maintenance and begin to move ahead without the thought or necessity that we are going to remodel everything again.

A Change in Command

Now, if I could speak plainly, I would say that I am thinking of all the committees. How many are there? Thirty? Or one hundred and thirty? I don't know. I don't know anybody who does know. If I were to guess I would guess it would be far above the higher number I mentioned. And the number of people employed on those committees— one hundred? one thousand? I don't know and I don't know anybody who does know. I think it may be above the higher number. And what are they doing precisely? I don't know. I'm not sure that there is anybody who knows.

As we turn now to maintenance and operation, I wonder if the image of the automobile I used may not be misleading because we must come to know that unlike automobiles we don't need to bring out a new model every year. We may have to take the vehicle we've got and be content with it for years to come.

Now, we note, and with some anxiety, the tendency to begin to restructure things that are hardly announced in the field. I remind you that Brother McConkie mentioned that in his remarks. Brother Monson mentioned it.

I would like to mention just two or three. There are no inferences in choosing these. I'm just using examples and there are many other examples. Consider the Bishop's Training Program. It's been out a year or two and they're just getting to it when we think of remodeling it. Likewise with the Teacher Development Program, library, reporting system, and many, many others that we could mention. They've been fielded, hardly out there, hardly settled in, when we see a little flaw or a little error. We get out the drawing boards, we call in the designers, and we say let's redo it, bring out another model.

I think that in the months and perhaps years ahead we will find that we'll have to use a little oil, a little grease here and there; we can tighten it a bit, we can loosen it a bit; but no major overhauling of programs. I repeat, that no change or improvement now is so vital as a respite from change. As we move out into the field and see the beleaguered stake presidents, quorum leaders, and bishops, we know we must cut down.

This Is for You

And so, suppose each of us in his assignment begins to look over his committees. If I can speak bluntly, we have a tendency in this Church

125

when we hear the doctrine preached, to say, "It's too bad Brother Jones isn't here. He sure needs this sermon." Now, this is for you and your organization.

Let me suggest this, for instance. Three years ago we talked about the restructuring of general boards. When the Sunday School General Board was reorganized, as a Presidency and the Twelve we came to the conclusion that as the Church doubled, we cannot double the size of general boards. We can't look forward to the time when we would have 200, 300, or 600 people on general boards as we were then proliferating them. And so the announcement was made for executives to choose a different kind of board member for different purposes. We began to gear down; yet we still have essentially the same large boards.

The travel for general boards now has been reduced fully by 90 percent. Fully 90 percent reduction in travel. Then came the announcement that Instructional Development will take over much of the writing and the preparation of the lessons in collaboration with the boards and the officers. Maybe many of the board members would find better employment in writing because they have had the experience in the organizations and understand them.

This Is His Church

Maybe we can begin to reduce and maybe we can get the courage to cut down and release some committees and some from boards. Where once we thought: "Well, we just can't release her, she's been here for so many years and she loves it so much." Or, "He's put so much into this committee." Or, "We feel an obligation to him." Or, "We feel an obligation to her." Or, "This one is well connected." We will now consider the needs of the Church first.

This is *His* church, not *a* church. This is *the* Church. The Church of Jesus Christ of Latter-day Saints. I suggest that the day is here when we say to many who have been employed to overhaul this Church "Thanks for a job well done." "Thank you." "The Lord bless you." "He'll find other spiritual employment for you." For these many people on hundreds of committees who are commissioned to restructure and remodel the programs of the Church a reorientation is necessary.

One other thought. We have employees—hundreds, indeed thousands of employees—many of them in creative fields. And there's the tendency, a natural tendency, for an employee to feel that he has failed unless the results of his work somehow are evidenced in change. It may be a change in programming or structure. It may be a change in procedure. But unless they've effected a change, they feel that they've failed.

I suggest that we are all under obligation to look at those who work under our direction fulltime. Begin to give the feeling to them that it's a maintenance and operation assignment now.

There are many plans; there are thousands of plans on hundreds of drawing boards with hundreds of architects looking over them. If I had the courage I would say, "Let's roll them up. Mark them for future reference. Put them up on the shelf. We can get them down if necessary."

If you have major changes and restructuring on the drawing board, I say you should look them over and perhaps discard them. Remember, it is your Church as much as it is ours, and He is your Lord as much as He is ours. We have now a driver heading this journey who is committed to principle, a procedures-and-programs principle.

John Taylor made this statement. This is from the *Millennial Star*, November 15, 1851.

> Concerning government: Some years ago, in Nauvoo, a gentleman in my hearing, a member of the legislature, asked Joseph Smith how it was that he was enabled to govern so many people, and to preserve such perfect order; remarking at the same time that it was impossible for them to do it anywhere else. Mr. Smith remarked that it was very easy to do that. "How?" responded the gentleman; "to us it is very difficult." Mr. Smith replied,

(And this reference we are all familiar with. It is common among us but in this generation it now needs to be employed.)

> I teach them correct principles, and they govern themselves.

The brethren in England in early days had many major problems finding their way. They wrote to the Prophet Joseph Smith. I quote part of his answer.

> There are many things of much importance, on which you ask counsel, but I think you will be perfectly able to decide upon, as you are more conversant with the peculiar circumstances than am I; and I feel great confidence in your united wisdom; therefore, you will excuse me for not

entering into detail. If I should see anything that is wrong, I would take the privilege of making known my mind to you and pointing out the evil. (*Teachings of the Prophet Joseph Smith,* p. 176.)

What does it all mean: programs and procedures, and restructuring, remodeling and renovating? We need to live in the house, as Brother Monson says, for a while. We might not be quite so quick to change that door, remove that window, or put in that partition after we have lived in it a bit.

Another Parable

I would like to cite from another parable. This, from the fifth chapter of Jacob. I think that the Lord is saying something to us in our day.

> And it came to pass that the servant said unto his master: How comest thou hither to plant this tree, or this branch of the tree? For behold, it was the poorest spot in all the land of the vineyard.
>
> And the Lord of the vineyard said unto him: Counsel me not; I knew that it was a poor spot of ground; wherefore, I said unto thee, I have nourished it this long time, and thou beholdest that it hath brought forth much fruit. (Jacob 5:21-22.)

And then they came back and

> Behold, the wild branches have grown and have overrun the roots thereof; and because that the wild branches have overcome the roots thereof it hath brought forth much evil fruit. (Jacob 5:37.)

And then the master of the vineyard

> wept, and said unto the servant: What could I have done more for my vineyard? (Jacob 5:41.)

And then,

> Now behold, notwithstanding all the care which we have taken of my vineyard, the trees thereof have become corrupted, that they bring forth no good fruit; and these I had hoped to preserve, to have laid up fruit thereof against the season, unto mine own self. But, behold, they have become like unto the wild olive-tree, (Jacob 5:46.)

(And need I mention anything more than grooming?)

> and they are of no worth but to be hewn down and cast into the fire; and it grieveth me that I should lose them. (Jacob 5:46.)

A Change in Command

> But what could I have done more in my vineyard? Have I slackened mine hand, that I have not nourished it? Nay, I have nourished it, and I have digged about it, and I have pruned it, and I have dunged it; and I have stretched forth mine hand almost all the day long, and the end draweth nigh. And it grieveth me that I should hew down all the trees of my vineyard, and cast them into the fire that they should be burned. Who is it that has corrupted my vineyard? (Jacob 5:47.)

Now, listen carefully:

> And it came to pass that the servant said unto his master: Is it not the loftiness of thy vineyard—have not the branches thereof overcome the roots which are good? And because the branches have overcome the roots thereof, behold they grew faster than the strength of the roots, taking strength unto themselves. Behold, I say, is not this the cause that the trees of thy vineyard have become corrupted? (Jacob 5:48.)

Now, the next verses:

> And it came to pass that the Lord of the vineyard said unto the servant: Let us go to and hew down the trees of the vineyard and cast them into the fire, that they shall not cumber the ground of my vineyard, for I have done all. What could I have done more for my vineyard?
>
> But, behold, the servant said unto the Lord of the vineyard: Spare it a little longer.
>
> And the Lord said: Yea, I will spare it a little longer, for it grieveth me that I should lose the trees of my vineyard. (Jacob 5:49-51.)
>
> For it grieveth me that I should lose the trees of my vineyard; wherefore ye shall clear away the bad according as the good shall grow, that the root and the top may be equal in strength, until the good shall overcome the bad, and the bad be hewn down and cast into the fire, that they cumber not the ground of my vineyard; and thus will I sweep away the bad out of my vineyard. (Jacob 5:66.)

The bigger we get, the bigger we get. We have a tendency to think that if one is good, two are better. If two are good, four would be superior, and so on. We get an assignment, and we think that unless it has touched every meeting, every activity, every worship service; unless it is seen on every bulletin board and on every schedule; unless it is on every agenda, we've failed.

We feel that unless we somehow convince the member of the Church that he should be a missionary, to the exclusion of everything; or a genealogist, to the exclusion of everything; or a youth leader, to the exclusion of everything; we think we have failed.

129

In Wisdom and in Order

There is one more scripture that comes to mind:

> And see that all these things are done in wisdom and order; for it is not requisite that a man should run faster than he has strength. And again, it is expedient that he should be diligent, that thereby he might win the prize; therefore, all things must be done in order. (Mosiah 4:27.)

We must do things in order with moderation and dignity and restraint.

Now, those feelings, brethren and sisters, have been on my mind constantly. I can confess sleepless nights as I have prayed and wondered and pondered over "why?" Why, I thought, when we needed President Lee the most, he who was familiar and conversant as no man ever had been with the programs of the Church, was he taken from us? But the peace was there immediately. There is no question, the Lord is in charge.

President Spencer W. Kimball

Now, one final thought. I was given an assignment to prepare an article for the *Ensign* on President Spencer W. Kimball of the Council of the Twelve. I went to work on it. I visited with him. I traveled with him and had some intimate conversations with him. But I couldn't get going. I tried, I built a file and I fussed with it. Finally I felt, well, is this article supposed to be something else?

As I look at President Kimball, I have the feeling that we move into a period where there will be more emphasis on principles and less emphasis on programs and procedures.

His whole life has been a preparation for the call that he now has received. He was tested even in the days of his childhood.

His father, who had been on an Indian mission for some twelve years, was sent to Arizona as a stake president. There were eleven children in the family and Sister Kimball, his mother, was expecting the twelfth child and was not well. Her husband took her to Salt Lake City where there was better medical attention available. One day word came to the school that the Kimball children were wanted at home. Racing from his classroom, little Spencer saw the other children coming from their rooms. They ran home expecting, no doubt, to hear the announcement of a new little brother or a new little sister. Old

Bishop Moody gathered them in his arms and said, "Your mother has died."

Then, before there came a loving stepmother, there was the typhoid fever. He lay near death for weeks. Nothing could be done. There was the labor of a father who was a stake president with precious little to live on. The cow and the garden were essential. It seemed nothing but work, work, work.

Finally as he moved forward there were other tests that only a few of us know, and many that none but him know, I am sure.

He was called to the Council of the Twelve. Six years later, stricken with heart attacks, he pushed against them until he was flattened. The doctor said he had to get away. He went to his Indians, to the Polacca family in Arizona, in the pines, there to spend the weeks necessary to recuperate.

One day they lost him. He wasn't there for breakfast. He had gone for a walk, they supposed. As the day wore on and he didn't show up, Brother Polacca got the other Navajos and with great concern for their ailing brother they began a circular search from the camp. When they found him he was sitting under a tree reading the scriptures. He had the Bible open to the gospel of John. It was obvious to them that he had been weeping. As they came and gathered around him, he looked up and in answer to their anxious expressions said simply, "Six years ago today I was called as a special witness of the Lord Jesus Christ, and I just wanted to spend the day with Him whose witness I am."

Then we've lived in our day to see him suffering with throat cancer. Elder Lee made the statement to the doctors in New York, "This is no ordinary man you're operating on." A little fiber of vocal cord was left that the doctor, under normal radical procedures, would have excised, and President Kimball's voice was saved.

And then there were other recurring heart attacks. He told me one day coming from the temple, "The doctor says it's like this," and he gestured with his hand a level course that turned sharply downward, meaning the end.

I said, "How long?"

And he said, "Months, maybe two."

I said, "If they operate, what then?"

He replied, "They don't know. They don't have statistics on seventy-seven-year-old men undergoing these procedures."

131

That All May Be Edified

And I said, "Should you survive, what then?"

He said, "Like this," and he gestured with a long level gesture.

I said, "How long?"

And he said, "Years."

There were other tests. Tests more terrible than any of these physical tests, not to be mentioned publicly, but he has told his brethren of the Twelve. On two occasions at stake quarterly conferences, not related to the incidents of business there, he was subject to what must have been the full might of the adversary. These experiences, not to be recorded here in detail, were not unlike that his grandfather recorded when he was opening the work in England. Nor were these experiences unlike those the Prophet Joseph Smith felt as he first knelt in the grove.

I'm not suggesting that these physical tests and his fine personality and all of the rest of his qualifications are his authority to act. I'm suggesting that the Lord is saying something to us and that if we have eyes to see and ears to hear and hearts that will be penetrated, we will understand. President Kimball's qualification comes because he is an Apostle—a prophet.

The Lord, as scripture records it,

> in those days... went out into a mountain to pray, and continued all night in prayer to God.
> And when it was day, he called unto him his disciples: and of them he chose twelve, whom also he named apostles. (Luke 6:12-13.)

Special Witnesses

They were to stand as servants, special witnesses, to set in order His church in all the world. As He called them in that day—Peter, James and John, Andrew, Philip and Bartholomew, Matthew, Thomas, and the others—power and authority were given them to guide His kingdom. In our day it is Spencer, Nathan, and Marion, Ezra, Mark, Delbert, and the others, holding precisely the same authority and possessed of the same witness and authorized with power to guide and direct His Church.

Those of us who are your advisers in Internal Communications are anxious over these things, and we pray that you will not take the instruction that you get lightly. It seems unsettling at times to set out on a course and then abruptly have it blunted and set in another direction. We can feel thwarted from doing something that seems so good at the moment. *But we must learn to accept direction.*

I have an idea that as the Lord has spoken and as His peace has come to us that we have received a signal and now we must climb aboard and move ahead. We must turn from manufacturing programs to the using of them. Turn from the mining of ideals to the refining of them. Turn from the overhauling and remodeling of programs and procedures to the maintenance and operation of them.

There is no power that can thwart this work. It is the Lord's work. He directs it. He is no stranger to His servants on this earth. He guides it and directs it. Of Him I bear witness, in the name of Jesus Christ, amen.

13

We Are Going to Find Him

My dear brothers and sisters, it is a great privilege to present a message in this historic and sacred meeting for the temple dedication. I hope we will be united by the Spirit at this time.

When I am in South America there is someone I always look for. I first met him fourteen years ago in Cuzco, Peru, the ancient city in the top of the Andes.

Brother Tuttle and I were attending a sacrament meeting in the Cuzco Branch. We were seated at one end of the room facing the congregation. Behind the congregation was a door which opened onto the street. Against the wall to our left was a small sacrament table. The room was full of people. The door to the street was open for the cool night air to enter.

The Boy

While Brother Tuttle was speaking, a little boy appeared in the doorway. He was perhaps six or seven years old. His only clothing was a tattered shirt which almost reached his knees. He was dirty and undernourished, with all the characteristics of a street orphan. Perhaps he entered the room to get warm, but then he saw the bread on the sacrament table.

He began to approach, carefully walking next to the wall. When he was just about to reach the sacrament table, one of the sisters saw him. Without saying a word, with only a movement of her head, she clearly communicated the message, "out." He hesitated an instant, turned around, and disappeared into the night. My heart wept for him. Undoubtedly the sister felt justified because this was a special meeting, with General Authorities present, and this was a dirty little boy who

---

Address given at the dedication of the Brazil Temple November 1978.

wasn't going to learn anything, and after all, he wasn't even a member of the Church.

In a short time he appeared in the doorway again, looking toward the bread. Again he began to quietly approach the table. He had almost reached the row where the woman was sitting when I got him to look at me. I held out my open arms. He came to me, and I picked him up to hold him in my arms.

They Are Ours

I felt that I had an entire people in my arms. It was a deeply moving experience. Dirty little boys and girls, in tatters, are not offensive to me, nor are their brave parents repugnant to me because they are ours.

In order to teach the members an important principle, I had the child sit in President Tuttle's seat. When the meeting ended, he got down from the seat and darted out into the night. I have looked for him since then.

Now he would be old enough to serve a mission, so I have looked for him in missionary meetings in Chile, Peru, Ecuador, Colombia, and Brazil.

Perhaps he is married now with his own child in tatters. I have hoped to see him in some conference or leadership meeting. I have looked for his face in the congregations. Many times I have thought I saw him in a crowd of people, or beside the road, or in the Indian market. He would be taller now, and would no longer appear in our doorway on his own. It must be harder now to enter. He was innocent then—but now?

Perhaps he has a sister. I have also looked everywhere for her. I have looked in our meetings among the sister missionaries—everywhere. Some must think it is a search in vain, but we are going to find them, because we are going to check all the souls in South America.

Perhaps we won't find him until his own children have grown in stature or have their own children, but we are going to find him. Perhaps someone may say that he has died, that he has gone away. We will find him anyway. We will sort through all the names, every soul who has lived in South America, to make sure we haven't overlooked him.

A Voice from the Dust

I felt something when I held that child in my arms. A voice from the dust, perhaps from the dust of those small feet, already rough, whispered to me that this was a child of the covenant, of the lineage of the prophets. When we find him, and we are going to find him, we will bring him here to the temple—clean, well nourished, and pure—to be endowed and to kneel for sacred sealings. If he has departed, his son will come here in his place.

I have been in Cuzco since that time, and now I see this people whom I held in my arms, coming to be baptized, to preach, to preside. They will find him. Some day perhaps he will be there in Cuzco in a sacrament meeting as one of the twelve chosen Apostles. He will bear witness as I bear witness, that the day of the children of Laman and Lemuel and Nephi has come, that the Book of Mormon, the voice from the dust, is true. He will bear witness as I bear special witness that Jesus is the Christ, the Son of God, the Only Begotten of the Father. In the name of Jesus Christ, amen.

14

Families and Fences

I come to this pulpit this Sabbath morning with a new obligation, anxious perhaps as never before for the sustaining influence of the Spirit of the Lord, for an interest in your faith and prayers for us here and for those who shall be listening, as I speak to the parents of wayward and lost children.

Sometime ago a father, worried about a serious problem with his son, was heard to remark, "When he leaves and we don't know where he is, there's pain in our hearts; but when he's here, there are times when he's a pain in the neck." It's about that pain in the heart that I want to speak. I speak to a very large audience, I fear.

Hardly is there a neighborhood without at least one mother whose last waking, anxious thoughts and prayers are for a son or a daughter wandering who knows where. Nor is there much distance between homes where an anxious father can hardly put in a day's work without being drawn within himself time after time, to wonder, *What have we done wrong? What can we do to get our child back?*

What Have We Done? What Can We Do?

Even parents with the best intentions—some who have really tried—now know that heartache. Many parents have tried in every way to protect their children—only now to find they are losing one. For the home and the family are under attack. Ponder these words, if you will:

> *Profanity*
> *Nudity*
> *Immorality*
> *Divorce*
> *Pornography*
> *Addiction*

Address given at general conference October 1970.

That All May Be Edified

Violence
Perversion

These words have taken on a new meaning in the last few years, haven't they?

You are within walking distance, at least within a few minutes' drive, of a theater in your own neighborhood. There will be shown, within the week, a film open to young and old alike that as recently as ten years ago would have been banned, the film confiscated, and the theater owner placed under indictment. But now it's there, and soon it will be seen at home on your television screens.

The Apostle Paul prophesied to Timothy:

> This know also, that in the last days perilous times shall come.
> For men shall be lovers of their own selves, covetous, boasters, proud, blasphemers, disobedient to parents. (2 Timothy 3:1-2.)

Disobedient to Parents

There is more to that scripture, but we stop on that phrase "disobedient to parents."

We have no desire to touch the subject that causes you so much pain, nor to condemn you as a failure. But you are failing, and that's what makes it hurt. If failure is to end, one must face squarely problems like this, however much it hurts.

A few years ago I was called in the wee hours of the morning to the side of my ailing mother, who was hospitalized for a series of tests.

"I'm going home," she said. "I'll not continue with these tests. I want you to take me home right now. I won't go through another day of this."

"But mother," I said, "you must go through with this. They have reason to believe that you have cancer, and if it is as they suppose, you have the worst kind."

There! It had been said. After all the evading, all the whispered conversations. After all the care never to say that word when she was around. It was out.

She sat quietly on her bed for a long time and then said, "Well, if that's what it is, that's what it is, and I'll fight it." Her Danish dander was up. And fight it she did, and winner she was.

Some may suppose she lost her battle to that disease, but she came away a glorious, successful winner. Her victory was assured when she faced the painful truth. Her courage began then.

Face the Painful Truth

Parents, can we first consider the most painful part of your problem? If you want to reclaim your son or daughter, why don't you leave off trying to alter your child just for a little while and concentrate on yourself. The changes must begin with you, not with your children.

You can't continue to do what you have been doing (even though you thought it was right) and expect to unproduce some behavior in your child, when your conduct was one of the things that produced it.

There! It's been said! After all the evading, all the concern for wayward children. After all the blaming of others, the care to be gentle with parents. It's out! It's you, not the child, who needs immediate attention.

Now, parents, there is substantial help for you if you will accept it. I add with emphasis that the help we propose is not easy, for the measures are equal to the seriousness of your problem. There is no patent medicine to effect an immediate cure.

And parents, if you seek for a cure that ignores faith and religious doctrine, you look for a cure where it never will be found. When we talk of religious principles and doctrines and quote scripture, interesting, isn't it, how many don't feel comfortable with talk like that? But when we talk about your problems with your family and offer a solution, then your interest is intense.

Know that you can't talk about one without talking about the other and expect to solve your problems. Once parents know that there is a God and that we are His children, they can face problems like this and win.

If you are helpless, He is not.

If you are lost, He is not.

If you don't know what to do next, He knows.

It would take a miracle, you say? Well, if it takes a miracle, why not. We urge you to move first on a course of prevention.

There is a poem entitled "The Fence or the Ambulance." It tells of

139

efforts to provide an ambulance at the bottom of a cliff and concludes with these two verses:

> Then an old sage remarked: "It's a marvel to me
> That people give far more attention
> To repairing results than to stopping the cause
> When they'd much better aim at prevention.
> Let us stop at its source all this mischief," cried he,
> "Come, neighbors and friends, let us rally;
> If the cliff we will fence, we might almost dispense
> With the ambulance down in the valley."
>
> Better guide well the young than reclaim them when old,
> For the voice of true wisdom is calling:
> "To rescue the fallen is good, but 'tis best
> To prevent other people from falling."
> Better close up the source of temptation and crime,
> Than deliver from dungeon or galley;
> Better put a strong fence round the top of the cliff,
> Than an ambulance down in the valley.
>
> (Joseph Malins.)

Prevention—the Strong Fence

We prevent physical disease by immunization. This heart pain you are suffering perhaps might likewise have been prevented with very simple measures at one time. Fortunately the very steps necessary for prevention are the ones that will produce the healing. In other words, prevention is the best cure, even in advanced cases.

I would like to show you a very practical and a very powerful place to begin, both to protect your children and, in the case of one you are losing, to redeem him.

I have in my hands the publication *Family Home Evenings*. It is the seventh in a series and is available across the world in seventeen languages. If you would go through it with me, you would find that this one is based on the New Testament. The theme is free agency. While it draws lessons from New Testament days, it does not content itself with them back then and there. It leaps across the centuries and concerns itself with you and here and now.

It is well illustrated, much of it in full color, and has many meaningful activities for families with children of any age.

There is here, for instance, a crossword puzzle. And here on this

140

colorful page is a game. Cut it out and make a spinner of cardboard, and the whole family can play. You'll find yourselves, depending on the moves you make, somewhere between "Heavenly Treasures" and "Earthly Pleasures."

There is a lesson entitled "How Our Family Came to Be." "Tell your children," it suggests, "how you met, fell in love, and married. Be sure both parents participate, and illustrate your story with pictures and mementoes you have saved—the wedding dress, the announcements; wedding pictures. It might be a good idea to tape your narrative and keep it for your children to play to their children some day."

Let me list some of the other titles: "Our Family Government," "Learning to Worship," "Speaking Words of Purity," "Family Finances," "Parenthood, a Sacred Opportunity," "Respect for Authority," "The Value of Humor," "So You're Going to Move," "When the Unexpected Happens," "The Birth and Infancy of the Savior."

Here is one entitled "A Call to Be Free." That's the siren call your child is following, you know. This lesson includes a page of very official-looking colored certificates with instructions to "choose for each family member some activity he has not learned to do; then give each member a certificate . . . signed by the father: 'This certificate gives the owner permission to play a tune on the piano as a part of family home evening.'" (Of course, the child has never had piano lessons.)

Other certificates may include (depending on the age of the child) "walking on one's hands, speaking in a foreign language, or painting an oil portrait." Then as each member says he cannot do the thing permitted, talk about why he is not free to do the thing he is permitted to do. The discussion will reveal that "each person must learn the laws that govern the development of an ability and then learn to obey those laws. Thus obedience leads to freedom."

Under special helps for families with small children, it suggests they put toy cars on the table top and feel free to run them anywhere they want and in any manner they like. Even little minds can see the results of this.

There is much more to this lesson and to all of these special lessons —subtle, powerful magnets that help to draw your child closer to the family circle.

This program is designed for a family meeting to be held once a week. In the Church, Monday night has been designated and set aside, Churchwide, for families to be at home together. Instruction has recently gone out, from which I quote:

> Those responsible for priesthood and auxiliary programs, including temple activities, youth athletic activities, student activities, etc., should take notice of this decision in order that Monday night will be uniformly observed throughout the Church and the families be left free from Church activities so that they can meet together in the family home evening. (*Priesthood Bulletin,* September 1970.)

The Promise

With this program comes the promise from the prophets, the living prophets, that if parents will gather their children about them once a week and teach the gospel, those children in such families will not go astray.

Some of you outside the Church, and unfortunately many within, hope that you could take a manual like this without accepting fully the gospel of Jesus Christ, the responsibilities of Church membership, and the scriptures upon which it is based. You are permitted to do that. (We could even give you a "certificate" to permit you to raise an ideal family.) You still would not be free to do so without obeying the laws. To take a program like this without the gospel would have you act as one who obtained a needle to immunize a child against a fatal disease but rejected the serum to go in it that could save him.

Parents, it is past time for you to assume spiritual leadership of your family. If there is no substance to your present belief, then have the courage to seek the truth.

There is living now the finest generation of youth that ever walked the earth. You have seen some of them serving on missions. Perhaps you have turned them away. You ought to seek them out. If they are nothing else, they are adequate evidence that youth can live in honor. And there are tens of thousands of them who are literal saints—Latter-day Saints.

Never Give Up

Now, parents, I desire to inspire you with hope. You who have heartache, you must never give up. No matter how dark it gets or no matter how far away or how far down your son or daughter has fallen, you must never give up. Never, never, never.

I desire to inspire you with hope.

> Soft as the voice of an angel, whispering a message unheard,
> Hope with a gentle persuasion whispers her comforting word.
> Wait till the darkness is over, wait till the coming of dawn,
> Hope for the sunshine tomorrow, after the shower is gone.
> Whispering hope, Oh how welcome thy voice.
>
> ("Whispering Hope," Alice Hawthorne.)

God bless you heartbroken parents. There is no pain so piercing as that caused by the loss of a child, nor joy so exquisite as the joy at his redemption.

I come to you now as one of the Twelve, each ordained as a special witness. I affirm to you that I have that witness. I know that God lives, that Jesus is the Christ. I know that though the world "seeth him not, neither knoweth him," that He lives. Heartbroken parents, lay claim upon His promise: "I will not leave you comfortless; I will come to you." (John 14:17-18.) In the name of Jesus Christ, amen.

15

A Tribute
to the Rank and File
of the Church

That day, 150 years ago, came and went quietly.

Those who met in that humble farmhouse to organize The Church of Jesus Christ of Latter-day Saints were not—indeed they were not—the prominent men of their day.

Only a few, and they of most humble prospect, were party to it. It was as Paul had told the Corinthians:

> Not many wise men after the flesh, not many mighty, not many noble, are called:
>   But God hath chosen the foolish things of the world to confound the wise; and God hath chosen the weak things of the world to confound the things which are mighty. (1 Corinthians 1:26-27.)

This sacred event, witnessed by those few, had been preceded by marvelous spiritual manifestations.

In preparation for it the Father and the Son had appeared to one of them. He had been called as the Prophet.

Angelic messengers had instructed them.

The principle of revelation, thought by most to have concluded in centuries past, was demonstrated to be ongoing.

The Book of Mormon had been published, and its pages carried a testimony of the prophet Moroni that angels have not "ceased to appear unto the children of men." Nor will they "so long as time shall last, or the earth shall stand, or there shall be one man upon the face thereof to be saved." (Moroni 7:36.)

These humble men from among the common folks of that day were to become Apostles of the Lord Jesus Christ, as surely as Peter, the

---

Address given at general conference April 1980.

fisherman, and the other common men had been made Apostles in ancient times.

And so the angels came, a continuation of them, to teach these men, to confer the priesthood upon them, to deliver keys of authority to them; for these were things that men could not assume, nor take to themselves.

Above all, the Lord Himself appeared and reappeared, "That the fulness of my gospel might be proclaimed by the weak and the simple unto the ends of the world." (D & C 1:23.)

Those Beginnings not so Far Away

Those days of beginning were not so far away as we sometimes think. There sits behind me on the stand Elder LeGrand Richards of the Quorum of the Twelve Apostles.

He remembers personally some of those who helped to open this work.

He attended the dedication of the Salt Lake Temple and remembers President Wilford Woodruff very clearly. He heard him speak on several occasions.

Yesterday Elder Faust mentioned the incident wherein Wilford Woodruff, leading a group of immigrants, was inspired not to take an ill-fated boat. Brother Richards heard Brother Woodruff give that sermon, name a number in the audience, and say to them, "If I had not followed that prompting, you would not be here today."

President Woodruff was only two years younger than the Prophet Joseph Smith, and he had been an Apostle for five years when the Prophet was martyred.

Hands we have touched have touched the hands that shaped the beginnings of this dispensation.

Some things have not changed very much over the years. Some things have not changed at all. This work has been brought through 150 years by ordinary men and women and children across the world.

The Rank and File

The rank and file of The Church of Jesus Christ of Latter-day Saints, present and past, who now number in the millions, have each carried their part.

That All May Be Edified

Lives are shaped through the influence of obscure, faithful members who carry the spirit of the gospel.

When once I tried to thank a great teacher and patriarch, William E. Berrett, he quickly passed the credit back to one who had taught him. An old convert from Norway was called to teach a group of mischievous Aaronic Priesthood boys. They were greatly amused by his broken English, but somehow the Spirit polished his words and soon the boys responded.

I have heard Brother Berrett testify on more than one occasion, "We could warm our hands by the fire of his faith."

President Heber J. Grant once heard Bishop Millen Atwood preach a sermon in the Thirteenth Ward:

> I was studying grammar at the time, and he made some grammatical errors in his talk.
>
> I wrote down his first sentence, smiled to myself, and said: "I am going to get...enough material to last me for the entire winter in my night school grammar class." We had to take...four sentences a week, that were not grammatically correct, together with our corrections.
>
> But I did not write anything more after that first sentence—not a word; and when Millen Atwood stopped preaching, tears were rolling down my cheeks, tears of gratitude and thanksgiving that welled up into my eyes because of the marvelous testimony which that man bore of the divine mission of Joseph Smith, the Prophet of God.
>
> Although it is now more than sixty-five years since I listened to that sermon, it is just as vivid today, and the sensations and feelings that I had are just as fixed with me, as they were the day I heard it.
>
> ...the one thing above all others that has impressed me has been the spirit, the inspiration of the living God that an individual had, when proclaiming the Gospel, and not the language....I have endeavored, from that day to this...to judge men and women by the spirit they have; for I have learned absolutely, that it is the spirit that giveth life and understanding, and not the letter—the letter killeth. (*Improvement Era*, April 1939, p. 201.)

Judging by the Spirit

Whenever we seek for true testimony we come, finally, to ordinary men and women and children.

Let me quote from the diary of Joseph Millett, a little-known missionary of an earlier time. Called on a mission to Canada, he went alone and on foot. In Canada, during the wintertime, he said:

"I felt my weakness. A poor, ill-clothed, ignorant boy in my teens, thousands of miles from home among strangers.

"The promise in my blessing and the encouraging words of President Young to me, with the faith I had in the gospel, kept me up.

"Many times I would turn into the woods... in some desolate place with a heart full, wet eyes, to call on my master for strength or aid.

"I believed the Gospel of Christ. I had never preached it. I knew not where to find it in the scriptures."

That didn't matter so much, for, "I had to give my Bible to the boatman at Digby for passage across the sound."

Years later, Joseph Millett, with his large family, was suffering through very, very difficult times. He wrote in his journal:

"One of my children came in and said that Brother Newton Hall's folks was out of bread, had none that day.

"I divided our flour in a sack to send up to Brother Hall. Just then Brother Hall came.

"Says I, 'Brother Hall, are you out of flour?'

" 'Brother Millett, we have none.'

" 'Well, Brother Hall, there is some in that sack. I have divided and was going to send it to you. Your children told mine that you was out.'

"Brother Hall began to cry. He said he had tried others, but could not get any. He went to the cedars and prayed to the Lord, and the Lord told him to go to Joseph Millett.

" 'Well, Brother Hall, you needn't bring this back. If the Lord sent you for it you don't owe me for it.' "

That night Joseph Millett recorded a remarkable sentence in his journal:

The Lord Knew Him

"You can't tell me how good it made me feel to know that the Lord knew there was such a person as Joseph Millett." (Diary of Joseph Millett, holograph, Archives of The Church of Jesus Christ of Latter-day Saints, Salt Lake City.)

The Lord knew Joseph Millett. And He knows all those men and women like him, and they are many. Theirs are the lives that are most worth recording.

This rank and file of the Church—150 years of them—have brought the truth to this generation. It is planted where it is most likely to bear an abundant harvest—in the hearts of the ordinary people.

When President Kimball first came here as a member of the

That All May Be Edified

Twelve, he was asked to sit for a portrait. (Those of us who know him well know how those hours of sitting still must have bothered him.) To keep him from daydreaming, the painter one day asked an abrupt question:

"Brother Kimball, have you ever been to heaven?"

His answer seemed to be a shock, as he said without hesitation, "Why, yes . . . certainly. I had a glimpse of heaven just before coming to your studio."

"I Had a Glimpse of Heaven"

He then told of an experience in the temple where he had performed a marriage:

> As the subdued congratulations were extended, a happy father . . . offered his hand and said, "Brother Kimball, my wife and I are common people and have never been successful, but we *are* immensely proud of our family. . . . This is the last of our eight children to come into this holy house for temple marriage. They, with their companions, are here to participate in the marriage of this, the youngest."
>
> I looked at his calloused hands, his rough exterior, and thought to myself, "Here is a real son of God fulfilling his destiny." (*Ensign*, December 1971, p. 36; also in *Conference Report*, October 1971, p. 152-53.)

They of the Last Wagon

President J. Reuben Clark told of pioneer members of the Church in these words:

> Day after day, they of the last wagon pressed forward, worn and tired, footsore, sometimes almost disheartened, borne up by their faith that God loved them, that the restored gospel was true, and that the Lord led and directed the Brethren out in front.

He then told of the morning:

> . . . when from out that last wagon floated the [cry] of the newborn babe, and mother love made a shrine, and Father bowed in reverence before it. But the train must move on. So out into the dust and dirt the last wagon moved again. . . .
>
> Who will dare to say that angels did not cluster round and guard her and ease her rude bed, for she had given another choice spirit its mortal body. (*Improvement Era*, November 1947, p. 705.)

148

Who would dare to say that angels do not now attend the rank and file of the Church who—
answer the calls to the mission fields,
teach the classes,
pay their tithes and offerings,
seek for the records of their forebears,
work in the temples,
raise their children in faith,
and have brought this work through 150 years?

There comes a witness, also, from some who have stumbled and fallen but have struggled back and have found the sweet, forgiving, cleansing influence of repentance. They now stand approved of the Lord, clean before Him; His Spirit has returned to them and they are guided by it. Without reviewing the hard lessons of the past they guide others to that Spirit.

Still a Day of Miracles

Who would dare to say that the day of miracles has ceased? Those things have not changed in 150 years, not changed at all.

For the power and inspiration of the Almighty rests upon this people today as surely as it did in those days of beginning:

"It is by faith that miracles are wrought; and it is by faith that angels appear and minister unto men; wherefore, if these things have ceased wo be unto the children of men, for it is because of unbelief." (Moroni 7:37.)

The prophet Moroni taught that angelic messengers would accomplish their work

> by declaring the word of Christ unto the chosen vessels of the Lord, that they may bear testimony of him.
>
> And by so doing, the Lord God prepareth the way that the residue of men may have faith in Christ, that the Holy Ghost may have place in their hearts." (Moroni 7:31-32.)

There has come, these last several years, a succession of announcements that show our day to be a day of intense revelation, equaled, perhaps, only in those days of beginning, 150 years ago.

But then, as now, the world did not believe. They say that ordinary men are not inspired; that there are no prophets, no Apostles; that angels do not minister unto men—not to ordinary men.

149

That All May Be Edified

Disbelief Cannot Change Truth

That doubt and disbelief have not changed. But now, as then, their disbelief cannot change the truth.

We lay no claim to being Apostles of the world—but of the Lord Jesus Christ. The test is not whether men will believe, but whether the Lord has called us—and of that there is no doubt!

We do not talk of those sacred interviews that qualify the servants of the Lord to bear a special witness of Him, for we have been commanded not to do so.

But we are free, indeed, we are obliged, to bear that special witness.

But that witness, the testimony of this work, is not reserved to those few of us who lead the Church. In proper order that witness comes to men and women and children all over the world.

Across the world the ordinary members, who might be described as obscure, bear witness that they were guided to this Church by revelation and that they are guided in their service in it.

Revelation that belongs to the prophet and president of the Church, to speak on matters for the entire Church, rests as well upon all who hold office, each within the limits of his calling.

It rests upon parents who preside over families, and if we will live for it, it will rest upon each of us.

Like all of my Brethren, I too come from among the ordinary people of the Church. I am the seventy-eighth man to be accepted by ordination into the Quorum of the Twelve Apostles in this dispensation.

Compared to the others who have been called, I am nowhere near their equal, save it be, perhaps, in the certainty of the witness we share.

I feel compelled, on this one hundred fiftieth anniversary of the Church, to certify to you that I know that the day of miracles has not ceased.

I know that angels minister unto men.

I am a witness to the truth that Jesus is the Christ, the Son of God, the Only Begotten of the Father; that He has a body of flesh and bone; that He knows those who are His servants here and that He is known of them.

I know that He directs this Church now, as He established it then, through a prophet of God. In the name of Jesus Christ, amen.

Windows of enlightenment *let in the light of faith.*

Enlightenment

"The many problems facing us are complex. There are no simple answers. The more I meditate upon them, the more they show themselves in their various forms and become almost too formidable to me to even approach. Except for those eight words, . . . 'having first obtained mine errand from the Lord,' except for that qualification, I would quickly recommend retreat and capitulation. But with that, I have no doubts . . . that within the foreseeable future we will give the lie to much that is taught in the world today." (From an address given to the seminary and institute faculty at BYU on July 15, 1958.)

That All May Be Edified

I t is my feeling that you will have to be very wise and discerning to know the path you should follow. For in no age are those seeking to be decent and to be honest subjected to so many counterfeits. Upon every path which the uninitiated will walk there will be advocates of evil. They will urge and entice to thoughts and practices that will ultimately bring the participant to shame, dishonor, and unhappiness. Substitute standards for integrity, morality, and family life are so blatantly written, preached, and displayed that even the best-intended and well-directed person must keep their own guard up during every waking hour. We must also seek to inform and protect the innocent; and must try to reclaim the deceived and the erring who have fallen along the way.

Added to the obvious counterfeits are the subtle, hard-to-detect and difficult-to-discern allurements. It takes a keen mind to penetrate through the nebulous, tentative, and the uncertain, and to bring out of the gray mist those values and guides which are positive, sure, and safe.

Be spiritually sensitive if you wish to identify those things or those persons that ring true.

(16) "Judge Not According to the Appearance" suggests a direction for those whose faith is temporarily shaken because of some alleged wrongdoing of a Church leader. It points the way toward that steady maturity which is required if we are to resolve critical dilemmas and keep our faith strong.

(17) In the atmosphere of conflicting theories and philosophies often found on college campuses, "What Every Freshman Should Know" gives some guidance to new or experienced students. It also gives criteria which we can use to measure the detractors of high moral standards, patriotism, and religion. To counter permissive atheistic free speech in the classroom, I desired to declare in favor of *full* academic freedom.

(18) The plaintive words of a dying boy, "Mama, you won't forget me, will you?" introduce the theme of "The Family and Eternity." The talk deals with the preservation of the family, one of the great missions of the Church. The purpose and the importance of the sealing ordinances to secure the eternal family, when understood, show how basically wrong abortion is and the attendant sorrows that always follow it.

153

(19) "Why Stay Morally Clean" probes the very depths of a crucial issue facing every youth. Its message is not limited to the youth, however, but is applicable to all people in physically tempting circumstances. While it is plain in its language, it combines delicacy with the power of truth. In no instance does it use the three-letter word that is commonly and revoltingly blasted forth in every form of the media. The instruction is clear. Its message is easily understood. While it has been reprinted and widely distributed, its ever-present need determined its inclusion here.

(20) I was asked on one occasion by President Kimball if I would care to talk to the students at Brigham Young University on the subject of perversion. I begged him to excuse me from doing it, for I thought myself incapable of talking on that subject to a mixed audience. Later I repented of having declined the invitation and worked with great care to do as he had asked me to do. While "To the One" was given before a large audience at a Brigham Young University fireside, I singled out the afflicted individual for help, and also tried to inform and guide anyone who might have responsibility to help "the one" find his way.

16

Judge Not According to the Appearance

I speak to that member of the Church who struggles with a test of faith that could touch any one of us.

If I can take the arm of that one and steady him when his faith is tottering, I do not hesitate to impose upon the rest of you for just a few minutes.

At times someone has come to me, their faith shaken by alleged wrongdoings of some leader in the Church.

For instance, one young man was being constantly ridiculed by his co-workers for his activity in the Church. They claimed to know of a bishop who had cheated someone in business; or a stake president who had misrepresented something on a contract; or a mission president who had borrowed money, giving false information.

Or, they told of a bishop who had discriminated against one member, refusing to give a temple recommend, but had shown favoritism by signing a recommend for another whose unworthiness was widely known.

Such incidents as these, which supposedly involve Church leaders, are described as evidence that the gospel is not true, that the Church is not divinely inspired, or that it is being misled.

He had no satisfactory answer to their charges. He felt defenseless and foolish and was being drawn to join them in their criticism of the Church.

Did he believe all of these stories? Well, he could not be sure. There must be something to some of them.

Address given at general conference April 1979.

155

The Test of Faith

If you also face such a test of faith, consider the questions he was asked:

"Have you ever in your life attended any Church meeting— priesthood meeting, sacrament meeting, Relief Society, Sunday School, a conference or fireside, a seminary class, a temple session, or any other meeting sponsored by the Church—where any encouragement or authorization was given to be dishonest, to cheat in business, or take advantage of anyone?"

He answered that he had not.

"Have you read, or do you know of anything in the literature of the Church, in the scriptures themselves, in lesson manuals, in Church magazines or books, in Church publications of any kind, which contains any consent to lie, or to steal, to misrepresent, to defraud, to be immoral or vulgar, to profane, to be brutal, or to abuse any living soul?"

Again he said, after thoughtful consideration, that he had not.

"Have you ever been encouraged in a training session, a leadership meeting, or an interview to transgress or misbehave in any way? Have you ever been encouraged to be extreme or unreasonable or intemperate?"

He had not.

"You are inside the Church where you can see at close hand the conduct of bishops or Relief Society presidents, of high councilors, stake presidents, or General Authorities. Could such conduct be described as being typical of them?"

He thought it could not.

"You are active and have held positions in the Church. Surely you would have noticed if the Church promoted any of these things in any way."

Yes, he thought he would have noticed.

"Why then," I asked him, "when you hear reports of this kind, should you feel that the Church is to blame?"

There is no provision in the teachings or doctrines of the Church for any member to be dishonest, or immoral, or irresponsible, or even careless.

"Have you not been taught all of your life that if a member of the Church, particularly one in a high position, is unworthy in any way, he

156

acts against the standards of the Church? He is not in harmony with the teachings, the doctrines, or with the leadership of the Church.

"Why, then, should your faith be shaken by this account, or that, of some alleged misconduct—most of them misrepresented or untrue?"

There are those who assume that if someone is depressed, the Church must have caused it. If there is a divorce, somehow the Church is to blame. And on and on.

A Backhanded Compliment

When something is published about someone in major difficulty, if he is a member of the Church, that fact is generally included as essential information.

But have you ever read of a robbery, a theft, an embezzlement, a murder or suicide, that listed the guilty party as a Baptist, or a Methodist, or a Catholic? I think you have not.

Why, then, do they find it worth the mention when the unfortunate person is a Mormon?

Really, that is something of a backhanded compliment. It is an acknowledgment that members of the Church are supposed to know better, and we're supposed to do better; and when we don't, they point at the Church.

Be careful of those who promote controversy and contention, "For verily, verily I say unto you, he that hath the spirit of contention is not of me," saith the Lord. (3 Nephi 11:29.)

This next question concerns those who are shaking your faith.

Evaluating the Detractor

Are they really being fair? Could it be that they point to alleged misconduct, insinuating that the Church is responsible, to excuse themselves from living the high standards of the Church or to cover some failure to do so? You think about that—carefully.

Now, does anyone holding a responsible position in the Church ever act unworthily?

The answer: of course, it happens. It is an exception, but it happens.

When we call a man to be a stake president or a bishop, for instance, we say, in effect:

"Here is a congregation. You are to preside over them. They are under constant temptation, and you are to see that they win that battle.

157

That All May Be Edified

Govern them in such a way that they can succeed. Devote yourself unselfishly to this cause.

"And, incidentally, while you preside, you are not excused from your own trials and temptations. They will, in fact, be increased because you are a leader. Win your own battle as best you can."

If a leader does conduct himself unworthily, his actions fly against everything the Church stands for, and he is subject to release.

It has even been our sad responsibility, on some few occasions, to excommunicate leaders from the Church who have been guilty of very serious illegal or immoral conduct.

That should increase, not shake, your faith in the Church, or of a nonmember toward it.

When I was a student, nothing tried my faith more than the falling away of the Three Witnesses. If ever there was a temptation, for the sake of appearances, for the Church to compromise Church principles, that was the time. It was not done; and therefore, what had shaken my faith, one day was transformed into an anchor to hold it steady.

When you hear stories, be wise. Unless you are in all the interviews, and hear all the evidence, you are not in a position to really know. Be careful, lest you jump to a confusion.

Unless you are a participant and have full knowledge, better:

"Judge not, that ye be not judged.

"For with what judgment ye judge, ye shall be judged." (Matthew 7:1-2.)

A Lesson About Judging

Years ago I learned a lesson about judging.

I was a city councilman in Brigham City and was also on the stake high council. Late one night I was returning home from a high council meeting, pondering on what had happened there.

There was a red light and a siren. I was given a ticket for going forty-five miles an hour in a thirty-mile-an-hour zone. I accepted the ticket without protest, for I had not been paying attention.

The city judge was always in his office very early, and I went to get the matter settled before going to teach seminary the next day.

The judge had recently made a request for some new furniture. It rested with me, as a councilman, to approve it and sign the voucher.

158

He looked at my ticket and smiled, saying, "There have, on occasions, been exceptions made."

I told him that in view of my position he was obliged to treat me like any other citizen. Reluctantly he consented.

"The going rate is a dollar a mile. That will be fifteen dollars."

I paid the fine.

Two nights later Councilman Bundy reported, in a meeting of the city council, that he had fired a policeman. When the mayor asked the cause, he was told, and I quote: "Well, he was always arresting the wrong people."

Later Councilman Bundy explained that there had been vandalism in the city. Late at night someone had gone down Forest Street in a recreation vehicle and snapped off all the young trees. There had been damage in the cemetery also.

Where were the police? He found they were hiding behind signboards waiting for some unwary motorist.

Councilman Bundy had tried over a period of weeks to get them to patrol the city at night. One young officer just did not seem to learn, and so he had been dismissed.

Here then, was a man who gave a traffic ticket to a city councilman. Two days later he was dismissed. And the cause, stated in a city council meeting, with several delegations as witness: "He was always arresting the wrong people."

Do you think he could be convinced that I did not cause him to be fired?

Had I known of it, I may have delayed or prevented his dismissal, just for appearances.

Appearances, however, convicted me of unworthy use of influence.

Appearances Not What They Seem

Another example: Years ago in one of our Church schools, a teacher was summarily dismissed. The general explanation given did not satisfy his colleagues.

A delegation went to the office of the principal and demanded that he be reinstated. The principal refused. He offered no further explanation.

That All May Be Edified

The delegation concluded, therefore, that the principal had acted for "political reasons," for he was known to have some deep philosophical differences with that teacher.

The teacher (and this is frequently the case) took the part of a mistreated soul. His actions encouraged his colleagues in their protest.

The truth, known to the members of the Church Board of Education, was that the teacher had been dismissed for some very serious misconduct. Should all be made public, it would be doubtful that he could be reemployed as a teacher.

The principal, however, had some faith. If things were not noised about, the teacher might, through repentance and restitution, make himself again worthy to teach—perhaps even in the Church school system.

This principal generously took much criticism, even abuse, over a long period of time. He felt that the good of a family and the rehabilitation of a teacher was more important than his own professional reputation for the moment.

I was inspired by his example. It has been repeated a thousand times or more in the wards and stakes of the Church.

Often actions of bishops and stake presidents and others are misread by people who are not in a position to know the full truth.

Neither the bishop nor the member he is judging is obliged to confide in us. The bishop must keep confidences.

When all is said and done, in most cases, it is clearly none of our business anyway.

Bishops Keep Confidences

Often someone will not go to his bishop with a problem. He wants to see a General Authority instead. He says the bishop will talk—for what about the time when someone in the ward went to him and soon everyone knew about the problem?

Follow these cases through, as I have done, and you will probably find that, first, the member confided in her neighbor who didn't know what to counsel her. Then she talked it over with her best friend, and then her sister, and received conflicting advice. Finally, her husband was told by the man he rides with that they'd better see the bishop.

Indeed, it was noised about, but not by the bishop. Bishops keep confidences.

John, the Apostle, counseled: "Judge not according to the appearance, but judge righteous judgment." (John 7:24.)

Stumbling Blocks to Stepping Stones

Now, then, stand steady. Keep your faith. I bear witness that the gospel of Jesus Christ is true. God lives and directs this work. The Church is on the right course. It is on schedule. And I bear witness that it is righteously led by a prophet of God.

Things that now are stumbling blocks may, one day soon, be stepping-stones for you.

But do not expect to see the day when this Church, or those in it, will be free from resistance, criticism, even persecution. That will never be.

Just remember:

> Blessed are ye, when men shall revile you, and persecute you, and shall say all manner of evil against you falsely, for my sake.
>
> Rejoice, and be exceeding glad: for great is your reward in heaven: for so persecuted they the prophets which were before you. (Matthew 5:11-12.)

In the name of Jesus Christ, amen.

17

What Every Freshman Should Know

To begin with, I think I should relieve you graduates of some anxiety by quoting a bit of verse appropriate for this occasion.

> The month of June approaches,
> And soon throughout the land,
> The graduation speakers
> Will tell us where we stand.
>
> We stand at Armageddon,
> In the vanguard of the press.
> We're standing at the crossroads,
> At the gateway to success.
>
> We're standing on the threshold
> Of careers all brightly lit,
> But in the midst of all this standing,
> We sit, and sit, and sit.
> (Laurence Eisenlohr.)

The genius who composed that entitled it, appropriately enough, "Oh, My Aching Baccalaureate." I thought it would help a little if you knew that I know what it means to be killing one's self by degrees!

Now we are convened as a baccalaureate service. The word *baccalaureate* has two meanings. It is the bachelor's degree, and it is likewise defined as "a sermon to a graduating class." I underline the word *sermon.* This is the part of your graduation program that invites attention to the spiritual nature of man; and well may we give attention to it, for it is the most neglected part of our nature.

I suppose my talk might be entitled "What Every Freshman Should Know." It may seem backward to be telling you now, as graduates,

---

Address given at Utah State University baccalaureate service June 8, 1973.

what every freshman should know, but perhaps it will test you to see if you know, as seniors, what a freshman should know. Then, of course, with this commencement you become freshmen again, in life.

With this commencement you graduate now from one of the finest universities in the world. Your lives have no doubt been influenced, as mine was here, by the excellent example of members of the faculty. For them I have the greatest respect.

Now, lest I be misunderstood, I emphasize that my remarks tonight refer to schools in general, to the universities throughout the world, and not to this one alone.

Standards Have Changed

Standards have changed much in our universities. Through the influence of a few, restrictions on dormitory living have been pulled down. Standards have been abandoned in favor of coeducational living in university housing.

New courses are being introduced in many universities, under the general heading "Alternatives to Marriage." Some of those alternatives, if accepted, would give our communities kinship with the ancient cities of Sodom and Gomorrah.

The trend sees enrollments declining, endowments withheld (some withdrawn), a loss of confidence in our system of higher education, and worse than that, the graduates from many institutions of higher learning are moving into private and public life well trained, technically proficient, even talented, but somehow without that attribute of character called *integrity.*

A Time for Assessment

Graduation is a time for assessment and appreciation for things gained at school. At the dorm and at the apartment you are sorting through things that have accumulated during your school days. Some, such as old work books and test papers, will be discarded. Others you will carry away with you.

The question I ask the graduate is this: In all the review of what you have gained, are you giving any attention to the things you may have lost? If you knew the value of some of the things you may have discarded, you would dig frantically through the wastebasket and trash can to rescue them before they were hauled away permanently.

That All May Be Edified

You came to college basically to gain an occupation, and likely you have earned it. But as always, there was a price to pay, and occasionally we pay an exorbitant price. Not infrequently a college student will jettison things essential to life and end up well occupied but unhappy.

Did you come as a freshman with idealism, and put it aside?

Did you come with faith, and carry away in its place skepticism?

Did you come with patriotism, and replace it with cynicism?

Did you come free from any binding habits, and now leave with an addiction?

Did you arrive aspiring for marriage, a home, and a family, and now have abandoned those aspirations?

And critically important, did you come with virtue and moral purity, and now must admit to yourself that while you were here you have lost it?

How did this happen? Was that an essential price to pay for an occupation or for broadened cultural horizons? The intangibles you carry away may not equal in value the intangibles you may be leaving behind.

If they are gone now, do you know how it happened? Did you give them up willingly? Did you set them aside, or were they taken from you? Have you been the victim of an academic confidence game?

The large body of university professors in the world today represent the finest standard of our civilization. However, some few professors (thank the Lord at this school there are but a few) delight in relieving the student of his basic spiritual values. Throughout the world more and more faculty members look forward to the coming of a new crop of green freshmen with a compulsive desire to "educate" them.

The Unsuspecting One

During my term as mission president in New England I was responsible for the Joseph Smith Memorial in Vermont. The visitors' center, with its lawns and gardens, is surrounded by woods.

A doe took up residence there and each spring brought twin fawns onto the lawn. They were tame enough that the caretaker, on occasion, could pick them up.

One fall a bow hunter came into the grounds and killed a half-grown fawn with an arrow. The unsuspecting doe stood watching a few feet away, interested in what he was doing.

164

There is no way that that man could be classed as a sportsman, or even a hunter. "Like shooting fish in a bucket" is the expression. No doubt both the trophy and the hunt became exaggerated in the conversation of the man, but there is no way his contemptible deed could give him any sense of achievement.

Each year, many fall victim in the colleges and universities. There, as captive audiences, their faith, their patriotism, and their morality are lined up against a wall and riddled by words shot from the mouths of irreverent professors.

Study the Professors Too

I hope that while you were taking courses you found time enough, after the study of your subject, to study the professors. One may well learn more from studying the professor than studying the subject.

Most of them, I repeat, have influenced your lives for good. But there are others, those few, who delight in destroying faith. I have found it generally true that a professor who ridicules faith and religious beliefs and downgrades patriotism, who continually presses for the loosening of standards of campus discipline for both faculty and students, is a very interesting subject for study. A student would do well to look him over. May I predict what you will find.

Be assured that one who strives to widen the breadth of accepted moral conduct does so to condone what he is doing. Not infrequently you will find such a one unworthy. If he derides spiritual development, it can generally be concluded that he failed in the subject. He defends himself by declaring it an unnecessary discipline. He is the one who ridicules faith and humility, who would smile in contempt when anyone mentions virtue, or reverence, or dedication, or morality.

The Clue

Let me give you a clue. There is something very interesting about a person who is anxious to forsake the standards of his church, particularly if he leaves them and encourages others to do likewise.

Have you ever wondered what it means when he can leave it, but he cannot leave it alone? Normal behavior would have him cancel his affiliation in the church and let that be that. Not so with this individual. He can leave it, but he cannot leave it alone. He becomes consumed with it and obsessed with it. That says something about him.

165

That All May Be Edified

And one might ask, Is he talking to students, or is he really talking to himself? You might ask also, and he might ask himself: Is he happy, really happy?

Let me alert you to one thing. The professor who is uptight about the subject of religion, the one who can't, just positively can't, seem to conduct a class without tossing a barb or two at the church, belittling the minister, the rabbi, the priest, the bishop, or the stake president, or at the standards they teach—he is not the major source of concern. His bald-faced brand of prejudice is obvious even to the unwary student. Even the freshman fawn will move aside when he strings his bow.

The Sly Innuendo

But there is another that I would like to describe to you. I can best make the point by referring to Shakespeare's *Othello.*

Othello claimed the two desires of his life. He became the general—he had arrived at the top—and he won the hand of the lovely Desdemona. Two other characters in the play complete the main cast: Cassio, his trusted lieutenant, and Iago, conspiring and jealous.

Two things Iago wanted in life—to be general and to have Desdemona. Othello had them both.

Motivated by malignant jealousy, Iago set out to destroy Othello—never openly, always careful and clever. He does not, in the play, tell an open, bald-faced lie. He works by innuendo and suggestion.

"Where is Desdemona tonight?" he would ask.

"Oh, she has gone to Relief Society." Othello would answer.

"Oh, *has* she?" Iago would question.

It was not the words—on paper they are harmless inquiry—but the inflection made them contagious with suspicion.

On one occasion Cassio came to Othello's home with a message. After a conversation with Desdemona, he left to attend to other matters. As he was leaving the home, Othello and Iago approached.

Iago perverted an innocent situation with his comment, "I cannot think it that he would steal away so guilty-like, seeing you coming."

And so it unfolds. Nothing to incriminate Iago, so innocent was he. Just a sly reference, a gesture, an inflection, the emphasis on the word or the sentence.

Othello is finally convinced that Desdemona is unfaithful, and he determines to destroy her. The tragedy concludes with Othello

166

threatening his innocent wife. She pleads for a week, for a day. Her final plea: "But while I say one prayer." But he denies her that. How terrible the tragedy of her death when he then finds proof of her innocence!

You may meet an Iago one day as you move forward through life. Through innuendo and sly remarks, through an inflection or a question, in mock innocence he might persuade you to kill your faith, to throttle your patriotism, to tamper with drugs, to kill your agency, to abandon morality and chastity and virtue. If you do, you have an awakening as terribly tragic as that of Othello.

This is the man who ridicules belief in a hereafter and says there is no such thing as God. He'd better hope he is right. For if, as some of us know, the opposite is true, the final scene will be his, and justice more than poetic and penalties adequate in every way will be exacted from him. Ultimately we are punished quite as much by our sins as we are for them.

Academic Freedom

Now you have completed your studies at this university. Here, theory has it, learning may be pursued in an atmosphere of academic freedom. Freedom, one might ask, for whom? Some interesting changes have occurred in the past generation.

Some years ago a plaintiff prospered in her grievance concerning the saying of prayers in public schools. The practice was declared unconstitutional by the United States Supreme Court. That decision was a partial decision, for the effect was, regardless of the intent, to offer great encouragement to those who would erase from our society every trace of reference to the Almighty.

She wanted to protect her son from any contact with religion, and now her son is protected from my type of religion—but my son is exposed to *hers*.

Atheism, a Negative Religion

There is a crying need for the identification of atheism for what it is, and that is, a religion—albeit a negative one, nevertheless it is a religious expression. It is the one extreme end of the spectrum of thought concerning the causation of things.

167

That All May Be Edified

Those who are spiritually sensitive recognize God as the cause, a living being who rules in the affairs of man. The so-called atheist declares that God is not—not just that He isn't the cause of things, but that He indeed is *not.*

We put sunshine and rain under the heading of weather. It would be a little ridiculous to talk about clear weather and cloudy and claim that the two are not related and could not be considered as part of the same discipline.

It is equally ridiculous to separate theism from atheism and claim that they are two separate matters, particularly when we condone, in some instances encourage, the atheist to preach his doctrine in the college classroom, and then at once move with great vigor to eliminate any positive reference to God. He is protected, as they say, by the principle of academic freedom.

The administrator in the university today who intends to maintain academic freedom had better see to it that he administers impartially. Otherwise he offends the very principle he claims to sustain. When university standards of discipline are dominated by the influence of the atheist, then the administrator is partial. With the Newman Club, Hillel, the institute of religion, or the Wesleyan Society off campus, how can he protect the teaching of atheism in the college classroom?

Atheism, as theism, is divided into many sects—communism, agnosticism, skepticism, humanism, pragmatism, and there are others.

The atheist proclaims his own dishonesty in accepting pay to teach psychology, sociology, history, or English, while he is indeed preaching his atheistic religious philosophy to his students. If the atheist wants to teach his doctrine at a public university, let him purchase property off campus and build himself a building and offer classes. Let him label them for what they are.

As a student in a public university, it should be my right to register for a course in English and be taught the subject of English, or to register for a course in history and be taught the subject of history, and not be exposed as a fish in a barrel to the atheistic philosophies of an unhappy professor.

The patrons of a university, the citizens who finance it, have the right to send their sons and daughters to school without the anxiety that they will be taught sectarian religion, including that of the atheist. They have the right to expect that the standards of campus discipline and dormitory living are not dictated by a few ultra-liberals who are confined by no moral standards whatsoever.

We are very particular to forbid anyone from preaching Catholicism, or Protestantism, or Mormonism, or Judaism in a public school classroom, but for some reason we are very patient with those who teach the negative expression of religion.

In the separation of church and state we ought to demand more protection from the agnostic, from the atheist, from the communist, from the skeptic, from the humanist and the pragmatist than we have yet been given.

I have had university administrators tell me that they would like to correct this situation in this school or that one, but they cannot act. The offending professor is protected in what he does. He hides behind tenure and draws support from professional societies.

Destruction of Faith Is Protected

I submit that the atheist has no more right to teach the fundamentals of his sect in the public school than does the theist. *Any system in the schools or in society that protects the destruction of faith and forbids, in turn, the defense of it must ultimately destroy the moral fiber of the people.*

Is any lesson more abundantly clear in our present society? We are coming apart at the seams. Anyone can see that. Just read any newspaper any day. Evil has unclothed herself and walks the streets in brazen, impudent defiance.

When you leave this university and go on to further studies in life, Iago will still be there—perhaps not under the title of professor, but he will be clamoring for your attention. It will be interesting for you to see what he will do, subtly, to destroy your faith.

You will have an invitation to compromise your integrity for position, political preference, or money. You have been tested in college, and I'm sure you've seen a student or two used up. So you will see many consumed in society by those proselyting for others to join them in their unhappiness.

Basic Rights and Wrongs

Remember, graduates, there are some rights and wrongs. We must come to understand that there are basic truths and basic principles, basic conformities, necessary to achieve happiness. There are some things that are false, that are wrong. For instance, we cannot be happy and at once be wicked—never, regardless of how generally accepted that course may be.

If it were printed in every book, run on every news press, set forth in every magazine; if it were broadcast on every frequency, televised from every station, declared from every pulpit, taught in every classroom, advocated in every conversation, still it would be wrong.

Wickedness never was happiness, neither indeed can it be, neither indeed ever will it be.

I declare in favor of full academic freedom. If prayer is to leave the public schools, let the ridicule of prayer leave also. I speak for humility, for faith, for reverence, for brotherhood, for charity, for patriotism. I speak for temperance, and I likewise speak for justice.

I yearn for the day when the rank and file of our college professors will assert themselves, when the moral fiber in them will set itself against the decay in our public universities.

I pay tribute to those professors, the great body of men and women, those who have taught you well, men and women of integrity who command a discipline and are able to teach it. They are the ones most worth studying. That is something that every freshman should know. They reflect a balance in development of the whole man. These are the men and women to be trusted, to be emulated.

God grant that they may soon look up from their books, set aside their papers, turn from their studies, and stand to be counted with those administrators who struggle to keep the moral foundation of our universities in place. May those men and women wield heavy influence and plant in the hearts and minds of the students a fundamental respect for truth and for integrity.

Look Through Your Luggage

Now, in conclusion, as you leave the campus satisfied at the things you have gained, go through your pockets, look through your luggage, see if something may have been lost—spiritual things—essential if there is to be happiness in your future.

Take with you your faith, your patriotism, your virtue. If they are battered a bit they can be repaired. Even virtue, if tarnished, can be polished again. Carry them away with you. They can be renewed. You will come to know in the years ahead that life has precious little to offer without them.

You have been taught, in the course of your university experience, to seek information from that professor who has inquired and studied a field—for instance, English, mathematics, sociology, the humanities, all subjects. I profess to you in this baccalaureate sermon that I have made inquiry into spiritual things. I have come to know that God lives and that ultimately He will rule in the affairs of men. I know that many of the treasures that you may have set aside will prove to be that which was of most worth to you.

God bless you as you leave this great institution. May His spirit attend you. May there be room somewhere in the things you carry away, for faith, for integrity, for patriotism, for virtue—for which I pray in the name of Jesus Christ, amen.

18

The Family and Eternity

Some time ago I was counseling a woman who had joined the Church following the breakup of her marriage and the loss of her only child, a boy who was nine years old at the time he passed away. She told me something that I remember very well because it touched me deeply.

After the separation in her marriage, while she was trying to make a living for herself and her son, he became afflicted with a terminal disease. Some time before he passed away, he became aware of the fact that he was not going to live. His mother said from that time on he had only one thing on his mind: over and over again he would say pleadingly, "Mama, you won't forget me, will you? I won't be forgotten, will I?"

"Mama, You Won't Forget Me!"

That pleading of a dying youngster speaks somehow for all of us, and expresses our yearning not to be forgotten.

When I was presiding over the mission in New England, I received a letter from a mother explaining that shortly after joining the Church, they had lost their only child, a little girl about five who was struck down by a car. For weeks after the funeral this brokenhearted mother brooded and mourned the loss of her child: then, in the agony of her bereavement, she wrote, asking two questions. First, "Tell me how it is. Did it all go dark? I can't stand the thought that it's all dark for my little girl." And the second question, "Will she be alone? Please tell me that my little girl won't be alone. I can't bear the thought that she's all alone now."

How grateful I am that we could offer comfort to this mother, and how grateful I am that we have received revelations in this dispensation

---

Address given at a genealogical seminar August 6, 1970.

The Family and Eternity

that give us a great deal of knowledge about what transpires and what we may expect as we go beyond the veil!

The Preservation of the Family

The preservation of the family is one of the great missions of the Church. The Lord has revealed a way for us to permanently establish the family. The work of priesthood genealogy prepares the way for temple ordinance work, which makes eternal the basic organization of the Church—the family.

We believe in revelation. As Latter-day Saints "We believe all that God has revealed, all that He does now reveal, and we believe that He will yet reveal many great and important things pertaining to the Kingdom of God." (Article of Faith 9.) I do not think many Latter-day Saints read the last phrase of that statement. They believe all that God has revealed, but I would like to discuss with you "all that He does now reveal."

Revelation is a principal subject in one of the most interesting books in Church literature, the biography *Wilford Woodruff,* by Matthias F. Cowley. This detailed history of the president of the Church and his times was made possible through his carefully written journal.

On April 5, 1894, President Woodruff recorded in his journal, "I met with the Brethren on the matters of adoptions and endowments and the following is a revelation to Wilford Woodruff." The next page was left blank. The revelation was not lost, however.

During a talk at a general conference of the Church in April 1894, he said: "Therefore, as the Lord commanded us not to speak only as we were moved by the Holy Ghost, I desire that, and in order to obtain it I want the prayers and faith of the Latter-day Saints.

"I have some things resting upon me that I wish to present before the Latter-day Saints, and in order to do this I will call upon President George Q. Cannon to read from the Book of the Doctrine and Covenants concerning the subject which I wish to speak upon."

Then George Q. Cannon, first counselor in the First Presidency, read concerning the preservation of family ties.

Following this, President Woodruff continued speaking: "Thus [referring to section 128] you have before you the subject which is resting upon us, and which we wish to present to the Latter-day Saints.

173

That All May Be Edified

... I wish to say to the Latter-day Saints that we live in a very important generation. We are blessed with power and authority, holding the Holy Priesthood by the commandment of God, to stand upon the earth and redeem both the living and the dead. If we did not do it, we should be damned and cut off from the earth, and the God of Israel would raise up a people who would do it. The Lord would not permit me to occupy this position one day of my life, unless I was susceptible to the Holy Spirit and to the revelations of God. It is too late in the day for this Church to stand without revelation. Not only the President of the Church should possess this gift and give it to the people, but his counselors and the Apostles and all men that bear the Holy Priesthood, if they magnify their calling, although they may not be called to give revelations to lead and direct the Church. The spirit of revelation belongs to the Priesthood.

"... You have acted up to all the light and knowledge that you have had [referring again to the matter of adoptions and endowments]; but you have now something more to do than you have done. We have not fully carried out those principles in fulfillment of the revelations of God to us, in the sealing of the hearts of the fathers to the children and the children to the fathers."

The Principle and Ordinance of Sealing

Then came the substance of the revelation in the simplicity of a single declarative sentence that has ushered in a most marvelous work in this dispensation: *"We want Latter-day Saints from this time to trace their genealogies as far as they can, and to be sealed to their fathers and mothers. Have children sealed to their parents, and run this chain through as far as you can get it."* (Italics added.)

President Woodruff said, "... In my prayers the Lord revealed to me, that it was my duty to say to all Israel to carry this principle out, and in fulfillment of that revelation, I lay it before this people. I say to all men who are laboring in these temples, carry out this principle, and then we shall make one step in advance of what we have had before. Myself and counselors conversed upon this and we were agreed upon it, and afterwards we laid it before all the Apostles who were here ... the Lord revealed to every one of these men—and they would bear testimony to it if they were to speak—that that was the word of the

Lord to them. I never met with anything in my life in this Church that there was more unity upon than there was upon that principle. They all feel right about it, and that it is our duty." (*Deseret Evening News,* May 19, 1894.)

Genealogical Society of Utah Organized

On November 13, 1894, a meeting was held in the Church Historian's Office in Salt Lake City. Attending that meeting were all members of the First Presidency: President Wilford Woodruff; his first counselor, George Q. Cannon; and his second counselor, Joseph F. Smith. Franklin D. Richards, president of the Council of the Twelve Apostles, and other members of the Council were present in that meeting when the Genealogical Society of Utah was organized for benevolent, educational, and religious purposes and for the preservation of family ties.

Today we have other organizations in the Church that are working on family ties. We have stakes and missions, wards, branches, and districts. Each is presided over by a priesthood officer. These organizations are temporarily essential; they are not eternal organizations. They can be organized or they can be dissolved. Stakes are often divided and boundaries changed in size and shape, and they may have an entirely different group of people than when they were organized.

These organizations are for convenience in administering priesthood authority. Officers are called to administer in the wards and stakes, but they serve temporarily. The bishops and stake presidents will be replaced one day. These are temporary assignments placed upon the shoulders of men.

The Family an Eternal Organization

But the family, on the other hand, can be an eternal organization. Though the family may move from one ward or stake to another, the family organization remains intact. It may even be transferred from mortality into the eternities in the spirit world. The family established under the priesthood in the temple is founded in what is perhaps the most profound of all ordinances. When a couple enters into the new and everlasting covenant, they have the possibility of entering full expression of their life powers, both spiritual and physical.

That All May Be Edified

This is a responsibility not to be regarded lightly. Those sacred life-giving physical powers which have been reserved and protected through the entire life of the individual are at last released for a sacred and pure and holy purpose, the begetting of a family.

These positions in the family, the positions of parenthood, should not be temporary; they should be permanent. Presiding officers in the Church are changed from time to time, but not so with the father and mother. What happens when a father is not diligent in his responsibility? Sometimes we may even think he ought to be replaced, but who has the authority to do that? A bishop can release a Sunday School superintendent, but he cannot release the father of a family. He has not that authority, nor has a stake president.

Do the General Authorities of the Church have that authority? I know that I cannot release a father from presiding over his family. His calling is special; it is permanent in the new and everlasting covenant, and no release is contemplated.

A release can come, of course, through transgression. Through authority reserved to the president and prophet himself, those binding ties can be dissolved. This comes, however, not at the instigation of the bishop and the stake president. It comes when the individual breaks the covenant, transgresses, and becomes unworthy.

When we catch a vision of what the family is, what those binding ties are, and what the marriage covenant is, then we must know that surely few things in our day offend the Lord more than the silly and whimsical way in which many people enter into and release themselves from the marriage covenant. Indeed, we have reached a point in history when the marriage covenant, considered through all generations of history as sacred and vital, is now declared by many to be useless.

The Tragedy of Abortion

As an outgrowth, those sacred life processes through which spirits may enter mortality are being tampered with. That path of life over which new spirits must cross to enter a mortal body is often walled up through contraceptive practice; and should, through some accidental means, those natural conditions be met and a body be generated, abortive procedures are now all too common, and the spirits are thrust back whence they came. These practices are looked upon as advancements for mankind. Both are founded upon selfishness.

176

Salvation for the Living and the Dead

When I read and reread section 128 of the Doctrine and Covenants, I am impressed with the fact that the Lord made many references not just to the dead and baptism for the dead, but he also talked about salvation for the living and the dead. When you read that section, you notice how they are together—the living and the dead, or the dead and the living. The same principles relate to both of them.

This binding of the families together through genealogical research, and the subsequent performance of the sealing ordinance in the temple, is being strengthened by the vital program to secure the family and bind its members together while they are living. Never before in the history of the Church have there been two programs that have come so close to interlocking for the living and the dead than we have in our day. We have the family home evening program and the home teaching program, both directed at stabilizing and strengthening the families. And we have the genealogical program and temple work, with the objective of making the family unit eternal and keeping it together in the spirit world. We have these programs because "we believe all that God has revealed, all that He does now reveal, and that He will yet reveal many great and important things pertaining to the Kingdom of God."

Something Worth Preserving

If we are to preserve families, everything must be done to see that there is something worthy of preserving. There is much to be said for the sustaining of a happy family life here in mortality, and in a very real way it ties very closely to what we know as priesthood genealogical work. Reference is made in section 128 to the coming of Elijah. This had been prophesied by Malachi four hundred years before Christ. The closing words of the Old Testament are:

> Behold, I will send you Elijah the prophet before the coming of the great and dreadful day of the Lord:
> And he shall turn the heart of the fathers to the children, and the heart of the children to their fathers, lest I come and smite the earth with a curse. (Malachi 4:5-6.)

Let me quote for you the words of President Harold B. Lee, delivered at the dedication of the Oakland Temple. "I ask you to

177

consider a Churchwide family teaching program about which we are talking today.... President Joseph F. Smith and his counselors promised Church members that if they would gather their children around them once a week and instruct them in the gospel, those children in such homes would not go astray.

"And so today there are being prepared instructions to do what? ... to turn here upon the earth the hearts of parents to children, and the hearts of children to parents. Can you conceive that when parents have passed beyond the veil that that is the only time when parents should have their hearts turned to their children, and children to their parents?

"I would have you consider seriously whether or not that binding with your family will be secure if you have waited until you have passed beyond the veil before your hearts then yearn for your children whom you have neglected to help along the way. It is time for us to think of turning the hearts of parents to children now while living, that there might be a bond between parents and children that will last beyond death. It is a very real principle, and we should consider it."

So today in the Church, priesthood genealogical work enjoys the status and receives an emphasis it has never previously enjoyed. The work in the temples and the organization through which wards and stakes do genealogical research constitute a modern-day implementation of that revelation given through President Woodruff.

We are all concerned as never before with the binding of families here upon the earth, that they might be bound together in eternity. What more marvelous experience is there than for members of all ages in a family to bind themselves together in genealogical research?

19

Why Stay Morally Clean

Surely all of us have been conscious of the fact that there has been a very powerful Spirit with us in this session this morning. Few times, I suppose, have I desired so much for the sustaining power of the Spirit as I discuss a very delicate and difficult subject.

There are many young people in our audience today. It is to them, particularly to the teenagers, that I speak. The subject should be of great interest to you—why stay morally clean.

I approach the subject with deepest reverence. This may surprise some, for this subject is the most talked about, sung about, and joked about of any subject. Almost always it is talked about immodestly.

I intend to sustain modesty, not to offend it, as I venture to speak on this most delicate subject.

Young people, my message is of very deep importance to you. It concerns your future happiness. Some things that I say may be new to you who have not read the scriptures.

In the Beginning

In the beginning, prior to your mortal birth, you lived with our Heavenly Father. He is real. He actually lives. There are those living upon the earth who bear witness of His existence. We have heard His servants do so in this session. He lives, and I bear testimony of it.

He knew you there. Because He loved you He was anxious for your happiness and for your eternal growth. He wanted you to be able to choose freely and to grow through the power of correct choice, so that you may become much as He is. To achieve this it was necessary for us to leave His presence. Something like going away to school. A plan was presented and each agreed to leave the presence of our Heavenly Father to experience life in mortality.

Address given at general conference April 1972.

That All May Be Edified

The Accepted Plan

Two great things were in store for us as we came into this world. One, we would receive a mortal body, created in the image of God. Through it, by proper control, we might achieve eternal life and happiness. Two, we would be tried and tested in such a way that we could grow in strength and in spiritual power.

Now this first purpose is wonderfully important, for this body given us will be resurrected and will serve us through the eternities.

Under the accepted plan, Adam and Eve were sent to the earth as our first parents. They could prepare physical bodies for the first spirits to be introduced into this life.

The Power of Creation Is Good

There was provided in our bodies, and this is sacred, a power of creation. A light, so to speak, that has the power to kindle other lights. This gift is to be used only within the sacred bonds of marriage. Through the exercise of this power of creation, a mortal body may be conceived, a spirit enter into it, and a new soul born into this life.

This power is good. It can create and sustain family life, and it is in family life that we find the fountains of happiness. It is given to virtually every individual who is born into mortality. It is a sacred and significant power, and I repeat, my young friends, that this power is good.

You who are teenagers, like every other son and daughter of Adam and Eve, have this power within you.

The power of creation, or may we say procreation, is not just an incidental part of the plan—it is essential to it. Without it the plan could not proceed. The misuse of it may disrupt the plan.

Much of the happiness that may come to you in this life will depend on how you use this sacred power of creation. The fact that you young men can become fathers and that you young women can become mothers is of utmost importance to you.

As this power develops within you, it will prompt you in the search for a companion and empower you to love and to hold him.

I repeat, this power to act in the creation of life is sacred. You can some day have a family of your own. Through the exercise of this power you can invite children to live with you—little boys and little

180

girls who will be your very own—created in a way in your own image. You can establish a home, a dominion of power and influence and opportunity. This carries with it great responsibility.

This creative power carries with it strong desires and urges. You have felt them already in the changing of your attitudes and your interests.

As you move into your teens, almost of a sudden a boy or a girl becomes something new and intensely interesting. You will notice the changing of form and feature in your own body and in others. You will experience the early whispering of physical desire.

The Power Is Strong and Constant

It was necessary that this power of creation have at least two dimensions: One, it must be strong, and two, it must be more or less constant.

This power must be strong; for most men by nature seek adventure. Except for the compelling persuasion of these feelings, men would be reluctant to accept the responsibility of sustaining a home and a family. This power must be constant too, for it becomes a binding tie in family life.

You are old enough, I think, to look around you in the animal kingdom. You soon realize that where this power of creation is a fleeting thing, where it expresses itself only in season, there is no family tie.

It is through this power that life continues. A world, full of trials and fears and disappointments, can be changed into a kingdom of hope and joy and happiness. Each time a child is born, the world somehow is renewed in innocence.

Again I want to tell you young people that this power within you is good. It is a gift from God our Father. In the righteous exercise of it, as in nothing else, we may come close to Him.

We can have, in a small way, much that our Father in Heaven has as He governs us, His children. No greater school or testing place can be imagined.

Temple Marriage

Is it any wonder then, that in the Church marriage is so sacred and so important? Can you understand why your marriage which releases these powers of creation for your use should be the most carefully planned, the most solemnly considered step in your life? Ought we to consider it unusual that the Lord directed that temples be constructed for the purpose of performing marriage ceremonies?

Allurements That Seek to Destroy

Now, there are other things that I will tell you as a warning. In the beginning there was one among us who rebelled at the plan of our Heavenly Father. He vowed to destroy and to disrupt the plan.

He was prevented from having a mortal body and was cast out—limited forever from establishing a kingdom of his own. He became satanically jealous. He knows that this power of creation is not just incident to the plan, but a key to it.

He knows that if he can entice you to use this power prematurely, to use it too soon, or to misuse it in any way, you may well lose your opportunities for eternal progression.

He is an actual being from the unseen world. He has great power. He will use it to persuade you to transgress those laws set up to protect the sacred powers of creation.

In former times he was too cunning to confront one with an open invitation to be immoral. But rather, sneakingly and quietly he would tempt young and old alike to think loosely of these sacred powers of creation. To bring down to a vulgar or to a common level that which is sacred and beautiful.

His tactics have changed now. He describes it as only an appetite to be satisfied. He teaches that there are no attendant responsibilities to the use of this power. Pleasure, he will tell you, is its sole purpose.

His devilish invitations appear on billboards. They are coined into jokes and written into the lyrics of songs. They are acted out on television and at theaters. They will stare at you now from most magazines. There are magazines—you know the word, *pornography*—open, wicked persuasions to pervert and misuse this sacred power.

You grow up in a society where before you is the constant invitation to tamper with these sacred powers.

I want to counsel you, and I want you to remember these words.

Do not let anyone at all touch or handle your body, not anyone. Those who tell you otherwise proselyte you to share their guilt. We teach you to maintain your innocence.

182

Maintain Your Innocence

Turn away from any who would persuade you to experiment with these life-giving powers.

That such indulgence is widely accepted in society today is not enough!

For both parties to willingly consent to such indulgence is not enough!

To imagine that it is a normal expression of affection is not enough to make it right.

The only righteous use of this sacred power is within the covenant of marriage.

Never misuse these sacred powers.

The Law Is Established

And now, my young friends, I must tell you soberly and seriously that God has declared in unmistakable language that misery and sorrow will follow the violation of the laws of chastity. "Wickedness never was happiness." (Alma 41:10.) These laws were set up to guide all of His children in the use of this gift.

He does not have to be spiteful or vengeful in order that punishment will come from the breaking of the moral code. The laws are established of themselves.

Crowning glory awaits you if you live worthily. The loss of the crown may well be punishment enough. Often, very often, we are punished as much by our sins as we are for them.

You Can Become Clean

I am sure that within the sound of my voice there is more than one young person who already has fallen into transgression. Some of you young people, I am sure, almost innocent of any intent but persuaded by the enticements and the temptations, already have misused this power.

Know then, my young friends, that there is a great cleansing power. And know that you can be clean.

If you are outside of the Church the covenant of baptism itself represents, among other things, a washing and a cleansing.

183

For those of you inside the Church there is a way, not entirely painless, but certainly possible. You can stand clean and spotless before Him. Guilt will be gone, and you can be at peace. Go to your bishop. He holds the key to this cleansing power.

Then one day you can know the full and righteous expression of these powers and the attendant happiness and joy in righteous family life. In due time, within the bonds of the marriage covenant, you can yield yourselves to those sacred expressions of love which have as their fulfillment the generation of life itself.

To Love Someone More Than Self

Someday you will hold a little boy or a little girl in your arms and know that two of you have acted in partnership with our Heavenly Father in the creation of life. Because the youngster belongs to you, you may then come to love someone more than you love yourself.

This experience can come, insofar as I know, only through having children of your own or perhaps through fostering children born of another and yet drawn close into family covenants.

Some of you may not experience the blessings of marriage. Protect nonetheless these sacred powers of creation, for there is a great power of compensation that may well apply to you.

Through this loving one more than you love yourself, you become truly Christian. Then you know, as few others know, what the word *father* means when it is spoken of in the scriptures. You may then feel something of the love and concern that He has for us.

It should have great meaning that of all the titles of respect and honor and admiration that could be given Him, that God Himself, He who is the highest of all, chose to be addressed simply as *Father.*

Protect and guard your gift. Your actual happiness is at stake. Eternal family life, now only in your anticipations and dreams, can be achieved because our Heavenly Father has bestowed this choicest gift of all upon you—this power of creation. It is the very key to happiness. Hold this gift as sacred and pure. Use it only as the Lord has directed.

My young friends, there is much happiness and joy to be found in this life. I can testify of that.

I picture you with a companion whom you love and who loves you. I picture you at the marriage altar, entering into covenants which are sacred. I picture you in a home where love has its fulfillment. I picture you with little children about you and see your love growing with them.

I cannot frame this picture. I would not if I could. For it has no bounds. Your happiness will have no ends if you obey His laws.

I pray God's blessings upon you, our youth. May our Heavenly Father watch over you and sustain you that in the expression of this sacred gift you may draw close to Him. He lives. He is our Father. Of this I bear witness in the name of Jesus Christ, amen.

20

To the One

W hat I say in this presentation will be serious and solemn. I will
not speak to everyone. I ask the indulgence of the "ninety and
nine" while I speak to "the one." I ask you, the ninety and nine, to sit
quietly if you will, reverently if you can, and to generously help create
an atmosphere where we can reach that one who desperately needs the
counsel that I will present. The cooperation of you of the ninety and
nine may not, after all, prove to be without some benefit to you. There
may be a time in the years ahead when you can use something of what I
say to help someone else, perhaps someone very close to you.

I have worried for fear that any treatment of the subject I approach
may be indelicate or immodest. I feel perhaps as did Jacob, the Book of
Mormon prophet, when he opened a sermon with these words:

> It grieveth me that I must use so much boldness of speech concerning you,
> before your wives and your children, many of whose feelings are exceed-
> ingly tender and chaste and delicate before God, which thing is pleasing
> unto God;
>   But, notwithstanding the greatness of the task, I must do according to
> the strict commands of God, and tell you concerning your wickedness and
> abominations, in the presence of the pure in heart, and the broken heart, and
> under the glance of the piercing eye of the Almighty God. (Jacob 2:7, 10.)

I understand those words of Jacob as I never have before. I see before
me the worthy youth of Zion. I must nevertheless touch upon a subject
such as he did and for the same reason.

One more sentence from Jacob: "Wherefore I, Jacob, gave unto
them these words as I taught them in the temple, *having first obtained
mine errand from the Lord.*" (Jacob 1:17; italics added.) Rest assured
that I have wrestled in prayer over this assignment.

And so, now to the subject. To introduce it I must use a word. I will
use it one time only. Please notice that I use it as an adjective, not as a

---

Address given at a Brigham Young University fireside March 5, 1978.

noun; I reject it as a noun. I speak to those few, those very few, who may be subject to homosexual temptations. I repeat, I accept that word as an adjective to describe a temporary condition. I reject it as a noun naming a permanent one.

Perversion Is Wrong

I have had on my mind three general questions concerning this subject. First: Is sexual perversion wrong?

There appears to be a consensus in the world that it is natural, to one degree or another, for a percentage of the population. Therefore, we must accept it as all right. When you put a moral instrument on it, however, the needle immediately flips to the side labeled "wrong." It may even register "dangerous." If there has been heavy indulgence, it registers clear over to "spiritually destructive."

The answer: It is not all right. It is wrong! It is not desirable; it is unnatural; it is abnormal; it is an affliction. When practiced, it is immoral. It is a transgression.

There is much in the scriptures that applies to this subject indirectly as well as a number of very direct references. In all of them, this and every other form of moral mischief is condemned. I read but two. This, from Romans, chapter one:

> For this cause God gave them up unto *vile* affections: for even their women did change the *natural* use into that which is *against nature:*
> And likewise also the men, leaving the natural use of the woman, burned in their *lust* one toward another; men with men working that which is unseemly, and receiving in themselves that recompence of their *error* which was meet. (Romans 1:26-27; italics added.)

Men Know Good from Evil

The Book of Mormon states: "And men are instructed sufficiently that they know good from evil." (2 Nephi 2:5.) Even one who is spiritually immature ought intuitively to sense that such actions are wrong, very wrong.

There is a reason why we in the Church do not talk more openly about this subject. Some matters are best handled very privately. With many things it is easy—very easy—to cause the very things we are trying to avoid. On one occasion, with a friend of mine, I went to the medical center of a large university to see another friend who was a doctor there. In the waiting room before us was a low table covered with pamphlets describing various diseases. My friend observed: "Well, there they are. Read enough about it and you'll think you've got it."

Do not be misled by those who whisper that it is part of your nature and therefore right for you. That is false doctrine!

Change Is Possible

The second question: Is this tendency impossible to change? Is it preset at the time of birth and locked in? Do you just have to live with it? For example, the shutter of an expensive camera is calibrated at the factory and cannot be adjusted in the field. If such a camera, by chance, is thrown out of calibration or damaged, it cannot be fixed locally. It must eventually go back to the factory, for only there can it be put in order. Is perversion like that? The answer is a conclusive *no*! It is not like that.

Some so-called experts, and many of those who have yielded to the practice, teach that it is congenital and incurable and that one just has to learn to live with it. They can point to a history of very little success in trying to put whatever mechanism that causes this back into proper adjustment. They have, to support them, some very convincing evidence. Much of the so-called scientific literature concludes that there really is not much that can be done about it.

I reject that conclusion out of hand. And there is a very sensible reason. How can a conclusion on a matter like this be valid when the studies have ignored the part of our nature most affected by it? It has not been fully studied as a moral and a spiritual disorder.

It is not unchangeable. It is not locked in. One does not just have to yield to it and live with it. Test it against moral law and you learn something very quickly. If a condition that draws both men and women into one of the ugliest and most debased of all physical performances is set and cannot be overcome, it would be a glaring exception to all moral law. If that were so (and it is not), it would stand out as a strange and peculiar exception, one that can be applied to none other of the kinds of mischief that relate to the power of procreation. Such a thing is totally inconsistent.

The Lord Works by Rules

The Lord does not work by exceptions. He works by rules. Put a moral or a spiritual test upon it and the needle flips conclusively to the indicator that says "correctable." Almost every major physical disease was once thought to be incurable, but yields now that the cause is fully known and the right combination of remedies is applied.

Now, back to the illustration of the camera. There is a reason why there has been so little success in putting this mechanism back into proper adjustment—we keep using the wrong manual of instruction. For the most part, experts refer to the pages written by those who are assigned to do corrective work, rather than to the instruction provided by the Maker who created us.

When we understand the fundamental moral law better than we do, we will be able to correct this condition routinely. The solution to this problem rests with the "thou shalts" and the "thou shalt nots."

Predators

If someone is heavily involved in perversion, it becomes very important to him to believe that it is incurable. Can you not see that those who preach that doctrine do so to justify themselves? Some who become tangled up in this disorder become predators. They proselyte the young or the inexperienced. It becomes very important for them to believe that everyone, to one degree or another, is "that way." You hear them claiming that a large percentage of the population is involved, in one way or another, with this activity. Do not be deceived. If you are one of the few who are subject to this temptation, do not be misled into believing that you are a captive to it. That is false doctrine!

What's to Be Done?

The third question is a very logical extension of the other two: If it is wrong, and if it is not incurable, how can it be corrected? What can be done for someone who has had a few thoughts in this direction? Or for one who has experienced a long and ugly history of indulgence? How can they be helped?

That All May Be Edified

First, understand that the power of procreation is good. It is the power to create life. Think of that! The power to generate life given to man! Through its employment a couple can unselfishly bring children into the world. This power becomes a binding tie in marriage. Those who employ this power in complete worthiness have the promise of eternal increase. Those who do not, face the possibility that it will be withdrawn from them.

In marriage a couple can unselfishly express their love to one another. They reap, as a result, a fulfillment and a completeness and a knowledge of their identity as sons and daughters of God.

The power of procreation is good—divinely good—and productive. Pervert it, and it can be bad—devilishly bad—and destructive.

This power is very different from our physical or emotional nature. We cannot toy with it, or employ it prematurely or unwisely, without being on some very dangerous ground.

Now, it is not all that unusual for a boy or a girl, in a moment of childish play with someone of the same gender, to enter into some mischief that should remain essentially innocent and meaningless and should be forgotten. And two young men or two young women, motivated by some attraction or responding to a desire for affection—any kind of affection—sometimes are drawn almost innocently into unnatural behavior. They can be drawn into some circumstance that makes them, for the moment, doubt their identity. Do not be deluded into thinking that such thoughts and feelings are normal for you. Just because you experience some period of confusion, do not make of that thing something that it is not. Do not order your life to conform to a transient thought or experience.

And just because someone has stubbed his toe a bit, or just because someone did not watch carefully where he was going and got off the track into some unnatural behavior, or just because he may have fallen victim to some clever predator, that is no reason to jump off the cliff into spiritual oblivion.

It is normal for a male to want to become more masculine, or for a female to want to become more feminine. But one cannot increase masculinity or femininity by deviate physical contact with one of his own gender. There are many variations of this disorder, some of them very difficult to identify and all of them difficult to understand. When one projects himself in some confused role-playing way with those of the same gender in an effort to become more masculine or more feminine, something flips over and precisely the opposite results. In a strange way, this amounts to trying to love yourself.

A male, in his feelings and emotions, can become less masculine and more feminine and confused. A female can become, in her emotions, less feminine and more masculine and confused. Because the body cannot change, the emotional part may struggle to transform itself into the opposite gender. Then an individual is on a hopeless, futile quest for identity where it can never be achieved.

There is even an extreme condition in which some individuals, in a futile search, will undergo so-called "change" operations in an effort to restructure their identity and become whole. Do not ever even consider that. That is no answer at all! That has eternal, permanent consequences. If an individual becomes trapped somewhere between masculinity and femininity, he can be captive of the adversary and under the threat of losing his potential godhood. And so we are brought once again to the doctrine of agency, which is fundamental to the very purpose of our coming into mortality.

If an individual tries to receive comfort, satisfaction, affection, or fulfillment from deviate physical interaction with someone of his own gender, it can become an addiction. At first it may fill a need and give comfort of some kind; but, when that has faded, feelings of guilt and depression follow. A greater need soon emerges. A cycle begins which sets that individual on a long, sad, destructive skid into emotional and physical disintegration and ultimately into spiritual oblivion.

For centuries men have sought to find the cause of this condition. This is an essential step in developing a cure. Perversion may have some very physical expressions, but it is not a physical disorder. A most extensive physical examination will not reveal one shred of evidence that it is. Physicians have never located any tangible control center in the body that can be adjusted by medical or surgical means to change this condition. The next obvious place to look is the emotional or psychological part of our nature. Here we come closer.

Psychologists and psychiatrists have struggled for generations to find the cause. Many have searched with resolute dedication and have studied everything that might have a bearing on it—parent-child relationships, inherited tendencies, environmental influences, and a hundred and one other things. These things and many, many more remain on the scope. They either have some important effect *on* this problem, or they are affected in important ways *by* this problem.

Counselors somehow seem always to be working on the symptoms. When they find something that works on one case and apply it to another, it may not work at all. They have not, as yet, found a remedy. This condition cannot, as yet, be uniformly corrected by emotional or physical or psychological or psychiatric treatment. Depending on the severity, some forms of these treatments are of substantial help in about 25 percent of the cases. And anything that does help, does help. But there must be a better answer.

Turn to the Spiritual Nature

Since perversion can have such an effect on the physical and on the emotional, it has been thought to be centered there. But where do we turn when the physical and the emotional treatments are only partly successful? To Latter-day Saints the answer ought to be obvious. We turn to the spiritual nature. The world may not regard that as important, but we do. When this is regarded as a moral matter and as a spiritual matter, there are answers not otherwise available.

The cause of this disorder has remained hidden for so long because we have been looking for it in the wrong place. When the cause is discovered, it may be nothing so mysterious after all. It may be hidden because it is so obvious.

I present a possibility. And I remind you—I am talking to the one. You, the ninety and nine, are merely listening in. I am conscious that when I mention it, the first reaction may be resistance, resentment, even hostility—that is to be expected—but hear me out.

Subtle Selfishness

Have you explored the possibility that the cause, when found, will turn out to be a very typical form of selfishness—selfishness in a very subtle form? Now—and understand this—I do not think for a minute that the form of selfishness at the root of the perversion is a conscious one, at least not to begin with. I am sure it is quite the opposite. Selfishness can attach itself to an individual without his being aware that he is afflicted with it. It can become imbedded so deeply and disguised so artfully as to be almost indistinguishable.

192

To the One

It is hard to believe that any individual would, by a clear, conscious decision or by a pattern of them, choose a course of deviation. It is much more subtle than that. If one could even experiment with the possibility that selfishness of a very subtle nature may be the cause of this disorder, that quickly clarifies many things. It opens the possibility of putting some very sick things in order.

The spiritual perspective for the cure of perversion emerges with the realization that the physical power of creation or procreation is different from every other part of our nature. It is so devised that the only employment of it calculated to bring happiness is in giving, not in receiving. Consider this: *One cannot procreate alone.* And this: *One cannot procreate with his own gender.* These are absolutes. And there is a third: *One cannot procreate without yielding or giving.*

When one has the humility to admit that a spiritual disorder is tied to perversion and that selfishness rests at the root of it, already the way is open to the treatment of the condition. It is a painful admission indeed that selfishness may be at the root of it, but we do not have much evidence that one can cure perversion by trying to cure perversion. If unselfishness can effect a cure, we ought to be desperate enough by now at least to experiment with the possibility. I repeat, we have had very little success in trying to remedy perversion by treating perversion. It is very possible to cure it by treating selfishness.

Some individuals, entangled in perversion, make a clear-cut decision to come out in the open, to stay that way, and to plunge further into it. That becomes a clear-cut act of selfishness. There is an inevitable result. From it we learn something important. Any individual is, of course, free to do that because each has his agency; but he cannot do that and produce any happiness for those who love him nor, ultimately, for himself.

There are bonds of love that tie human beings together. How sad when signals of love are sent across this network of communication from one human being to another and there comes back in return static, rejection, heartbreak, and agony! That kind of signal generates very quickly from selfishness. That is a selfish signal.

Individuals guilty of very selfish acts inevitably hurt those around them. No person ever made a conscious decision to make unnatural behavior his life-style without sending brutal, destructive, selfish signals to those who love him.

193

If you cannot understand perversion—and I admit that I cannot understand it—you can understand unselfishness and selfishness. And you can learn to cure perversion.

Now, before we go any further, let me point out that anything can be perverted—even unselfishness. So don't come up with some rationalization that participation in an act of sexual deviation is a generous and an unselfish gesture. Don't claim that it is an unselfish thing to relieve the craving of someone who is similarly affected. Any thinking soul ought to know better than that. And don't argue that in natural relationships, even in marriage, there can be complete and brutal selfishness. That may be true, but that is not our subject. And in any case, that is no justification for any immoral or selfish act of any kind.

Submit to True Healing

The admission that one may suffer from selfishness cuts to the very quick. That is how deep the cut must be to repair many physical disorders. And yet our hospitals are full to overflowing with patients. They count it quite worthwhile to submit to treatment, however painful. They struggle through long periods of recuperation and sometimes must be content with a limited life-style thereafter, in some cases in order just to live. Is it not reasonable that recuperation from this disorder might be somewhat comparable? If unselfishness can cure it—if it has to be applied for a long period of time, and thereafter continually—is it not worth it?

The Certain Cure

We can do many things that are very personal, but these need not be selfish. For instance, it need not be a selfish thing to study and improve your mind, to develop your talents, or to perfect the physical body. These can be very unselfish if the motive is ultimately to bless others. But there is something different about the power of procreation. There is something that has never been fully explained that makes it dangerous indeed to regard it as something given to us, for us.

Now, I hope I will not disappoint you too much if I say at once that I do not know of any quick spiritual cure-all. Setting aside miracles for the moment, in which I firmly believe, generally I do not know of some spiritual shock treatment that will sear the soul of an individual and instantly kill this kind of temptation—or any other kind, for that matter. No spiritual wonder drug that I know of will do it. The cure rests in following for a long period of time, and thereafter continually, some very basic, simple rules for moral and spiritual health. A lesson from the prophet Elisha is in order here.

"Wash and Be Clean"

Naaman was the general of the Syrian army. "He was also a mighty man in valour, but he was a leper." There was in his house a slave girl from Israel. She told of prophets in Israel who "would recover him of his leprosy." The king of Syria, wanting to save his valued general, sent a letter to the king of Israel saying that he had sent Naaman, "that thou mayest recover him of his leprosy."

The king of Israel was frightened and said, "Am I God, to kill and to make alive, that this man doth send unto me to recover a man of his leprosy?" Elisha heard of the letter and told the king, "Let him come now to me, and he shall know that there is a prophet in Israel." When Naaman arrived, Elisha sent a messenger to him saying, "Go and wash in Jordan seven times, and thy flesh shall come again to thee, and thou shalt be clean."

At this Naaman was furious. He thought he would at least come out and "call on the name of the Lord his God, and strike his hand over the place, and recover the leper." And the Bible records that Naaman "went away in a rage."

But then his servant (it seems that, always, there has to be a servant) "came near, and spake unto him, and said, . . . If the prophet had bid thee do some great thing, wouldest thou not have done it? how much rather then, when he saith to thee, Wash, and be clean?" Naaman stood rebuked by his humble servant, and the incident concludes in these words: "Then went he down, and dipped himself seven times in Jordan, according to the saying of the man of God: and his flesh came again like unto the flesh of a little child, and he was clean." (See 2 Kings 5:1-14.)

If I could announce to you some dramatic, even bizarre, cure for this condition, I am sure many would move without hesitation to accept it, but when we talk of little things, most, I fear, will receive it just as Naaman first received the message from the prophet Elisha. If I should tell you to do some great thing and you would be cured, would you not do it? How much better, then, for you to do the little things! Then *your* flesh can become again as a little child, and you will be clean. Think very seriously on that.

The Private Battle

You must learn this: Overcoming moral temptation is a very private battle, an internal battle. There are many around you who want to help and who can help—parents, branch president, bishop, for a few a marriage partner. And after that, if necessary, there are counselors and professionals to help you. But do not start with them. Others can lend moral support and help establish an environment for your protection. But this is an individual battle.

Establish a resolute conviction that you will resist for a lifetime, if necessary, any deviate thought or deviate action. Do not respond to those feelings; suppress them. Suppression is not a very popular word with many psychologists. Look what happened to society when it became unpopular!

The Right to Be Free

You have a God-given right to be free and to choose. Refuse the unnatural; choose the moral way. You will know, then, where you are going. Ahead is but the struggle to get there.

Do not try merely to *discard* a bad habit or a bad thought. *Replace* it. When you try to eliminate a bad habit, if the spot where it used to be is left open it will sneak back and crawl again into that empty space. It grew there; it will struggle to stay there. When you discard it, fill up the spot where it was. Replace it with something good. Replace it with unselfish thoughts, with unselfish acts. Then, if an evil habit or addiction tries to return, it will have to fight for attention. Sometimes it may win. Bad thoughts often have to be evicted a hundred times, or a thousand. But if they have to be evicted ten thousand times, never surrender to them. You are in charge of you. I repeat, it is very, very difficult to eliminate a bad habit just by trying to discard it. Replace it. Read in Matthew, chapter 12, verses 43 to 45, the parable of the empty house. There is a message in it for you.

Break All Perverse Connections

Now to you, the one, some very direct counsel. If you are subject to this kind of temptation, it is essential that you break all connections with those who for one reason or another encourage it. Do not go back to places where you were tempted. Do not frequent those places where people with like attractions gather. This may require an adjustment socially, occupationally, even geographically.

If you are involved in a liaison, no matter how innocent it may appear, break it up right now. Some things tie you to this kind of temptation. Quit them. Avoid the very appearance of evil. This may be very painful if you are entangled in a relationship with deep emotional ties. Cut those ties and encourage the other person to do likewise. Get it done soon, and get it done completely and finally.

Freedom from this kind of enslavement is up a trail that an individual must walk alone. If you stumble, get up and move on. Soon your bruises will heal. You will grow stronger. Your battle is two-thirds won, or three-fourths or four-fifths won, when you take charge of your identity.

Accept yourself as belonging in the tabernacle that God has provided for you. Your body was provided as an instrument of your mind. It has the purpose to bless others. Don't be mixed up in this twisted kind of self-love.

Undeviating Determination

With physical ailments we always want a quick cure. If a prescription hasn't worked by sundown, we want to get another one. For this ailment there is no other prescription that I know about. You will have to grow away from your problem with undeviating—notice that word—*undeviating* determination. The longer you have been afflicted, or the more deeply you have been involved, the more difficult and the longer the cure. Any relapse is a setback. But if this should happen, refuse to be discouraged. Take your medicine, however bitter it tastes.

There is great power in the scriptures. Study the gospel—live it. Read the revelations. Every prescription against selfishness of any kind will bring some control of this disease. Every routine of unselfishness will give you more strength.

Look forward to being well and clean and happy. Even if you are guilty, there is no life sentence imposed or pronounced upon you. Keep that in mind.

Now I want to express my gratitude to you of the ninety and nine who have listened patiently, I think even intently, to a message that has been directed, primarily, at the one. I think your time may not have been misspent. The principles that we have talked about apply to any moral temptation, and you may likewise have been reinforced and forewarned.

A Personal Message

I want to tell you, all of you, pointedly that I have thought this to be a very personal message. No good purpose will be served if you make this message the subject of chatter in the dormitories, or in classes, or in Church meetings. I repeat, I have thought this to be a very personal message, and I have already said that we can very foolishly cause things we are trying to prevent by talking too much about them.

Now, what I have to say on this subject, I have said. And that is all I would say to you if you wrote to me, or if you came to see me personally. I am not the one to treat you. *You* are the one to treat you. If you are worried about this problem, if you need help, it should come first from your parents, then from your branch president or bishop or from others that he may enlist to assist you. But you yourself can call upon a power that can renew your body. You yourself can draw upon a power that will reinforce your will. If you have this temptation—fight it!

Oh, if I could only convince you that you are a son or a daughter of Almighty God! You have a righteous spiritual power—an inheritance that you have hardly touched. You have an Elder Brother who is your Advocate, your Strength, your Protector, your Mediator, your Physician. Of Him I bear witness. The Lord loves you! You are a child of God. Face the sunlight of truth. The shadows of discouragement, of disappointment, of deviation will be cast behind you.

I came into the Quorum of the Twelve Apostles to fill the vacancy when Joseph Fielding Smith became the President of the Church. He was a good and a great man, a prophet. He wrote these words with which I conclude, speaking to you, the one.

To the One

Does the journey seem long,
The path rugged and steep?
Are there briars and thorns on the way?
Do sharp stones cut your feet
As you struggle to rise
To the heights through the heat of the day?

Is your heart faint and sad,
Your soul weary within,
As you toil 'neath your burden of care?
Does the load heavy seem
You are forced now to lift?
Is there no one your burden to share?

Are you weighed down with grief,
Is there pain in your breast,
As you wearily journey along?
Are you looking behind
To the valley below
Do you wish you were back in the throng?

Let your heart be not faint
Now the journey's begun;
There is One who still beckons to you.
Look upward in gladness
And take hold of his hand,
He will lead you to heights that are new,

A land holy and pure
Where all trouble doth end,
And your life shall be free from all sin,
Where no tears shall be shed
For no sorrows remain;
Take his hand and with him enter in.
("Does the Journey Seem Long," *Hymns,* no. 245.)

God bless you, the one. You are loved of Him and of His servants. I bear witness that God lives, and that great healing, cleansing power is extended now to you. And that great power is set against that intruding power of perversion which now raises its head in society. Come away from it, and one day you will be in His presence. He will welcome you with outstretched arms, and you and He will weep for joy over the one who has returned. In the name of Jesus Christ, amen.

A closed door symbolizes a warning, *for there are some places that we must not enter if we are to be protected against danger.*

Warning

"There are dangers all around. Some of you may say, 'If things get really tough, we will move here, or we will move back there, and then we will be safe; everything will be all right there.' If you do not fix it so that you are safe and in good company when you are alone, or when you are with your own husband or your own wife and your own children, you will not be safe or find happiness anywhere. There is no such thing as geographical security." (From an address given at the Box Elder High School graduation on May 23, 1974.)

That All May Be Edified

W hen the Teton dam collapsed and unleashed seventeen miles of backed-up water and accumulated debris upon the towns and farms beneath it, only eleven of nearly thirty-five thousand people in the path of the flood died. Why? Because they were warned; and more importantly, because they heeded the warning *instantly*. The result—a miracle of tremendous proportions made up of a myriad of small miracles.

What is happening in the world is much like a flood. A great wave of evil and wickedness has been loosed. It seeps around us and gets deeper and deeper. Our lives are in danger. Our property is in danger. Our freedoms are in danger.

We, too, have been warned. It seems almost against our natures to accept warning or guidance from others. There are, however, times when, regardless of how much we know, our very existence depends upon paying attention to those who guide us.

Knowing this, and as one who stands among those who have been commissioned by the Lord, I sense deeply the responsibility not only to teach, encourage, comfort, and enlighten, but to *warn*. I learned something about warning from an experience as a flight cadet training to be a pilot in World War II—it nearly cost me my life. A clumsy over-correction as I attempted to recover a plane from a spin caused it to shudder violently, stall, and then flip over into a secondary spin. I felt such panic as I had never known before or experienced since. I clawed at the controls. Finally, I think, I must have let go of them, for the plane pulled out in a long sweeping skid just feet above the desert floor. What had I done wrong? Later I was to learn a frightening fact. The plane was prone to do what it did. My instructor had failed to teach, to demonstrate, or to warn us against this singular danger. Other instructors had been more responsible.

Although terrifying to a young cadet, the experience was a valuable lesson. It brought to me a full realization that in my present calling I have the obligation not only to instruct, but also to *warn* of dangers. As with the Book of Mormon prophet Jacob, the Brethren of today must take upon their own heads the sins of the people if they fail to labor with their might to teach and to warn. (See Jacob 1:17-19.)

In spite of perilous conditions described, hope is a part of all dark prophecy. I quote the following to show the protecting power of the Lord. "The heavens shall be darkened, and a veil of darkness shall cover the earth; and the heavens shall shake, and also the earth; and great tribulation shall be among the children of men, *but my people I will preserve."* (Moses 7:61; italics added.)

Leaders and teachers in the priesthood and in the auxiliaries should never leave their listeners in doubt as to what they are being warned against. Nor should they be without instruction on how to meet the dangers which threaten them.

(21) General conference talks usually require long hours of work far in advance of the conferences. On this occasion I had been traveling constantly and had little time to prepare. Just before general conference I was in London, staying at a little hotel, and I had an afternoon and evening to spare before some meetings. I had determined I wanted to talk to the youth of the Church, to warn them. I remembered an experience in South Africa where the breakdown of a car turned to a most profitable lesson for us. A ranger showed us how crocodiles can hide in the mud. I thought of the "spiritual crocodiles" and determined to warn our youth about them. It didn't take long to write the talk which was delivered in general conference the following week.

(22) The first area conference was held in Manchester, England, in 1971. As supervisor of England at the time, I had some responsibility for the arrangements for the conference. Manchester was chosen because it had the largest hall in all of England and could accommodate the largest number of Saints in the meetings. This fact provided an important moment in Church history. Only twice in the history of the Church has there been a meeting of the Quorum of the Twelve Apostles in another land. The first in 1837 in Manchester, England, when the majority of the Twelve were on missions there. The second, again in Manchester, England, in connection with this conference. President Joseph Fielding Smith, who was present, called a meeting of the Twelve for the evening before the conference. Six of us were present. Another, Elder Thomas S. Monson, was to have arrived from the Orient. All afternoon I was greatly concerned about him for reasons that I could not understand. My intense worry was greatly relieved when he arrived just as the meeting convened. He later told of a harrowing plane trip across Europe. The plane had been struck by lightning; he had indeed been in danger. Seldom have I been so happy to see

anyone as I was to see Elder Monson on that occasion. It was in this setting that I spoke of "God's Sacred Word Among Us."

(23) At an area general conference in Copenhagen, I told of a painting by Christian Dalsgaard which hangs in the Royal Museum of Denmark. I had long admired the painting which depicts missionary Elders teaching a rural carpenter and his family. It has meaning to me because my grandfather, Peter S. Jensen, was taught the gospel in just such a rural setting in the countryside south of Copenhagen. I used that painting, and the experience of the Idaho flood to warn the people of Denmark today of the dangers that confront them. Following the conference, one of the high councilors from the Copenhagen Stake brought to our hotel room an etching of the painting, done about the time the painting was first shown. It is beautiful in its detail. Even the tract "A Voice of Truth" is discernable. I keep it in my office as a reminder of our obligation.

(24) "Prove Up to Your Blessings" was given at an Education Week devotional in 1963. The audience, although it was held at Brigham Young University, was not made up entirely of college students. The Education Weeks in those years attracted members from all over the Church. It had been my privilege from the time I was ordained a General Authority to perform sealings in the temple; we did many of them. Hardly a day would go by but that we were at the temple to perform sealings. Now it is not possible for us to do that. The Church has grown so much bigger, and the First Presidency has counseled the General Authorities to perform sealings only for their own families or some few who may be particularly close to them. Since in those days we performed a great many of them; this was constantly on my mind. I told the audience in attendance much of what I would tell a young couple as they came to be sealed in the temple.

(25) Sometime prior to the years when A. Theodore Tuttle and I were appointed as supervisors of the seminaries and institutes of religion, there had not been a close relationship between the seminary and institute teachers and the local stake presidencies and bishoprics. To the degree that this was true, the program was weakened. We held conventions about the Church to which stake presidents were invited. And the cooperation began. Some few teachers wanted to be a bit independent from their local leaders. At the beginning of one

new school year, we discussed our work and determined to settle on a theme that would follow as we traveled in our supervisory assignments. We cancelled assignments for a day and determined that we would spend the day in the office in prayer and discussion. After a day of going over and over again the objectives of the program and how we might achieve them, we came from that long day's effort with three small words, *follow the Brethren.*

21

Spiritual Crocodiles

I have always been interested in animals and birds, and when I was
a little boy and the other children wanted to play cowboy, I wanted
to go on safari to Africa and would pretend I was hunting the wild
animals.

When I learned to read, I found books about birds and animals and
came to know much about them. By the time I was in my teens I could
identify most of the African animals. I could tell a klipspringer from an
impala, or a gemsbok from a wildebeest.

I always wanted to go to Africa and see the animals, and finally that
opportunity came. Sister Packer and I were assigned to tour the South
Africa Mission with President and Sister Howard Badger. We had a
very strenuous schedule and had dedicated eight chapels in seven days,
scattered across that broad continent.

President Badger was vague about the schedule for September 10.
(That happens to be my birthday.) We were in Rhodesia, planning, I
thought, to return to Johannesburg, South Africa. But he had other
plans, and we landed at Victoria Falls.

"There is a game reserve some distance from here," he explained,
"and I have rented a car, and tomorrow, your birthday, we are going to
spend seeing the African animals."

The Animals Run Free

Now, I might explain that the game reserves in Africa are unusual.
The people are put in cages, and the animals are left to run free. That
is, there are compounds where the park visitors check in at night and
are locked behind high fences until after daylight when they are
allowed to drive about, but no one is allowed out of his car.

Address given at general conference April 1976.

That All May Be Edified

We arrived in the park in the late afternoon. By some mistake, there were not enough cabins for all the visitors, and they were all taken when we arrived. The head ranger indicated that they had a cabin in an isolated area about eight miles from the compound and we could spend the night there.

Because of a delay in getting our evening meal, it was long after dark when we left the compound. We found the turnoff and had gone up the narrow road just a short distance when the engine stalled. We found a flashlight and I stepped out to check under the hood, thinking that there must be a loose connection or something. As the light flashed on the dusty road, the first thing I saw was lion tracks.

Back in the car, we determined to content ourselves with spending the night there. Fortunately, however, an hour or two later we were rescued by the driver of a gas truck who had left the compound late because of a problem. We awakened the head ranger and in due time we were settled in our cabin. In the morning they brought us back to the compound.

We had no automobile, and without telephones there was no way to get a replacement until late in the day. We faced the disappointment of sitting around the compound all day. Our one day in the park was ruined and, for me, the dream of a lifetime was gone.

I talked with a young ranger, and he was surprised that I knew many of the African birds. Then he volunteered to rescue us.

Rescue

"We are building a new lookout over a water hole about twenty miles from the compound," he said. "It is not quite finished, but it is safe. I will take you out there with a lunch, and when your car comes late this afternoon we will bring it out to you. You may see as many animals, or even more, than if you were driving around."

On the way to the lookout he volunteered to show us some lions. He turned off through the brush and before long located a group of seventeen lions all sprawled out asleep and drove right up among them.

We stopped at a water hole to watch the animals come to drink. It was very dry that season and there was not much water, really just muddy spots. When the elephants stepped into the soft mud the water would seep into the depression and the animals would drink from the elephant tracks.

Spiritual Crocodiles

The antelope, particularly, were very nervous. They would approach the mud hole, only to turn and run away in great fright. I could see there were no lions about and asked the guide why they didn't drink. His answer, and this is the lesson, was "crocodiles."

Crocodiles

I knew he must be joking and asked him seriously, "What is the problem?" The answer again: "Crocodiles."

"Nonsense," I said. "There are no crocodiles out there. Anyone can see that."

I thought he was having some fun at the expense of his foreign game expert, and finally I asked him to tell us the truth. Now, I remind you that I was not uninformed. I had read many books. Besides, anyone would know that you can't hide a crocodile in an elephant track.

He could tell I did not believe him and determined, I suppose, to teach me a lesson. We drove to another location where the car was on an embankment above the muddy hole where we could look down. "There," he said. "See for yourself."

I couldn't see anything except the mud, a little water, and the nervous animals in the distance. Then all at once I saw it—a large crocodile, settled in the mud, waiting for some unsuspecting animal to get thirsty enough to come for a drink.

Suddenly I became a believer. When he could see I was willing to listen, he continued with the lesson. "There are crocodiles all over the park," he said, "not just in the rivers. We don't have any water without a crocodile somewhere near it, and you'd better count on it."

The guide was kinder to me than I deserved. My know-it-all challenge to his first statement, "crocodiles," might have brought an invitation, "Well, go out and see for yourself!"

I could see for myself that there were no crocodiles. I was so sure of myself I think I might have walked out just to see what was there. Such an arrogant approach could have been fatal! But he was patient enough to teach me.

My young friends, I hope you'll be wiser in talking to your guides than I was on that occasion. That smart-aleck idea that I knew everything really wasn't worthy of me, nor is it worthy of you. I'm not very proud of it, and I think I'd be ashamed to tell you about it except that telling you may help you.

209

That All May Be Edified

Spiritual Crocodiles

Those ahead of you in life have probed about the water holes a bit and raise a voice of warning about crocodiles. Not just the big, gray lizards that can bite you to pieces, but *spiritual crocodiles,* infinitely more dangerous, and more deceptive and less visible, even, than those well-camouflaged reptiles of Africa.

These spiritual crocodiles can kill or mutilate your souls. They can destroy your peace of mind and the peace of mind of those who love you. Those are the ones to be warned against, and there is hardly a watering place in all of mortality now that is not infested with them.

On another trip to Africa I discussed this experience with a game ranger in another park. He assured me that you can *indeed* hide a crocodile in an elephant track—one big enough to bite a man in two.

He then showed me a place where a tragedy had occurred. A young man from England was working in the hotel for the season. In spite of constant and repeated warnings, he went through the compound fence to check something across a shallow splash of water that didn't cover his tennis shoes.

"He wasn't two steps in," the ranger said, "before a crocodile had him, and we could do nothing to save him."

Pay Attention to Guides

It seems almost to be against our natures, particularly when we are young, to accept much guidance from others. But, young people, there are times when, regardless of how much we think we know or how much we think we want to do something, that our very existence depends on paying attention to the guides.

Now, it is a gruesome thing to think about that young man who was eaten by the crocodile. But that is not, by any means, the worst thing that could happen. There are moral and spiritual things far worse even than the thought of being chewed to pieces by a monstrous lizard.

Fortunately, there are guides enough in life to prevent these things from happening if we are willing to take counsel now and again.

Some of us are appointed now, as you will be soon, to be guides and rangers. Now, we don't use those titles very much. We go under the titles of parents—father and mother—bishop, leader, adviser. Our assignment is to see that you get through mortality without being injured by these spiritual crocodiles.

210

All of the training and activity in the Church has as its central purpose a desire to see you, our young people, free and independent and secure, both spiritually and temporally.

If you will listen to the counsel of your parents and your teachers and your leaders when you are young, you can learn how to follow the best guide of all—the whisperings of the Holy Spirit. That is individual revelation. There is a process through which we can be alerted to spiritual dangers. Just as surely as that guide warned me, you can receive signals alerting you to the spiritual crocodiles that lurk ahead.

Listen to Spiritual Communications

If we can train you to listen to these spiritual communications, you will be protected from these crocodiles of life. You can learn what it feels like to be guided from on high. This inspiration can come to you now, in all of your activities, in school, and dating—not just in your Church assignments.

Learn how to pray and how to receive answers to your prayers. When you pray over some things, you must patiently wait a long, long time before you will receive an answer. Some prayers, for your own safety, must be answered immediately, and some promptings will even come when you haven't prayed at all.

Once you really determine to follow that guide, your testimony will grow and you will find provisions set out along the way in unexpected places, as evidence that someone knew that you would be traveling that way.

The basic exercise for you to perform in your youth to become spiritually strong and to become independent lies in obedience to your guides. If you will follow them and do it willingly, you can learn to trust those delicate, sensitive spiritual promptings. You will learn that they always, invariably, lead you to do that which is righteous.

Now, my young friends, I would like to make reference to another experience, one I think of often but one I seldom talk about. I shall not mention it in detail; I only want to refer to it. It happened many years ago when I was perhaps not quite as young as you are now, and it had to do with my decision to follow that guide.

Agency

I knew what agency was and knew how important it was to be

211

individual and to be independent, to be free. I somehow knew there was one thing the Lord would never take from me, and that was my free agency. I would not surrender my agency to any being but to Him. I determined that I would *give* Him the one thing that He would never take—my agency. I decided, by myself, that from that time on I would do things His way.

That was a great trial for me, for I thought I was giving away the most precious thing I possessed. I was not wise enough in my youth to know that because I exercised my agency and decided myself, I was not *losing* it. It was *strengthened!*

I learned from that experience the meaning of the scripture: "If ye continue in my word, then are ye my disciples indeed;

"And ye shall know the truth, and the truth shall make you free." (John 8:31-32.)

I have not been quite as frightened of spiritual crocodiles since then, because I have been alerted on many occasions as to where they were lurking.

Spiritual First Aid

I have been nipped a time or two and on occasion have needed some spiritual first aid, but have been otherwise saved because I have been warned.

Fortunately, there is spiritual first aid for those who have been bitten. The bishop of the ward is the guide in charge of this first aid. He can also treat those who have been badly morally mauled by these spiritual crocodiles—and see them completely healed.

. That experience in Africa was another reminder for me to follow the Guide. I follow Him because I want to. Through the other experience I came to know the Guide. I bear witness that He lives, that Jesus is the Christ. I know that He has a body of flesh and bones, and He directs this Church, and His purpose is to see all of us guided safely back into His presence. In the name of Jesus Christ, amen.

22

God's Sacred Word Among Us

I t has been my privilege over the past number of years to be a frequent visitor to this land, the last part of that period as director of missionary work in the British Isles.

There are currently seven missions in the British Isles, with a membership (as of the first of the year) of 42,618, and nine stakes with a membership of 26,840, for a total of 69,458.

We presently have 1,248 full-time missionaries serving in the British Isles. During the past twelve months they have brought into the Church as converts, 4,172.

The history of the Church in this land is an inspiring history to read. Other speakers, I am sure, will recount some of that history.

Something that has always been the source of great amazement to me has been the influence of the relatively few people in the British Isles on the history of the world. It's very improbable when you look at it, that the people from this little island should move out across the world and eventually build the largest empire ever assembled.

It's an improbable thing that the language of these relatively few people should become the language of great nations in distant parts of the world—Canada, the United States, Australia, South Africa.

Though I do not speak a language other than English (I'm sure you would call it "American" here in England), I have, nevertheless, never found any difficulty in communicating. Whether it be in the Orient, in Latin America, in continental Europe, or in the islands of the Pacific— English is always spoken by many; and in many places it is spoken by most. That it should be spoken so widely in virtually every nation of the

Address given at the Manchester area conference August 1971.

earth and that the influence and dominion of these people should have touched so many places of the earth is a marvelous thing.

When you figure that so many of the members of the Church elsewhere trace their ancestry to these islands and to these people, again there is some meaning. I think most of the General Authorities assembled on this stand are from English ancestry.

A Guided History

I've always been fascinated by reading the history of England. There were, it seems, metes and bounds set by the Almighty to the activities of men in your history. Your history, in my mind, is a guided history.

Did you know that every missionary of the Church, no matter where he serves, carries with him two pages of English history.

Oh, I wish there were time to explore this in depth. Incidents that went unnoticed by the participants in ancient days, when revealed against the backdrop of history, emerge to reveal some guidance in the affairs of man and are an echo of the divine expression, "Lo, I am with you alway, even unto the end of the world." (Matthew 28:20.)

The king wanted a male heir. His wife did not bear one. He sought another wife and was confronted by the powers of the church. He put his wife away, and the church with her. He took a new wife, and there was a new church.

When he died he was, after a brief reign of an invalid son, succeeded by the daughter of the wife he had cast off. Mary set about to restore her church with such determination that in her short reign she is known in the pages of your history as Bloody Mary.

Upon her death there came to the throne Elizabeth I, daughter of Henry VIII and the woman for whom his first wife had been set aside. The tides of the church changed again.

An Englishman in those days who followed the allegiance of his sovereign, and in those days it was more than less compulsory, would have been Catholic under Henry VIII, Protestant under Henry VIII, Catholic under Mary Tudor, and then Protestant under Elizabeth I.

Elizabeth's reign was long. She had produced no heir, and one of the more famous episodes in English history relates to concern over who would succeed her.

214

God's Sacred Word Among Us

The one who stood first in the minds of many was Mary—once queen of France, queen of Scotland, pious and devout in Catholicism. Would England change churches again? The question was settled in Fotheringay Castle on the block.

When the years had moved on and Elizabeth's star had set, there came, by an irony of human history, James VI of Scotland, to become James I of England. He, the son and heir of Mary Queen of Scots who went to the block when all the other things were set aside because she believed as she did and belonged to the church that she did. In spite of all that, her son had not been raised in her faith.

The King James Version

This brings us to those interesting pages in the King James Version of the Bible that our missionaries carry across the world. I read a few sentences from an almost never considered introduction, words that relate to this land.

> To the most high and mighty Prince James, by the grace of God, King of Great Britain, France, and Ireland, defender of the Faith, etc.
>
> Great and manifold were the blessings, most dread Sovereign, which Almighty God, the Father of all mercies, bestowed upon us the people of England, when first he sent Your Majesty's Royal Person to rule and reign over us. For whereas it was the expectation of many,... that upon the setting of that bright Occidental Star, Queen Elizabeth of most happy memory, some thick and palpable clouds of darkness would so have over-shadowed this Land, that men should have been in doubt which way they were to walk; and that it should hardly be known, who was to direct the unsettled State; the appearance of Your Majesty... instantly dispelled those supposed and surmised mists, and gave...exceeding cause of comfort; especially when we beheld the Government established... by an undoubted Title, and this also accompanied with peace and tranquility at home and abroad.

And these interesting words:

> But among all our joys, there was no one that more filled our hearts, than the blessed continuance of the preaching of God's sacred Word among us; which is that inestimable treasure, which excelleth all the riches of the earth;
>
> Then, not to suffer this to fall to the ground, but rather to take it up, and to continue it in that state, wherein the famous Predecessor of Your Highness did leave it: nay, to go forward with the confidence and resolution of a Man in maintaining the truth of Christ, and propagating it far and near.
>
> (The Epistle Dedicatory.)

215

That All May Be Edified

And so the King James Version of the Bible, carried across the world by missionaries, is a page in English history.

There are other examples that lead one to believe that your history is a guided history.

In the days when Philip of Spain determined to conquer these islands, his motivation, his determination—the size and scope of his preparations—all summed, made certain the outcome. The British Isles would be conquered.

The armada sailed; the results a foregone conclusion. Yet tiny things weighed the outcome. Small miscalculations—a general commanding the fleet instead of an admiral—other things.

When it was over, Queen Elizabeth sought to honor those who had defended these islands. A medal was struck taking note of two things: a change in the weather and the hand of God.

An unexpected wind in an unusual place at the precise time and the outcome of the whole war was settled. Engraved on the face of the medal were the words, "God breathed, and they were scattered."

Sir Winston Churchill

The next example is of more recent vintage. In our generation there stood, a few miles from here across the English Channel, one described by Sir Winston Churchill as a "Maniac of ferocious genius, the repository and expression of the most virulent hatreds that have ever corroded the human breast—Corporal Hitler."

He too was capable of conquering these islands. Again the metes and bounds had been set. Little miscalculations, coupled with the indomitable, resilient spirit of the British people, their supporters from the Commonwealth and elsewhere, and the invasion was thwarted.

I recall the poignant words of Sir Winston Churchill following Dunkirk, at a moment when the war clouds hung heavily over these islands and the prediction for the fate of this nation was ominous. He concluded his address with these words:

> Even if, which I do not for a moment believe, these islands or a large part of it were subjugated and starving, then our empire beyond the seas, armed and guarded by the British Fleet, would carry on the struggle, until, in God's good time, the New World, with all its power and might, steps forth to the rescue and the liberation of the Old.

God's Sacred Word Among Us

Dependent Upon God

Now, all of this I have said by way of introduction to my purpose in raising a voice of warning. As one reads English history, one reads the history of a Christian people. Dependent upon God, determined for the most part to be reverent and live the gospel as they've understood it.

The English have been a church-building, a church-attending people, and now we are faced with another invasion.

This invasion confronts not only the British. You are not singled out among nations. But are in company with them in the most terrible of all invasions.

Paul wrote to Timothy:

> This know also, that in the last days perilous times shall come.
>
> For men shall be lovers of their own selves, covetous, boasters, proud, blasphemers, disobedient to parents, unthankful, unholy.
>
> Without natural affection, trucebreakers, false accusers, incontinent, fierce, despisers of those that are good,
>
> Traitors, heady, highminded, lovers of pleasures more than lovers of God;

And then strangely enough he adds,

> Having a form of godliness, but denying the power thereof. (2 Timothy 3:1-5.)

This terrible invasion that we meet across the world, not just here, but everywhere, makes great moment of the preaching of the gospel and makes great moment of the need for Latter-day Saints everywhere, particularly here in these islands, to live the gospel of Jesus Christ.

It is up to the Latter-day Saint to leaven the loaf. We are they who should be honest and responsible and moral people. We are they who should be devout and reverent. We are they who should be a church-going people and a church-building people. We are they who should pray, who should render service, who should preach the gospel to our fellowmen. We should give of ourselves and our means to sustain missionaries and to carry on the work of the Lord. We are they who should be honest in our dealings with our fellowmen; and look upon the basic principles of morality and integrity as worth holding.

Will the Lord Guide Our History?

In this way, perhaps, the Lord will guide our history, that metes and bounds will yet be set and that this invasion will be thwarted and conquered and that we might live freely from the domination of the adversary.

We are they who should look to our homes, each Monday night assembled as families. We should look upon our marriage covenants as sacred, even eternal. We should look upon our responsibilities as parents as being a sacred obligation to ourselves, to our Church, to our Father in Heaven.

I want to express my love for you, our brethren here in the British Isles, to you and to your families. We love you. We've been very proud of what you've done in connection with the preparations for this great conference. We pray that the blesings of the Lord might attend you. All things won't go easy. Living the gospel is never easy, but the Lord has said,

> Blessed are ye, when men shall revile you, and persecute you, and shall say all manner of evil against you falsely, for my name sake.
> Rejoice, and be exceeding glad: for great is your reward in heaven: for so persecuted they the prophets which were before you. (Matthew 5:11-12.)

May you be blessed with the leaven of the loaf. May you be blessed by following the counsel of those who come now to speak to you. Knowing that this assignment would come early in the conference, I've had the feeling to encourage and urge you to listen to the voice of the prophets and apostles and general officers now as they speak. Listen to them, my brethren and sisters, they preach the truth, the gospel of Jesus Christ.

He lives. Of Him I bear witness. The gospel is true. The Church of Jesus Christ of Latter-day Saints is, by His own declaration, "the only true and living church upon the face of the whole earth." (D&C 1:30.) In the name of Jesus Christ, amen.

23

A Voice of Warning

I desire greatly, my brothers and sisters, to be sustained by the Spirit of the Lord in this assignment. Yesterday we visited the State Museum of Art here in Copenhagen. I saw a painting that I have wanted to see for many years. It was painted 120 years ago by Christian Dalsgaard and is titled simply, "Mormon Preachers Visiting a Rural Carpenter's Home." It depicts in great detail the missionary elder preaching from the Book of Mormon. He stands with a carpenter's rest as an improvised pulpit and teaches the carpenter and his family. The other missionary, an older man, no doubt a local missionary, stands with a sheaf of tracts in his hand. On the floor is a tall hat, and in the hat is another tract. The title is clearly visible: "A Voice of Truth." This was the first tract published in Danish in 1850. It was written and published by Elder Erastus Snow, a member of the Twelve, when the mission was opened here. He had been sent to warn the people.

Danish Background

That painting is very beautiful to me, and it touches my heart. In a scene very much like this painting depicts, down in Travelsee, missionaries taught another family, Andrew Peter Simon Jensen and his Swedish wife, Amelia Salen Anderson Jensen—my grandparents. In 1882, grandfather sailed for America with one baby and left his wife here with the second one. He worked in a smelter in order to pay her passage.

They started their young life in America. But she was not to live very long; she died in a typhoid epidemic. She was buried in the winter in an unmarked grave and left him with six little children.

Address given at the Copenhagen area conference August 1976.

That All May Be Edified

My mother, one of the older children, was six years old. The family was divided, and my mother went to live with an adopted grandmother. This grandmother spoke no English, and so my mother grew up speaking Danish.

As a boy, when we would go to grandfather's house, the conversations would be in Danish. How grateful I am for that grandfather who heeded the voice of warning and for my wife's grandparents in Aalborg who likewise were taught the gospel and heeded that voice of warning! The Lord has said, "the voice of warning shall be unto all people, by the mouths of my disciples, whom I have chosen in these last days." (D&C 1:4.) And as President Kimball has rehearsed, it behooves all of us who have been warned to warn our neighbors. That is an obligation that is upon us.

Voice of Warning

That voice of warning is what I would speak about.

I would like to mention in more detail the flood in Idaho. President Kimball has mentioned our visit there. When that earthwork dam collapsed, there was seventeen miles of water backed up behind it. All of that water was released on the valleys below. It was a quiet Saturday morning, a beautiful sunny day. There were seventy-eight hundred people living just in the immediate path of the flood, and another twenty-five or thirty thousand further down the valley. Almost all of them are Latter-day Saints.

Wilford Ward, which was at the mouth of the canyon, was washed away, all of it—all of the houses, all of the barns, all of the gardens, everything—a whole ward gone. The chapel was gone. A mile or two downstream, Sugar City was washed away. The stake center and a few houses stood, but they were subject to terrible destruction. In all, 790 homes were completely destroyed. Most of them disappeared without a trace, except for the cement foundation. Eight hundred other homes were severely damaged, along with churches and schools and houses of business.

President Kimball has mentioned what happened to the people. Of the few who died, only six died by drowning—six of about thirty-five thousand. How could there be such a terrible destruction with such little loss of life? They couldn't go up on the roof and be saved because the houses were washed away. Most of them had several miles to go to high ground. Now, why did they live? Because they were warned! They didn't have very long, but they were warned; and every man who was warned, warned his neighbor. They didn't go casually over and knock on the front door and say, "Would you like to go over to the college this morning? It's on high ground. You think about it, and I will come and get you later if you want to go." No, that isn't the way the warning went. People went frantically from neighbor to neighbor. They honked their horns; they called and they screamed, "The flood is coming!" What about the six that drowned? One of them was just below the dam and had no choice. Two of them wouldn't believe the warning until it was too late. They later found them both in their car, but they hadn't heeded the warning. Three of them went back to get some material possessions, and they lost their lives.

But it was a miracle of tremendous proportion. As Latter-day Saints we learn to heed warnings. When there is a terrible destruction, we will warn our neighbor. There is page after page of miracles. Of how a father heard of the warning, but his children were scattered over the farm. He was in town, and his wife had no car. But they were saved. Miracles of how the aged and the infirm and the children were rescued. One expert said that there should have been about fifty-three hundred people killed. But there were only six. The others had been warned, and they had heeded the warning.

Now, I see a great similarity in what is happening in the world, a great tidal wave of evil and wickedness in the world. It just seeps around us and gets deeper and deeper. Our lives are in danger. Our property is in danger. Our freedoms are in danger, and yet we casually go about our work unable to understand that it behooves every man that has been warned to warn his neighbor.

Now, what warning have we received? President Kimball has talked to us about our missionary obligation—that we are to preach the gospel. And how are we to preach it? We are to preach it by living it. What part of the gospel are we to live? We are to live the Word of Wisdom—no tea, liquor, nor tobacco. Particularly, our young people must be taught that principle by our example. We have been taught a very rigid moral standard. We are to live that standard.

The world is amused when we talk about morality in that way, but let them be amused. We hold to the standard that the Lord has established, and we will not vary from it.

221

That All May Be Edified

"If Ye Are Prepared..."

What do we do then in this tidal wave of wickedness? How do we protect ourselves? How are we able to live the gospel? The Lord has said that all will find safety in His church, and He said, "...if ye are prepared ye shall not fear." (D&C 38:30.)

Two or three years ago Elder Neal A. Maxwell and I were in Denmark. He is one of the Assistants to the Council of the Twelve and was then the Commissioner of Education for the Church. We visited with the Minister of Education in Denmark. We talked about what was being taught in the public schools and how it varied from the standards that we taught in the Church, and what we are to do about it.

It isn't possible for us to come out of the world.

The Lord, when He taught His disciples, prayed for them. And He said, "I pray not that thou shouldest take them out of the world, but that thou shouldest keep them from evil." (John 17:15.) We have as much obligation to stay in the world as we do to stay away from sin. Why? Because we are to warn the world.

We can't establish Church schools all over the world. We don't have the funds. There just isn't enough money. Well, then, what do we do? We teach the gospel of Jesus Christ in our homes. We warn our own families. We teach our own children. Make sure that your children know that there is only one stand of morality, and that is that we remain moral and chaste, that we remain free from all indulgence. The world thinks all of that is all right, but we are not of the world. This is the church of Jesus Christ, the only true and living church upon the face of the whole earth.

And so, how can we heed the warning? We can live the gospel of Jesus Christ and then we can tell others about it. And we don't just casually go and knock on the door and say, "Sometime maybe you would like to go to Church with me. If not next week, the next. And if not then, thereafter."

The Power of Persistence

When President Hugh B. Brown was a missionary in England about sixty years ago, he had met one woman and wanted to teach her the gospel. She wasn't interested. Finally he was to return home. He went back for one more visit. There was a light on in the little home, so he knew she was there. But she wouldn't answer the door. She knew it was the missionaries, and she did not want to listen to them. In those days they carried canes. Elder Brown went around to the back door and knocked. Still no answer. Then he pounded vigorously on the door with the cane until it echoed through the house. Finally she opened the door, and he said, "I've come these thousands of miles to give this message and to warn you of the calamities that will come, and you're to hear my message." She and her children's children are in the Church, because he was raising a voice of warning.

President Kimball mentioned the work for our kindred dead. Did you know that in section 124 of the Doctrine and Covenants the Lord explains that we are given a period of time to do this work, mentioning specifically baptism for the dead? And then the Lord says that if we do not complete this work, we will be rejected as a Church and as a people. We have been warned about that. Now, what will we do about it?

Yesterday we went to the Ministry of Records, the Folk Register, to look for some information on my wife's ancestors. We found what we were looking for. Are you keeping the records on your life? You have been warned by a prophet to do so. Are you going to heed that voice of warning? You were told to see that your young people marry in the temple. That's the same counsel that's given across the world.

Lord, Is It I?

You were warned by a prophet. Will you heed the warning, or will you be as those six in Idaho who thought the warning was not for them? When you sit in church or in conference, do you hear that message and then say, "It's too bad Brother Jacobson isn't here. He surely should have heard that." Or do you take the message yourself?

There is a great lesson in the twenty-sixth chapter of Matthew. The Lord said, "One of you shall betray me." (Matthew 26:21.) I remind you these were apostles. They didn't say, "I'll bet that's Judas; he's been acting queer lately." The record very clearly shows that they said, "Lord, is it I?" (Matthew 26:22.)

Now, brothers and sisters, we had the experience this morning of being warned by a prophet. Who needs that warning? Lord, is it I? Yes it is—it's Brother Packer and it's Sister Packer and it's Brother Benthin and Sister Benthin and Brother Wennerlund and Sister Wennerlund and Brother Everybody and Sister Everybody. And it behooves every one of us who have been warned to warn his neighbors.

Now, I conclude with a testimony. I know the gospel is true. I know that Jesus is the Christ, that He lives, that He has a body of flesh and bone. The world teaches that He's but an influence or that He's only an ideal. But we know Him to be Jesus Christ, the Son of God, the Only Begotten of the Father, and that this is His church—that He presides over it, and through His earthly prophet, He directs it. And when He speaks for the Church, He speaks through His prophet. And His prophet raises a voice of warning, and we have been warned. And it behooves every man who has been warned to warn his neighbor. That we will be blessed in so doing, I pray in the name of Jesus Christ, amen.

24

Prove Up to the Blessings

There is conferred upon certain designated Church leaders a particularly significant and sacred authority in the sealing power. Through this power is given the authority to seal husband and wife, wife to husband, and, on some occasions subsequent to a civil marriage, children to parents. I look upon no portion of my responsibility with any more reverence, or maybe even equal reverence and the same sense of obligation, as I do this power. The sealing power is also delegated to the presidents of the temples and to some few selected brethren who officiate in the temples. The sealing power in the temple is the beginning of eternal togetherness.

It is not unusual for us to have the opportunity in the temple and sometimes in our offices to meet young couples who are about to be married and to counsel with them on the significant responsibility which comes in marriage and family life.

Tell Us What Lies Ahead

I wonder if you would imagine with me that there is such a young couple before us and that they have asked this question, "Tell us, will you please, what lies ahead? And give us, if you please, some words of counsel and guidance with reference to the marriage that now we will share."

Now, I readily can see that counsel to a new bride and groom would be belated for some of you here in this congregation. I hope that you may, in reference to what is said, make some estimate or appraisal not of the road ahead but of the road that you have traveled and take from these suggestions some great satisfaction or maybe find in them a suggestion or two for your children or your children's children in order that

---

Address given at Brigham Young University Education Week devotional June 13, 1963.

225

they might prove up to the blessings that come to them as they are married in the temple.

What I say to this young couple I would say not just as counsel or address but as warning.

First of all, your engagement is now over with. Your courtship, strangely enough, is just beginning. As you kneel at the altar and the words of the sealing ordinances are spoken, you officially are sealed one to another as husband and wife for time and for all eternity. There are several basic responsibilities that you very seriously ought to consider.

First of all, I want to emphasize to you that this is a religious ordinance—an ordinance of religion. It is only incidentally a civil ordinance. It complies with all that is necessary according to the civil statutes, but marriage was ordained in heaven. You will remember the Lord's promise to His authorized servants that when the proper authority is exercised "whatsoever you bind on earth may be bound in heaven; whatsoever you loose on earth may be loosed in heaven." (D&C 127:7.) As you accept the responsibility for this great opportunity, this great adventure, then you must realize that this is a religious ordinance.

I would suggest to you, since you are now a bride and groom on the threshold of all life's experiences, that you come back to the temple soon when you are not quite so emotionally involved. I am sure you will not gather much of the significance of your own marriage ceremony, but will you return as a witness sometime, with a friend or a relative, when you can a little more matter-of-factly, perhaps with a little more prayer, listen very carefully as the sealing ordinance is performed? Then I think you will find something that is not fully appreciated even by most of those who have been participants.

I am going to talk plainly to the two of you, and I think that some of the things I say will be a little difficult for you to take. There will be the temptation for you, as most of us do, to think, *Well, in our case it is an exception, and we will want to adjust the rules just a little bit to fit our circumstances,* rather than have the courage and the faith to adjust your circumstances to fit the rules that the Lord has set down.

First of all, today, as you are sealed for time and for all eternity, you become a separate family on the records of the Church, and that is a separation in a very real sense. All of the ties that have bound you to your father and mother to this point we undo today. We untie them all, and we rearrange a few of them. Many of them we leave permanently untied. That is why your mothers will be crying today. Mothers always weep at weddings. This is one of the reasons. They have others, but this is probably the more significant of them all because they know, in a very real sense, that they are losing and that they should lose you as you become a separate family on the records of the Church.

For Parents Only

I would urge parents to use considerable restraint in reference to the two of you as they learn to regard you as a separate family. I hope they will see you splashing around in the water—not drowning, but splashing—and have the courage and restraint so as not to encumber you with help, but to just let you find your own way. If you are drowning, that is a different matter. I should hope that they would throw you a lifeline and tie it to the shore somewhere and then not forever stand around to try to direct your activities.

I have noticed that a considerable amount of difficulty among our young people is occasioned from the oversupervision of parents in the selection of a mate for their children. They need to be very wise and very delicate in this matter. But all of that selection now is made, and as you accept one another, remember that now you belong to one another.

My young sister, you have had some very choice, intimate, cherished times with your mother, talking over things that are sacred and personal. Now all of these moments belong to your husband, and only rarely and on superficial things would you have to run back to mother—maybe for an occasional recipe or a remedy, but on all of the sacred and deep and important problems you belong to one another and you solve them between the two of you.

I would like to mention a statement by President Hugh B. Brown, from the book *You and Your Marriage.* Let me read a quotation of interest to the two of you, and you might call this to the attention of your in-laws, who not infrequently become out-laws with reference to the marital happiness of a young couple.

> As each new marriage craft sets sail, there should be a warning call which is familiar to all ocean travelers: "All ashore that's going ashore," whereupon all in-laws should get off the matrimonial boat and return only at infrequent intervals and then only as invited guests for brief visits. (Salt Lake City: Bookcraft, Inc., 1960, p. 138.)

227

The Lord has said that for this cause, "Therefore shall a man leave his father and his mother and shall cleave unto his wife; and they shall be one flesh." (Genesis 2:24.) So this day you become a separate family on the records of the Church, and that separation and the degree to which it is respected by parents and friends is basic with reference to your future happiness.

Sacred Powers of Creation

I would like to talk to you too, while we have the two of you here, about the sacred powers of creation. This day, as you become husband and wife, those powers of creation are released for your use. Herein lie the most cherished, sacred, and beautiful experiences in this life, that you might act in the creation of bodies for little spirits to inhabit. Now on this there is never any joking. It might have been appropriate as you were courting to tease one another a little bit, to joke about the third party, or to try to introduce into the relationship the strange powers of jealousy. But now as you accept this sealing ordinance, if it ever was appropriate (and this I question), after marriage it certainly has no place. There should never be any joking or jesting or teasing about these most personal and sacred of all human relationships.

Now, again, you belong to one another, and it would not be appropriate to talk about such intimate things with your friends. If on occasions there may develop a problem, you might then return and talk to your mother or to your father, or perhaps to your bishop or your family doctor, if the question was of that nature, but never would you discuss these most sacred of all things with just anyone—with someone at work, or with the neighbor woman. These are sacred and, of all things, most personal.

Fidelity

Young man, you have got to be worthy of faith. If your bride is to have faith in gospel things, it must start basically with you; and it does not matter where you are, how long you have been gone, or with whom you may be associating. Never once, at any time, is it your privilege to give this lovely little bride any reason to lack faith in you. She must know implicitly that under no circumstance ever would you be guilty of any infidelity. And the same with you, my young sister. You must realize that no matter how far away he is or how lonely it is for you, or what the difficulties are, never must there be one word, one inflection, one joke, one comment, one suspicion that would permit him to lack faith in you.

With reference to these sacred relationships, as you understand the sealing ordinance you will know that the Lord wills that you live together naturally, and that of this relationship children will be born. You are under the obligation—it is not just a privilege—of multiplying to replenish the earth, and in consequence of this the Lord has promised all of the basic essential joys. Let me quote from the prophet, the President of the Church, David O. McKay:

> Love realizes his sweetest happiness and his most divine consummation in a home where the coming of children is not restricted, where they are made most welcome, and where the duties of parenthood are accepted as a co-partnership with the eternal Creator. (*Gospel Ideals,* Salt Lake City: The Improvement Era, 1953, p. 469.)

I am fully aware what the pattern is in the world, but we are not of the world; and here is the temptation, I suppose, above any other temptation that you will face in your married life—to follow the pattern of the world and to adjust the standards of the Church to fit your so-called "special needs." I say to you solemnly and boldly that to do so places you under the responsibility of doing that which the Lord does not approve. You must understand that you are under disapproval of the Lord to follow such worldly practices. Again from the prophet:

> Some young people enter into marriage and procrastinate the bringing of children into their homes. They are running a great risk. Marriage is for the purpose of rearing a family, and youth is the time to do it. I admire these young mothers with four or five children around them, still young, happy. (*Gospel Ideals,* p. 466.)

As Timothy stated:

> I will therefore that the younger women marry, bear children, guide the house, give none occasion to the adversary to speak reproachfully. (1 Timothy 5:14.)

And then he said in his day, as is true of our day:

> For some are already turned aside after Satan. (1 Timothy 5:15.)

Lo, children are an heritage of the Lord:...

As arrows are in the hand of a mighty man; so are the children of the youth.

Happy is the man that hath his quiver full of them: they shall not be ashamed, but they shall speak with the enemies in the gate. (Psalm 127:3-5.)

The Order of the Home

There is another area that is important for each of you to consider. The husband, the holder of the household, is established this day in this marriage covenant as the head of the family and the breadwinner. It may be hard for you to recognize this role, young lady, but your happiness is conditioned upon it. I will say to you plainly, you show me a woman who is in charge of a home, who directs the management of all affairs, including those of her husband—you show me such a woman—and I will show you an unhappy woman. I would hope that you would make a solemn resolution with reference to this marriage covenant. It does not negate democracy in marriage. When the final decision is to be made, when particularly it has reference to prayer and the need of special guidance, then you, as the wife, defer to your husband who holds the priesthood and place the responsibility upon his shoulders, and then you follow where he leads.

With this, I say to you, young man, that never would you ever be brutal or unkind in any way—verbally, or in any other way—with this lovely young girl who will be your wife and the mother of your children. It is inconsistent with the priesthood that has been conferred upon you, and to the degree that you are an unworthy husband and an unworthy father, you likewise are an unworthy holder of the priesthood.

There will be the temptation for you, when the budget is pinched, when the budget is small, and the children are small in size but many in number, for you to want to join your husband on the breadwinning line. This is the poorest of all economies. If you will do what the Lord would have you do, you will resist the temptation to leave the home and the children, and you will manage on the budget that the father and husband is able to provide.

I emphasize this by mentioning an experience of just a day or two ago. I was in one of the mission fields. The president of the mission had called with reference to a critically serious problem. The fate of a missionary was under judgment; his Church membership was at stake.

Prove Up to the Blessings

The president asked that I interview the boy. I did, at great length. Finally, in great disappointment and wondering, I said, "Why did you do it?"

"I don't know," he said.

As I inquired into his background, about his youth, his childhood, his attitudes, his thoughts and actions, finally I came to a question. And then—since the pattern was so ordinary, since we see it so much, since it manifests itself on so many occasions—instead of asking the question, I simply made a declaration. "Your mother works, doesn't she?"

"Yes," he said in surprise.

"She has worked since you were a tiny boy, hasn't she?"

"Yes," again he said in surprise.

How did I know? This is the same pattern that we meet so often. In my heart I held the boy innocent and his parents guilty. During those tender years when he needed so much to be nurtured, when he needed a mother to love him and to tend him, particularly when he did not deserve it, she was out earnestly working to provide him with material "necessities." She probably said, "We must keep up appearances," and so was anxious that he should have music lessons and bicycles and tennis rackets and all of the rest. But what he needed in those tender years was love from a mama. A baby-sitter would not do, and a grandma would not do. He was deprived of that when he was a tiny boy, and as teenagers will, when he had a little freedom, he set about to fill that need. And as teenagers often will, he found the ugliest of all substitutes and now had disqualified himself from service in the ministry and had opened the door for unspeakable tragedy to come upon his parents.

So I say this to you, my young bride and groom, so that you may guard against the temptation to trade material achievement for the most sacred and beautiful and important things that you might bring to your children as they come to join your family.

I quote from the Doctrine and Covenants and ask that you read this occasionally as you plan your life's pattern:

> And again, verily I say unto you, that every man who is obliged to provide for his own family, let him provide [I insert parenthetically in here for your benefit that the Lord does not say, "Let her help him."], and he shall in nowise lose his crown; [And then a significantly important expression] and let him labor in the church. (D&C 75:28.)

231

That All May Be Edified

You, my beautiful, young sister, will be the heart of the home. It will be your responsibility to be the mother, and you will have a good deal more influence on your children over the years than will your husband, for you shall have so much more time exposure with them.

It is important for young women to be trained in the event that the husband and breadwinner is taken in death. Under such circumstances a wife and mother perhaps has no alternative but to leave the home and seek employment, but I urge you, strongly urge you, to resist the temptation to join your husband in the breadwinning line.

I read a few words taken, interestingly enough, from the Primary's *Children's Friend*. This is entitled "My Mother."

> Sometimes when I get home from school
> And mother isn't there,
> And though I know she'll be back soon
> And I don't really care,
> Still, all the furniture looks queer,
> The house seems hushed and sad.
> And then I hear her coming in,
> An, oh boy, am I glad!

Sister, stay as the heart of the home.

Honoring Priesthood

The activity of your husband in the priesthood will be largely dependent upon you. We accord to you, sister, the power to make a leader of your husband, and a woman should know that with the poorest of raw material, with the most ordinary of men, she can build a leader, if she will.

You should know, sister, that your husband will likely be called into positions of leadership. Let us suppose that next year he is called into the bishopric of your ward. It is Wednesday night and you were going forty miles to another city to visit with your mother. Your sister whom you had not seen for several years was coming from out of town and the three of you were going to have a lovely evening together. Then the phone rings. It is the bishop on the phone. "The president has called, there is a special bishopric's meeting tonight."

Your husband comes home. "Are you ready to go?" he says.

"I've changed my mind. I'm not going tonight. The bishop called and there is a special bishopric's meeting."

You will see him put his hand down on the table with real emphasis and say in a solemn declaration, "Well, I'm not going to go."

You say, "Oh, yes, honey. Yes, you are."

You will smile and get his meal on the table, fuss around him a little bit, encourage him, and get him in the car and off to the meeting, and then you will go in the bedroom and cry. You should know that if you let that one tear slip down your cheek, or if you look just a little cross, or if you let your disappointment show, on many occasions when it may well show, you will incline him away from his duty and obligation to the priesthood toward you.

I think I ought to predict also that you are going to be a widow now and again, but there are lots of kinds of widows. There are poolhall widows; there are hobby widows, golf widows, hunting widows, boating widows, archery widows, and, if you have a preference, I think as you grow older, you will be mighty grateful that you have only been, on occasions, a Church widow. That loneliness that you suffered as he has been about his priesthood duty has, in a large measure, brought him closer to you.

Occupation

Now, with reference to your occupation, you are just graduating from college, I understand. You have had some preparation. You have a great interest in your work. I might predict that you will succeed and that you will be a good breadwinner, but let me give you just this one word of warning. Your occupation must become a contributing factor toward the more important objective of building your home and family and not the major objective around which all else must revolve. We readily admit that there are occasions when you must be transferred by your employment and that many of the important things of family life must be geared in a measure to your occupation as the breadwinner, but it ought not to be the all-consuming, the single sole hub around which all that is important to you revolves.

Let me talk to you, too, as the husband, about hobbies. I bring this up and talk to you as the husband more specifically than the wife because it is more often the husband who is the offender here. You will surely have an interest in some hobby; you ought to. But why don't you use moderation? I get a little impatient when I see a man who collects something, or raises something, or is involved in something, and this is more consuming than anything about him, including his family. If it is golfing, flying, boating, horses, or any other hobby, my friend, I urge you to look upon it in moderation so that it does not become an avocation, for it is way down the list with reference to the important things in life. I see many men involved in hobbies, and they are important and useful. Life may well be quite dull without them. But not infrequently we see a man possessed by his hobby, and it is similar to a man who eats teaspoonful of salt, or pepper, or ginger, or cloves, or nutmeg, or chili powder, and then just tastes now and again of mashed potatoes and the basics. Let your hobby be the flavoring, the spice, the thing that makes life interesting; but do not be possessed by it.

I see I have another appointment in just a moment or two, and there will not be time to counsel you further. Just one or two words by way of conclusion.

When Troubles Come

You are going to have some troubles in your life. You know, if I had all the power that the Almighty has, and it was within my province to make your way so straight that there would be never a bend and to make it so smooth that there would be never a rut and to make it so clear that there would be never an obstacle, for your sakes I would not do it; for from your troubles there will come growth. You will find moments of disappointment, even despair. You will not be free from illness or even death, and even stark tragedy may visit you in this great adventure of family living. But from these things your love will deepen, your testimony will increase, your faith will grow, your knowledge of the Lord will become more firm. In no other way can man or woman win the approval of the Lord; and in no other way can man or woman become as God is quite so quickly as in family living.

I invoke the blessings of the Lord upon you, all of you here, with reference to your home and your families. It is the choicest of all life's experiences. I urge you to put it first. The center core of the Church is not the stake house; it is not the chapel; that is not the center of Mormonism. And, strangely enough, the most sacred place on earth may not be the temple, necessarily. The chapel, the stake house, and the temple are sacred as they contribute to the building of the most sacred institution in the Church—the home—and to the blessing of the most sacred relationships in the Church, the family.

I bear witness that the Lord lives and that the gospel of Jesus Christ is centered in family togetherness, in the name of Jesus Christ, amen.

25

Follow the Brethren

T his is a devotional assembly. As we come here to speak to you, representing the General Authorities of the Church, we are under much more of an obligation than to merely be informative. I sense that many of you come here with the expectation that you may draw forth from us answers to some questions that you may have.

Since this is a devotional assembly, you have the right to expect some inspiration from your attendance here. But I think that it is important that you know this: The inspiration you may draw from the General Authorities as they come here to speak to you depends only partly on the effort they have expended in the preparation *of* their sermons; it depends much more considerably on what preparation you have made *for* their message. In this I make no differentiation between the members of the faculty and the student body.

Resistance to Instruction

There is a tendency always for us to be a little resistant to instruction. We hear a stirring sermon and we are always wont to say, "I wish Brother Jones were here. He surely needed that instruction." Or we may even hear a sermon and consent to the truth of the words and yet be unwilling to change.

A poet framed this:

> The sermon was ended,
> The priest had descended.
> Much delighted were they,
> But preferred the old way.

With that much said by way of introduction, the whole burden of my message today can be said in three simple words: *Follow the*

Address given at Brigham Young University March 23, 1965.

Brethren. Though I may elaborate and attempt to illustrate and emphasize, there is the fact, the disarmingly simple fact, that in the three words *Follow the Brethren* rests the most important counsel that I could give to you.

There is a lesson to be drawn from the twenty-sixth chapter of Matthew. The occasion, the Last Supper.

> And as they did eat, he said, Verily I say unto you, that one of you shall betray me. (Matthew 26:21.)

I remind you that these men were apostles. They were of apostolic stature. It has always been interesting to me that they did not on that occasion nudge one another and say, "I'll bet that is old Judas. He has surely been acting queer lately." It reflects something of their stature. Rather it is recorded that:

> They were exceeding sorrowful, and began every one of them to say unto him, Lord, is it I? (Matthew 26:22.)

This Message Is for Me

Would you, I plead, overrule the tendency to disregard counsel and assume for just a moment something apostolic in attitude at least and ask yourself these questions: *Do I need to improve myself? Should I take this counsel to heart and act upon it? If there is one weak or failing, unwilling to follow the Brethren, Lord, is it I?*

In The Church of Jesus Christ of Latter-day Saints there is no paid ministry, no professional clergy, as is common in other churches. More significant even than this is that there is no laity, no lay membership as such; men are eligible to hold the priesthood and to carry on the ministry of the Church, and both men and women serve in many auxiliary capacities. This responsibility comes to men in all walks of life, and with this responsibility also comes the authority. There are many who would deny, and others who would disregard it; nevertheless, the measure of that authority does not depend on whether men sustain that authority, but rather depends on whether God will recognize and honor that authority.

Called of God

The fifth article of faith reads:

> We believe that a man *must* be called of God, by prophecy, and by the laying on of hands by those who are in authority, to preach the Gospel and administer in the ordinances thereof. (Italics added.)

In this article of faith lies a significant evidence of the truth of the gospel. I am interested in the word *must*: "We believe that a man *must* be called of God." You know, we do not ordinarily use that word in the Church. I question whether there has ever been a stake president receive a directive from the Brethren saying, "You are hereby ordered and directed that you must do such and such." Rather, I think the spirit of the communication would be, "After consideration it is suggested that..."

Unfortunately many of us will read it as it is written, but we act as though it read something like this:

> We believe in some circumstances, not usually, inadvertently perhaps, there may have been some inspiration with reference to the call of some men to office, possibly maybe to the higher offices of the Church, but ordinarily it is the natural thought processes leading to the appointment of the officials of the Church.

This position seems to be supported in the minds of those who are looking for weaknesses when they see the humanity of the leadership of the Church—bishops, stake presidents, and General Authorities. They sometimes notice haphazard and occasionally inadequate demonstrations of leadership and seize upon these as evidence that the human element predominates.

Sustaining Our Leaders

Others among us are willing to sustain part of the leadership of the Church and question and criticize others of us.

Some of us suppose that if we were called to a high office in the Church immediately, we would be loyal and would show the dedication necessary. We would step forward and valiantly commit ourselves to this service.

But (you can put it down in your little black book) if you will not be loyal in the small things, you will not be loyal in the large things. If you will not respond to the so-called insignificant or menial tasks which need to be performed in the Church and kingdom, there will be no opportunity for service in the so-called greater challenges.

A man who says he will sustain the President of the Church or the General Authorities, but cannot sustain his own bishop is deceiving himself. The man who will not sustain the bishop of his ward and the president of his stake will not sustain the President of the Church.

Accepting Counsel

I have learned from experience that those people who come to us for counsel saying they cannot go to their bishops are unwilling to accept counsel from their bishops. They are unwilling or unable to accept counsel from the General Authorities. Actually, the inspiration of the Lord will come to their bishop, and he can counsel them correctly.

Oh, how frustrating it is, my brethren and sisters, when some members of the Church come to us for counsel! One may receive an impression—an inspiration, if you will—as to what they should do. They listen, and then we see them turn aside from that counsel in favor of some desire of their own that will certainly lead them astray.

Some of us are very jealous of our prerogatives and feel that obedience to priesthood authority is to forfeit one's agency. If we only knew, my brethren and sisters, that it is through obedience that we gain freedom.

Freedom Through Obedience

No one loves freedom more than the holder of the priesthood. President John Taylor spoke very vigorously on this subject:

> I was not born a slave! I cannot, will not be a slave. I would not be a slave to God! I would be His servant, friend, His son. I would go at His behest; but would not be His slave. I would rather be extinct than be a slave. His friend I feel I am, and He is mine:—a slave! The manacles would pierce my very bones—the clanking chains would grate against my soul—a poor, lost, servile, crawling wretch, to lick the dust and fawn and smile upon the thing who gave the lash! . . . But stop! I am God's free man; I will not, cannot be a slave! (*Oil for Their Lamps* [Salt Lake City: LDS Department of Education, 1943], p. 73.)

The Lord said:

> If ye continue in my word, then are ye my disciples indeed;
> And ye shall know the truth, and the truth shall make you free. (John 8:31-32.)

239

That All May Be Edified

It is not an easy thing to be amenable always to priesthood authority. I recite the experience of the founder of this University, Dr. Karl G. Maeser. He had been the headmaster of a school in Dresden—a man of distinction, a man of high station. In 1856 Brother Maeser and his wife and small son, together with a Brother Schoenfeld and several other converts, left Germany bound for Zion.

When they arrived in England, Brother Maeser was surprised to be called on a mission in England. Much to their disappointment the families were separated and the Schoenfelds continued on to America. While the Maesers remained in England to fill the call from the Church authorities, the proud professor was often required to perform menial tasks to which in his former station he had never stooped.

It was customary among the higher German people that a man of Brother Maeser's standing never should be seen on the street carrying packages, but when the elders were going to the train they told him to bring their carpet bags. Brother Maeser paced the floor of his room, his pride deeply hurt. The idea of carrying the suitcases was almost more than he could stand, and his wife was also deeply hurt and upset to think that he had to do so.

Finally he said, "Well, they hold the priesthood; they have told me to go, and I will go." He surrendered his pride and carried the bags.

While the men who preside over you in the wards and stakes of the Church may seem like very ordinary men, there is something extraordinary about them. It is the mantle of priesthood authority and the inspiration of the call which they have answered.

The Gospel Is True

I wish you could accompany the General Authorities some time on an assignment to reorganize a stake. It has been my experience on a number of occasions to assist in these reorganizations. It never fails to be a remarkable experience. Some time ago late one Sunday night, returning with Elder Marion G. Romney after the reorganization of a stake, we were riding along silently—too weary, I suppose, to be interested in conversation—when he said, "Boyd, this gospel is true!" (An interesting statement from a member of the Twelve.) And then he added, "You couldn't go through what we have been through in the last forty-eight hours without knowing that for sure."

I then rehearsed in my mind the events of the previous hours; the interviews we held, the decisions made. We had interviewed the priesthood leadership of the stake and invited each of them to make suggestions with reference to a new stake president. Virtually all of them mentioned the same man. They indicated him to be an ideal man for a stake president with appropriate experience, a fine family, sensible and sound, worthy in every way. Near the end of our interviewing, with just two or three left, we interviewed this man and found him equal to all of the estimates that had been made of him during the day. As he left the room at the conclusion of the interview, Brother Romney said, "Well, what do you think?"

I answered that it was my feeling that we had not seen the new president yet.

This confirmed the feelings of Brother Romney who then said, "Perhaps we should get some more men in here. It may be that the new president is not among the present priesthood leadership of the stake." Then he said, "But suppose we interview the remaining few before we take that course."

There was another interview held, as ordinary as all of the others had been during the day—the same questions, same answers—but at the conclusion of this interview, Brother Romney said, "Well, now how do you feel?"

"As far as I am concerned," I said, "we can quit interviewing." Again this confirmed Brother Romney, for the feeling had come that this was the man that the Lord had set His hand upon to preside over that stake.

How did we know? Because we knew, both of us—together, at once, without any doubt. In reality our assignment was not to *choose* a stake president, but rather to *find* the man that the Lord had chosen. The Lord speaks in an unmistakable way. *Men are called by prophecy.*

It is in the way we answer the call that we show the measure of our devotion.

The Test of Faith

The faith of the members of the Church in earlier days was tested many, many times. In a conference report for 1856, we find the following. Heber C. Kimball, a counselor in the First Presidency, is speaking:

I will present to this congregation the names of those whom we have selected to go on missions. Some are appointed to go to Europe, Australia, and the East Indies. And several will be sent to Las Vegas, to the north, and to Fort Supply, to strengthen the settlements there.

Such announcements often came as a complete surprise to members of the Church sitting in the audience. Because of their faith, I suppose the only question they had on their minds in response to such a call was "When?" "When shall we go?" I am not so sure but that a similar call made today would call forth the response from many among us, not "When?" but "Why?" "Why should *I* go?"

On one occasion I was in the office of President Henry D. Moyle when a phone call he had placed earlier in the day came through. After greeting the caller, he said, "I wonder if your business affairs would bring you into Salt Lake City sometime in the near future? I would like to meet with you and your wife, for I have a matter of some importance that I would like to discuss with you."

Well, though it was many miles away, that man all of a sudden discovered that his business would bring him to Salt Lake City the very next morning. I was in the same office the following day when President Moyle announced to this man that he had been called to preside over one of the missions of the Church. "Now," he said, "we don't want to rush you into this decision. Would you call me in a day or two, as soon as you are able to make a determination as to your feelings concerning this call?"

The man looked at his wife and she looked at him, and without saying a word there was that silent conversation between husband and wife and that gentle almost imperceptible nod. He turned back to President Moyle and said, "Well, President, what is there to say. What could we tell you in a few days that we couldn't tell you now? We have been called. What answer is there? Of course we will respond to the call."

Then President Moyle said rather gently, "Well, if you feel that way about it, actually there is some urgency about this matter. I wonder if you could be prepared to leave by ship from the west coast on the thirteenth of March."

The man gulped, for that was just eleven days away. He glanced at his wife. There was another silent conversation, and he said, "Yes, President, we can meet that appointment."

242

"What about your business?" said the President. "What about your grain elevator? What about your livestock? What about your other holdings?"

"I don't know," said the man, "but we will make arrangements somehow. All of those things will be all right."

The Miracle of Faith

Such is the great miracle that we see repeated over and over, day after day, among the faithful. And yet there are many among us who have not the faith to respond to the call or to sustain those who have been so called.

There are some specific things that you can do. Search your soul. How do you regard the leadership of the Church? Do you sustain your bishop? Do you sustain your stake president and the General Authorities of the Church? Or are you among those who are neutral, or critical, who speak evilly, or who refuse calls? Better ask, "Lord, is it I?"

Avoid being critical of those serving in responsible priesthood callings. Show yourself to be loyal. Cultivate the disposition to sustain and to bless. Pray. Pray continually for your leaders.

Never say no to an opportunity to serve in the Church. If you are called to an assignment by one who has authority, there is but one answer. It is, of course, expected that you set forth clearly what your circumstances are, but any assignment that comes under call from your bishop or your stake president is a call that comes from the Lord. An article of our faith defines it so, and I bear witness that it is so.

Once called to such positions, do not presume to set your own date of release. A release is in effect another call. Men do not call themselves to offices in the Church. Why must we presume that we have the authority to release ourselves? A release should come by the same authority from whence came the call.

Act in the office to which you are called with all diligence. Do not be a slothful servant. Be punctual and dependable and faithful.

You have the right to *know* concerning calls that come to you. Be humble and reverent and prayerful concerning responsibilities that are placed upon your shoulders. Keep those standards of worthiness so that the Lord can communicate with you concerning the responsibilities that are yours in the call that you have answered.

That All May Be Edified

The Lord has said:

> Wherefore, lift up your hearts and rejoice, and gird up your loins, and take upon you my whole armor, that ye may be able to withstand the evil day, having done all, that ye may be able to stand.
>
> Stand, therefore, having your loins girt about with truth, having on the breastplate of righteousness, and your feet shod with the preparation of the gospel of peace, which I have sent mine angels to commit unto you;
>
> Taking the shield of faith wherewith ye shall be able to quench all the fiery darts of the wicked;
>
> And take the helmet of salvation, and the sword of my Spirit, which I will pour out upon you, and my word which I reveal unto you, and be agreed as touching all things whatsoever ye ask of me, and be faithful until I come, and ye shall be caught up, that where I am ye shall be also. (D&C 27:15-18.)

The Brethren Are Safe Guides

In closing, I say again, *follow the Brethren.* In a few days there opens another general conference of the Church. The servants of the Lord will counsel us. You may listen with anxious ears and hearts, or you may turn that counsel aside. What you shall gain will depend not so much upon their preparation *of* the messages as upon your preparation *for* them.

Remember the verses from the Doctrine and Covenants:

> What I the Lord have spoken, I have spoken, and I excuse not myself; and though the heavens and the earth pass away, my word shall not pass away, but shall all be fulfilled, whether by mine own voice or by the voice of my servants, it is the same.
>
> For behold, and lo, the Lord is God, and the Spirit beareth record, and the record is true, and the truth abideth forever and ever. (D&C 1:38-39.)

Returning again to Karl G. Maeser, on one occasion he was leading a party of young missionaries across the Alps. As they slowly ascended the steep slope, he looked back and saw a row of sticks thrust into the glacial snow to mark the one safe path across the otherwise treacherous mountains.

Something about those sticks impressed him, and halting the company of missionaries he gestured toward them and said, "Brethren, there stands the priesthood. They are just common sticks like the rest of us—some of them may even seem to be a little crooked, but the position they hold makes them what they are. If we step aside from the path they mark, we are lost."

Follow the Brethren

I bear witness, my brethren and sisters, that in this Church men are as they indeed must be—called of God by prophecy. May we learn in our youth this lesson; it will see us faithful through all of the challenges of our lives. May we learn to follow the Brethren, I pray, in the name of Jesus Christ, amen.

An exhortation *is a buttress to correct error and strengthen the structure.*

Exhortation

"There is a position of truth—strong, powerful, steady. Somebody has to stand, face the storm, declare the truth, let the winds blow, and be serene, composed, and steady in the doing of it. Who are we anyway? Are we the ones who were born to be immune from persecution or from any penalties in connection with living and preaching the gospel? (From an address given to seminary and institute personnel at BYU on June 19, 1970.)

That All May Be Edified

In today's world, unless we are on guard, we will join the many people who are comfort-seekers. We will, thereafter, try to find some place where there is 72°F. temperature, where we can lie relaxed, with no effort, be fed, tended, and protected. The Lord never told us that life was supposed to be easy, comfortable, or convenient. Life is all upstream. It is all uphill. If we quit the struggle, we will be washed downstream. We face ahead some narrow places, both as individuals and as a church. We are "shot at" with criticism and opposition from many directions.

If you feel that you must answer every criticism and challenge that comes your way, a single critic or one heckler can occupy your full time. I have learned that there is one place to search for approval and that is up—to be approved of our Lord and of our Heavenly Father.

When I have received a prompting that something needed to be said, I have tried to say it as diplomatically and as wisely as possible. But I have tried to have the courage to say things that are difficult to say even though they may make some uncomfortable. I know only one place to get instruction on what I am to talk about, and that is through the Spirit.

Many years ago I returned from a stake conference to report in a meeting of the General Authorities a serious problem. President Joseph Fielding Smith, then of the Quorum of the Twelve, listened intently to my report and then asked, "Brother Packer, what did you do about the problem?" I told him that I had come to report it. President Smith responded very quietly, "That doesn't do much good, does it?" I determined never to do that again. Thereafter, when I have found a problem and it was in my capability to resolve it, I would do so. Then it became a problem solved rather than a problem found and reported.

This life is short enough that it is silly to do less in the few brief hours of mortality when we have the intelligence and power to do more. To do less would reduce the power to do more in the eternity. So we must stand ready and serene even when it's raining or even when the lightning strikes very close. The Lord has said, "Behold, I will fight your battles." (D&C 105:14.)

On one occasion when I, along with President Benson, was the subject of a great deal of criticism by the local and national media, he sent me a card which read:

That All May Be Edified

> No weapon that is formed against thee shall prosper; and every tongue that shall revile against thee in judgment thou shalt condemn. This is the heritage of the servants of the Lord, and their righteousness is of me, saith the Lord. (3 Nephi 22:17.)

I was greatly strengthened by the message.

Fear and faith are antagonistic to one another. There is always the temptation to want to fight the challenges that come our way. It is often wise to turn the other cheek. When I was president of the Eastern States Mission I had an experience which is given in greater detail in one of the talks in this section. The missionaries got excited about a newspaper article which contained scurrilous and false attacks against the Church. Two elders drove a hundred miles to bring me a copy. I read it and said, "Thanks. Go back now and preach the gospel."

They did not understand. "What shall we do?" they asked.

I said, "Go about your work; preach the gospel."

"But aren't we going to call the editor? Aren't you going to demand equal space and answer this?"

"No," I said, "because I don't have time. I've learned that when we respond immediately to every criticism we may do so unwisely." Finally I did something about the article. Quietly after the heat of the battle, I sent two humble elders to see the editor; they accomplished much good.

So we do well to do what the missionaries were told to do. Stand steady. Go about our work. Preach the gospel. Serve the Lord. The talks in this section deal with one aspect or another of three basic elements of the gospel: authority, obedience, and agency.

(26) "Obedience" in a way sets the stage for the other four talks. There is a balance between authority and individual freedom. It is a hard lesson to learn. I am *free* to be obedient. That is a profound idea. When this idea is operative, obedience to God becomes the very highest expression of our independence.

(27) In more than twenty years as a General Authority, I have never seen the Brethren frightened. I have seen them concerned and determined, but I have never seen them frightened. Early in my days as a General Authority, I heard on the radio as I drove to the office, that a bomb had destroyed the large doors of the Salt Lake Temple. Because of construction, we then parked a block away from the administration

building. As I hurried to the office, I saw across the street at the temple, the cars, the policemen, and so forth. But I had a meeting to attend, so I did not go over to inspect. Late that evening as I returned along the same street I saw the temporary covering of the doors, and all was quiet. It occurred to me then that in meetings during the day with different combinations of the Brethren, I had not heard the subject mentioned. There were other things to do. There was a ministry to perform. How could our attention be diverted from that?

"Stand Steady" was given as counsel to follow at those times when we face difficulty, disruption, or actual danger.

(28) I have learned that the Spirit of the Lord will be where it will be. I have learned that you find it more often in quiet, homey moments as contrasted to classic moments of exultation. I have noticed over the years that many gifted people in the Church have something of a contempt for the homespun effort of the artist, the poet, the musician, who hold closely to the message of the restoration of the gospel. Often in these ordinary works the Spirit of the Lord is very evident. It can be evident, likewise, in the work of the artist of consummate skill, but only, I believe, when they have a profound respect for the ordinary experiences of life, where the Spirit of the Lord is wont to be. "The Arts and the Spirit of the Lord" speaks of these things.

(29) To willfully destroy a marriage, either your own or that of another couple, is to offend God. Marriage is sacred. The talk "Marriage" is pointed and plain and was given at a time when marriage was under attack from many worldly directions.

(30) "Some One Up There Loves You" cuts through the technical complexities of genealogical research and narrows a perplexing subject to simple terms so that beginners and young people can understand and enjoy it. But words of urgency, of obligation, are here. They are coupled with the assurance that genealogical research is not an all-or-nothing pursuit, but *another* responsibility which all can meet without neglecting other work one has to do.

26

Obedience

I would like to speak this morning about a subject that the Lord has returned to again and again in ancient and in modern scripture—a matter that is of critical importance to young people, of importance to students who are seeking to learn secular and, particularly, spiritual things. That is the matter of obedience. You do not talk about obedience unless you talk about authority, and you do not talk about obedience and authority unless you talk about agency.

The finest statement that I have ever read on the balance of authority and individual freedom in the Church comes, interestingly enough, from the preface of the *General Handbook of Instructions,* which is signed by the First Presidency of the Church. I would like to read a quote from that preface:

> A distinguishing characteristic of the Church organization lies in its balance of authority and individual rights. Priesthood is a brotherhood, and in its operation the highest capacities of man—his capacity to act as a free agent and his capacity to be spiritual—must be respected and enlarged. Leaders invite, persuade, encourage, and recommend in a spirit of gentleness and meekness. Members respond freely as the Spirit guides. Only this kind of response has moral value. An act is moral only if it expresses the character and disposition of the person, that is, if it arises out of knowledge, faith, love, or religious intent. Fear and force have no place in the kingdom because they do not produce moral actions and are contrary to God's gift of free agency. (*General Handbook of Instructions,* 1963.)

Authority Versus Individual Freedom

That statement explains how authority and individual freedom ought to be, and are, managed in the Church. This morning I would like to discuss an even higher expression of that—how it works with

---

Address given at Brigham Young University December 1971.

the individual, with you. Surely we have had enough demonstrations of the fact that young people are really agents unto themselves. You can do just exactly what you will do. You may face some restrictions and constraints, sometimes even force, but not from the Church—because the prophet said:

> Remember, my brethren...ye are free; ye are permitted to act for your-selves; for behold, God hath given unto you a knowledge and he hath made you free. (Helaman 14:30.)

If you feel pressed in and pressured and not free, it may be for one of two reasons. One, if you have lost freedom, possibly it has been through some irresponsible act of your own. Now you must regain it. You may be indentured—indentured to some habits of laziness or indolence; some even become slaves to addiction. The other reason is that maybe if you are not free you have not earned it. Freedom is not a self-preserving gift. It has to be earned, and it has to be protected.

For instance, I am not free to play the piano, for I do not know how. I cannot play the piano. I could quickly prove that, but I think it may be a mistake on your part if you ask me to. The ability to play the piano, the freedom to do that, has to be earned. It is a relatively expensive freedom. It takes an investment of time and of discipline. This discipline begins, as discipline usually does, from without. I hope that you do not have contempt for discipline that originates from without. That is the beginning. A parent usually presses a youngster to practice the piano. But somewhere, it is hoped, practice grows into self-discipline, which is really the *only* kind of discipline. The discipline that comes from within is that which makes a young person decide that he wants to be free to play the piano and play it well. Therefore, he is willing to pay the price. Then he can be free from supervision, from pressure, from whatever forms of persuasion parents use.

In our family I have a key that I use, a kind of fatherly key. With my children I know when it is time to lift supervision. As I meet young people around the Church, they are always saying, "When will my parents ever think I have enough maturity to act for myself?" I know when with my family. I have employed this key. I know that they are ready for full freedom in any field of endeavor the very minute they stop resenting supervision. At that moment I can back off, let them go alone, and really just be there to respond if they come for help.

Free to Choose

We are all free to choose. We are making choices. I chose to be a teacher. I wanted to be a teacher. I remember when I decided that—I was overseas in the military. As I sat one day pondering, I made the decision that I was going to be a teacher. I really wanted to be a teacher. Now, because of that choice, I am not free today to act as a surgeon or an architect or many other things. But that does not matter to me. It matters very little—it is not critical at all. I think young people might be surprised to learn how little, relatively speaking, some of these decisions are: whether you are going to be a mailman, a clerk, an architect, a lawyer, or whatever. These decisions are relatively unimportant.

There are some decisions, however, that affect all of those decisions or any of them. These are the decisions that are critical and basic. These are the decisions in which one must be free to be an agent unto himself to choose.

Freedom to Be Obedient

I am free, and I am very jealous of my independence. I am quick to declare my independence and my freedom. Choice among my freedoms is my freedom to be obedient. I obey because I want to: I choose to.

Some people are always suspicious that one is only obedient because he is compelled to be. They indict themselves with the very thought that one is only obedient because he is compelled to be. They feel that one would obey only through compulsion. They speak for themselves. I am *free* to be obedient, and I decided that—all by myself. I pondered on it; I reasoned it; I even experimented a little. I learned some sad lessons from disobedience. Then I tested it in the great laboratory of spiritual inquiry—the most sophisticated, accurate, and refined test that we can make of any principle. So I am not hesitant to say that I want to be obedient to the principles of the gospel. *I want to.* I have decided that. My volition, my agency, has been turned in that direction. The Lord knows that.

Some say that obedience nullifies agency. I would like to point out that obedience is a righteous principle. We read from the Doctrine and Covenants:

255

That All May Be Edified

Whatever principle of intelligence we attain unto in this life, it will rise with us in the resurrection.

And if a person gains more knowledge and intelligence in this life through his diligence and obedience than another, he will have so much the advantage in the world to come.

There is a law, irrevocably decreed in heaven before the foundations of this world, upon which all blessings are predicated—

And when we obtain any blessing from God, it is by *obedience* to that law upon which it is predicated. (D&C 130:18-21; italics added.)

Obedience to God can be the very highest expression of independence. Just think of giving to Him the one thing, the one gift, that He would never take. Think of giving Him that one thing that He would never wrest from you. You know these lines of the poet:

> Know this, that every soul is free
> To choose his life and what he'll be,
> For this eternal truth is given
> That God will force no man to heav'n.
>
> He'll call, persuade, direct aright,
> And bless with wisdom, love, and light,
> In nameless ways be good and kind,
> But never force the human mind.

("Know This, That Every Soul Is Free" *Hymns,* no. 90.)

I quote again from the Doctrine and Covenants:

And again, I say unto you, I give unto you a new commandment, that you may understand my will concerning you;

Or, in other words, I give unto you directions how you may act before me, that it may turn to you for your salvation.

I, the Lord, am bound when ye do what I say; but when ye do not what I say, ye have no promise. (D&C 82:8-10.)

Obedience—that which God will never take by force—He will accept when freely given. And He will then return to you freedom that you can hardly dream of—the freedom to feel and to know, the freedom to do, and the freedom to *be,* at least a thousandfold more than we offer Him. Strangely enough, the key to freedom is obedience.

I would expose you this morning to some tender, innermost feelings on this matter of agency. Perhaps the greatest discovery of my life, without question the greatest commitment, came when finally I had the confidence in God that I would loan or yield my agency to Him—without compulsion or pressure, without any duress, as a single individual alone, by myself, no counterfeiting, nothing expected other than the privilege. In a sense, speaking figuratively, to take one's agency, that precious gift which the scriptures make plain is essential to life itself, and say, "I will do as thou directs," is afterward to learn that in so doing you possess it all the more.

I Want to Do What You Want Me to Do

I illustrate with an experience. When I was president of the New England Mission, the Tabernacle Choir was to sing at the world's fair in Montreal. The choir had one day unscheduled and suggested a concert in New England. One of the industrial leaders there asked for the privilege of sponsoring the concert.

Brother Condie and Brother Stewart came to Boston to discuss this matter. We met at the Boston airport and then drove to Attleboro, Massachusetts. Along the way Mr. Yeager asked about the concert. He said, "I would like to have a reception for the choir members. I could have it either at my home or at my club." He wanted to invite his friends who were, of course, the prominent people of New England— indeed, of the nation. He talked of this, and then he asked about serving alcoholic beverages.

In answering, Brother Stewart said, "Well, Mr. Yeager, since it is your home and you are the host, I suppose you could do just as you want to do."

"That isn't what I had in mind," this wonderful man said. "I don't want to do what I want to do. I want to do what you want me to do."

The Key to Freedom

Somewhere in that spirit is the key to freedom. We should put ourselves in a position before our Father in Heaven and say, individually, "I do not want to do what I want to do. I want to do what Thou wouldst have me do." Suddenly, like any father, the Lord could say, "Well, there is one more of my children almost free from the need of constant supervison."

I know that I am free to do as I will. If the First Presidency or the president of the Twelve were to assign me to attend a conference north in the winter or south in the summer, I could have my own way concerning that. I could settle that with two words. I could just say, "I won't." In fact, I could say it in one word, "No." I could have my way every single time.

But I will it to be the other way. I want to do what they want me to do. Why? Because I have the witness, the conviction, that they are the servants of the Lord. They are placed as my leaders. I feel remorse when I disappoint them by failure to measure up to their high expectations or by some clumsy action.

Why do I feel that way? They are just men, you might argue. No, they are *not just men*. They are chosen above all other men, and they are the servants of the Lord.

A Continual Pattern of Choices

Life is a continual pattern of choices. We are always free. How vital it is as youth that we learn that there is something important about letting the Lord know that we have made that great decision and can say, "I do not want to do what I want to do. I want to do that which Thou wouldst have me do!"

I am continually anxious over my failures. Occasionally I am hurt by the actions of others, by the pain of being misused by somebody else. That happens to all of us, you know. But I know only one *agony,* and that is to know that I have hurt or offended someone else.

We have one boy who has a twinkle in his eye and all that goes with it. He is just full of humor and innocent mischief all the time. I came home one day to discover that there had been an infraction of family discipline. Circumstantial evidence was complete, so I disciplined him. He protested his innocence, but I knew he was guilty because he was always guilty of that kind of thing. That night I learned that he was innocent. I went to his room to apologize. I told him I was sorry and asked his forgiveness. Then I added another lesson. I said, "Son, I hope you're big enough to take this, because life has a way of doing that to us. Life has a way of serving up some judgments that we may not deserve or think we do not deserve. If you're not big enough to face a few of those in life, you've got a mighty long row to hoe, and there are some mighty deep ruts in it. So, your great concern, my boy, isn't when you're misused now and again. Your great concern ought to be when you hurt or offend another."

I Want to Be Good

There is one principle of safety that I would like to share. There is another decision that I have made. I am free to decide—I am free to be obedient if I will. I desire to be good. Some people would be ashamed to say that, but I am not. I want to be good. I want to be a good father. I want to be a good servant of our Heavenly Father. I want to be a good brother, a good husband. That is not easy. I sometimes fall short; but when I do, I have a steady grip for which I reach. I cling to one rod that relates to the decision about wanting to be good.

When the judgments are rendered and I stand there for my accounting with the list of infractions to be reviewed, there is one thing that I can cling to. From the day of that commitment the element of intent is absent. Intent cannot be introduced if I really want to obey and I want to be good.

I live in the hope that when I stand before God that fundamental truth relating to obedience and agency will be operative. When it is, it opens the great portals of mercy.

Theodore Roosevelt invented a rather favorite epithet once. He was not the greatest admirer of Woodrow Wilson. Wilson made a statement in reference to governmental policy, and Theodore Roosevelt said that he was using "weasel words." I quote:

> When a weasel sucks eggs the meat is sucked out of the egg. If you use a "weasel word" after another there is nothing left of the other. (Noel F. Busch, *T.R., the Story of Theodore Roosevelt and His Influence on Our Times* [New York, 1963], p. 305.)

The "weasel words" Roosevelt was referring to related to Wilson's statement on universal, voluntary military training. In response, Theodore Roosevelt stated, "If it's universal, it isn't voluntary; and if it's voluntary, it never will be universal. The one word cancels out the other one."

Liberty Jail

I know a place where some might think there are such words in our Church history, for one word seemingly cancels out the meaning of the other. Those two words are *Liberty Jail.* Isn't that interesting, *Liberty Jail.* The Prophet and others were confined in the Liberty Jail. A jail,

That All May Be Edified

yes—but at that moment he was most free of all men. A few verses from the Doctrine and Covenants catch the spirit of Joseph's pleadings:

> O God, where art thou? And where is the pavilion that covereth thy hiding place?
> How long shall thy hand be stayed, and thine eye, yea thy pure eye, behold from the eternal heavens the wrongs of thy people and of thy servants, and thine ear be penetrated with their cries?
> Yea, O Lord, how long shall they suffer these wrongs and unlawful oppressions, before thine heart shall be softened toward them, and thy bowels be moved with compassion toward them? (D&C 121:1-3.)

Then, as Joseph's prayer continued, the Lord spoke:

> My son, peace be unto thy soul; thine adversity and thine afflictions shall be but a small moment;
> And then, if thou endure it well, God shall exalt thee on high; thou shalt triumph over all thy foes. (D&C 121:7-8.)

Then, the conclusion of that section:

> No power or influence can or ought to be maintained by virtue of the priesthood, only by persuasion, by long-suffering, by gentleness and meekness, and by love unfeigned;
> By kindness, and pure knowledge, which shall greatly enlarge the soul without hypocrisy, and without guile—
> Reproving betimes with sharpness, when moved upon by the Holy Ghost; and then showing forth afterwards an increase of love toward him whom thou has reproved, lest he esteem thee to be his enemy;
> That he may know that thy faithfulness is stronger than the cords of death.
> Let thy bowels also be full of charity towards all men, and to the household of faith, and let virtue garnish thy thoughts unceasingly; then shall thy confidence wax strong in the presence of God. (D&C 121:41-45.)

I Want to Obey

Then, my fellow students, somehow you will come to know that God lives. You can come before Him—by yourself, no compulsion, no force, no coercion—and say, "I want to obey." In yielding that divinest of all possessions, you gain it all the more.

> And the doctrine of the priesthood shall distill upon thy soul as the dews from heaven.
> The Holy Ghost shall be thy constant companion, and thy scepter an unchanging scepter of righteousness and truth; and thy dominion shall be an

everlasting dominion, and without compulsory means it shall flow unto thee forever and ever. (D&C 121:45-46.)

God bless you. May you somehow know that obedience is a key to agency, that obedience is the doorway to freedom. God grant that you can come to know that Jesus is the Christ, that He lives. I know that He lives! I pray that you will know that He has a body of flesh and bones, that this is His Church, that He presides over the Church. May you know that there stands at His direction a prophet of God, a First Presidency, and others called to associate with them in the ministry. May you know that across the Church are His servants—bishops, stake presidents, quorum leaders—who have the spirit of persuasion, long-suffering, meekness, and love unfeigned. They desire to invoke that outward discipline as the beginning of self-discipline. Self-discipline, obedience, opens the portals of life eternal.

I bear witness that the gospel is true. I testify again that I want to obey it—that is the key to my agency. In the name of Jesus Christ, amen.

27

Stand Steady

This is the first time I have come before you as one of the members of the Council of the Twelve. I can't get used to that, although the preparation for it and the testing prior to it is something that one doesn't forget at all, nor I suppose would one want to submit to that twice in one lifetime. But I want you to know that I know without any doubt, from personal experience, that The Church of Jesus Christ of Latter-day Saints is as He has declared, the only true and living Church upon the face of the whole earth; that the Lord Jesus Christ in person directs this work. His servants here upon the earth come and go at His bidding, and His inspiration is constantly with us; so I come humbly and seek an interest in your faith and prayers.

You are all familiar with these words of Timothy in the New Testament:

> This know also, that in the last days perilous times shall come.
> For men shall be lovers of their own selves, covetous, boasters, proud, blasphemers, disobedient to parents, unthankful, unholy,
> Without natural affection, trucebreakers, false accusers, incontinent, fierce, despisers of those that are good.

Let me read that one again.

> ....despisers of those that are good,
> Traitors, heady, highminded, lovers of pleasures more than lovers of God;
> Having a form of godliness, but denying the power thereof: from such turn away.
> For of this sort are they which creep into houses, and lead captive silly women laden with sins, led away by divers lusts,
> Ever learning, and never able to come to the knowledge of the truth.
> Now as Jannes and Jambres withstood Moses, so do these also resist the truth: men of corrupt minds, reprobate concerning the faith.

Address given at Brigham Young University to seminary and institute personnel June 1970.

And then this injunction:

> But continue thou in the things which thou hast learned and hast been assured of, knowing of whom thou hast learned them.
>
> That the man of God may be perfect, thoroughly furnished unto all good works. (2 Timothy 3:1-8; 14, 17.)

"Continue Thou"

We move into perilous, troublesome times, and there is unrest everywhere. I was in Seattle attending a conference a few weeks ago; and in the meeting with the bishops and high councilors, the first question that came up was, "When should we move to the Salt Lake Valley?" Things are getting rough up there, and economic problems are compounding their fears. In California not too long ago, one of the stake leaders said, "What are the Brethren doing in the Salt Lake Valley, the valley of the mountains, to prepare industry, to invite industry, and to store supplies so that when things get too bad here we can move there?"

And after some thought I said, "Nothing. Why should we? There is no answer there."

Let me suggest what you do when there is or could be civil unrest or violence on the campus where you work in the institute or in the community where you are teaching seminary. First, instructions on what to do to protect Church-owned property and to secure the persons—yourself, your students, and so on—will come from President Berrett. He is acquainted with proper procedures and is giving instruction as necessary. You will find that these instructions tie you very closely with the stake presidents in the area who in turn have and will receive instruction on this; so I don't want to talk about that part of it. I want to talk about things that are more important.

There Was Work to Do

I think the uneasiness, by and large, is there. It's in Seattle and Los Angeles and other places, but I don't think you notice much great concern on the part of the Brethren. I recall not too many years ago riding to the office one morning and turning on the radio as they were excitedly announcing that the front doors of the temple had been "destroyed." Remember that? Most of you don't because it is just not that important—it isn't worth remembering. We were then using the

That All May Be Edified

parking lot north of the Relief Society building; and as I went to the office, I glanced across the street. There was a lot of action around the temple—people, police cars, fire trucks, and everything. But I was late to a meeting; so I had to resist the temptation to go over and see what was going on. I was in meetings with a combination of the Brethren all day. As I went back that night about 6:30 or 7:00, there was no one at the temple; but there were some big sheets of plywood over the place where the doors had been. And then it struck me that all day long in meeting with the Brethren, not once, for one second, was that thing ever brought up. It wasn't even mentioned. And why? Because there was work to do, you know. Why be concerned about that?

Samuel Johnson wrote something that I think has an application here that we ought to remember. "A fly can sting a stately horse and make it wince, but one is still a stately horse and the other, well."

There is the temptation always to get excited and, like the old Indian, jump on your horse and ride away in all directions. Don't, don't do that. Just stand steady. If there is anything that the youth of the Church need in perilous times like these, it is somebody who can stand secure and steady and serene, even when it's raining, and even if the lightning begins to strike right close. So my second suggestion is to stand steady, don't be in a panic, be secure. The Lord has said, "Behold, I will fight your battles." (D&C 105:14.)

Fear and Faith Antagonistic

Fear and faith are antagonistic to one another, and it is our obligation to promote faith, not fear; so stand steady. There is always the temptation—it's true in Church schools, it's true in seminaries and institutes, it's true of the missionaries out in the mission field, it's true of the bishops and stake presidents—there is the temptation always to want to fight. We have much to gain by learning to turn the other cheek. The Lord had something there for us when He said that.

Let me give you an example. When I was mission president one of the newspapers in the area in New England published an article about the Church. It had picked it up from another paper that was scurrilous. It was filthy; it was evil; it was entirely wrong. It had headlines across an inner page of the paper about the Church, and the article was a kind of hark back to some of the untruths to which we were subjected a few generations ago.

The missionaries got all excited about it. Some of them drove a hundred miles to bring that newspaper for me to see what had happened. I read it and said, "Thanks. Go back now and preach the gospel." They couldn't understand why I wasn't excited about it. They couldn't understand that I was excited about it and tried not to show it, I guess.

They said, "What shall we do?"

And I said, "Go about your work; preach the gospel."

"But aren't you going to call the editor, and aren't you going to demand equal space and answer this?" The answer was no, because I didn't have time.

All it takes is one critic or one heckler to take you right out of commission if you feel the necessity of answering everything that comes your way. Why don't you teach the students that? Why don't you teach the students to relax; and if they are bitten by a fly, to scratch the bite and go back to work? You see, if I had called that editor and said, "Now, look," and, "We demand," and so on, I suppose it's possible that we could have had him print a retraction of it—maybe a two-line retraction on the last corner of that last page in the want ads where nobody would see it. He might have been persuaded to do that much.

We did nothing until later; then we began to cultivate his help and suggestions. All we did was have two missionaries go to see him and say, "We are two missionaries, and we don't know very much. We're here without any compensation, paying our own way. We are supposed to preach the gospel in this town, and nobody seems to want to hear us. Now, you are a newspaper editor, and you're in touch with the people and know how they feel and how to communicate with them. Tell us what to do to get our job done. Will you help us?"

Who could resist that? And he didn't. So the day came within the year when there was another article in that same newspaper, headlined, "Latter-day Saints Have Dual Reason for Celebrating Christmas." Then in columns side by side were quotations from the New Testament and quotations from the Book of Mormon that sustain and bear witness of Christ; there was an explanation of the fact that we had a double reason for our worship, a double reason for our witness that Jesus is the Christ.

That All May Be Edified

Stay at Your Posts

Why don't you stay at your posts and just not get excited? When the kids come running to you all upset about this and that, why don't you just say, "What else is new?" You know, we have a good deal more to gain by staying on course, standing steady, than we have by trying to put out brush fires. So that would be my first element of counsel to you—just be there, be secure, have faith, and be steady. Be the anchor, and all will be well.

I have a feeling of reverence and awe when I think of education, when I think of the power you have. If we took each one of you and multiplied you by the number of students you taught this year and if we added these numbers, we would have quite a congregation. The thought is that we can speak through you to all those students, and then every year a new crop comes along; so the power of education is a monumental power. There is the possibility always present that it may be used perversely or that it may not be used to full intensity for righteous purposes. We are committed and biased.

A few years ago I attended a breakfast meeting in Boston, and Dr. Christiana, the president of the Boston University, was there. He had been newly appointed as president of the university, and he made his statement of his position as university president: "We can best serve as a neutral territory, a kind of arbiter where people can come to reason." When I wrote that down as he was speaking, I wrote on the same little card, "Heaven help us if we ever degrade to that!" Now, let me read it again, because a lot of people think this is quite a fine statement. "We can best serve as a neutral territory, a kind of arbiter where people can come to reason."

You Are on the Lord's Side

In other words he'll put good and evil in an arena, throw the student in the middle, and let him referee it; then just hope for the best. As we now know, those hopes in many cases are ill founded. So while you are staying at your post and while you are standing steady, make sure that you are committed, that you are nonneutral, that you are biased, that you are one sided, that you are on the Lord's side. We do not consent in any way to have the voice of the adversary or the other side speak in your classes. Can't you see that?

Some of you tend to say, "But our students have to see both sides of this picture." They surely do; and from a thousand pulpits, a thousand voices, they are hearing it from one side. And it is just your voice now, particularly on the university campuses, it is just your voice that's speaking the right side; so yours is not a playing field where good and evil can come and joust with one another until one side may win. Evil will find no invitation to contest in your classes. You are a training ground for one team, you are the coach, you are giving signals preparatory to the game of life; and you just don't welcome the scouts from the other team.

Maintain Faith

Your job is to maintain a form of faith. Faith is the only voice to speak from your platform. There is, of course, the thought to say (and I have seen this a time or two as I have been traveling about), "Let's invite in some people who can kind of bring us up to date and put us next to the issues, and let's have some resource visitors come in and take over our classes."

When I was in junior high school, I took a class in health. We thought it was a nuisance class. It was given on alternate days with physical education where we would swim and play basketball or something—but health was required. I remember reading in our health book an account of a mother.

In those days communicable diseases were a good deal more than just the nuisance that we find them now. More often than not in those days, for instance, diphtheria was fatal. I knew a woman once, a little old lady who was always nervous. She never could sit still; she always wrung her hands and looked sad. I could never understand why she seemed so sad until one day someone told me about the early years of her marriage, when she lived in a tiny ranching community. In two days during a diphtheria epidemic she had seen all five of her children carried out one at a time to be buried on the hillside of the ranch.

Listen carefully to the story I tell, because this applies to you:

A mother in the early part of the century was raising her family in a large community. She was concerned about their health and anxious about their physical well-being. She was hopeful that she could protect her family, particularly through the early years of life.

267

That All May Be Edified

A Mrs. Sullivan let her know that the Sullivan children had chicken pox. Because this mother was resourceful and because she was progressive and forward looking, she thought this was a good time to get that one over with; so she took her children to visit the Sullivans. The exposure would take place, of course, and within a few weeks at least they would have that one disease out of the way. Well, there is a lot to that account. She thought the season was right and the circumstances were right, but the ending of that story I won't forget. It was a few days later when word was brought from the Sullivans. The doctor had been summoned because one of the children was deathly sick. Can you imagine how the mother felt when she heard the verdict the doctor had pronounced upon the dying child? "It is not chicken pox, Mrs. Sullivan; it's smallpox that your children are afflicted with."

Do Not Yield the Pulpit

In your classes I seriously question that much good comes from the so-called resource visitors, save they come for one purpose—to reinforce you, to sustain you in bearing witness, in building faith, in sustaining the doctrines of The Church of Jesus Christ of Latter-day Saints. If you yield the pulpit, as it were, in your classes to someone, let it be to the stake president, to the bishop, to the Regional Representative of the Twelve, to the patriarch, to the man of faith, or to another member of the Church who is firm in his faith and who will confirm by another voice the witness that you are trying to establish in the minds and hearts of Latter-day Saint young people.

I am sure in one case I found this year that it was smallpox, not chicken pox, to which a progressive teacher was exposing his children. You have a great responsibility; and, of course, there comes with that a great opportunity. You have the responsibility to be the anchor; you have the responsibility to stand steady. Somewhere on earth in our day our youth must, positively must, be able to tie to someone who is not confused and who is secure in his faith.

Just a short time ago, I had a young couple come to see me in company with their bishop who had made the appointment. She, a student, wife of a student, had measles afflict their two-year-old daughter; and it was a very severe case of measles. She contracted it and underwent the usual adult experience of having it hit her harder than it had the youngster. It was only when she was recovering that she found she was pregnant. Her doctor immediately recommended an abortion. She was concerned about it and sought other counsel. Two other doctors confirmed the recommendation. Two of the three doctors were members of the Church.

And there came a Gethsemane to that young husband and wife— what to do? The best medical advice they could get agreed in counsel, but she said, "What does the Church teach?" The doctor alleged to her that the Church approved it. Finally, after their Gethsemane, this young couple determined that they would take the course of living with whatever problems presented themselves; but that they would keep their child. And they had come for a special blessing.

I told this young mother that not too long ago I had seen someone who fifteen years ago had been in the same situation, but who had taken the other course. With the best knowledge and information that the world could provide and considering some supposedly very important ethical principles involved, they had decided that it would be better for all concerned not to bring into the world a possibly handicapped child. And I said to this young mother, "You can imagine what happened to that mother when they moved to another city and became close to another family. One day as they were talking about moments of crisis, the other mother, pointing to a laughing, beautiful, healthy child, said, "We were really afraid about our little girl. We weren't sure she would be normal because I had the measles just after I got pregnant, and the doctors...." You know the rest.

There is a kind of personal hell that a lot of people live in. This young couple stood at the crossroad, and they didn't know which way to turn except that they wanted to know the position of the Church on this. Somebody has to stand, face the storm, declare the truth, and let the winds blow, and be serene and composed and steady in the doing of it. That is your responsibility and your obligation as teachers; so don't yield the pulpit to supposedly resource visitors, save it be to those who will build faith.

A Position of Truth

There is a position of truth—strong, powerful, steady. There is a road, and there is a borrow pit on either side of it. Do you know what I mean by that? If you get too far to the left of your lane of traffic, you'll end up in the borrow pit. I suppose there isn't anybody here in doubt that if you get too far in the other direction there's one just as deep.

I used to be a pilot. In those days before radar we used to fly on radio beams; and they had that beam sent out in just one line. On one side the letter *A* was continually broadcast; on the other side the letter *N* was continually broadcast; and then in the middle there was a steady beam so that there was solid sound. The only place you were really safe was right on the beam where there was a steady sound, steady communication. That was vital.

I remember in Tokyo, for instance, they had a beam that went out over Tokyo Bay; and it was a very perilous place to come in because there was an island there. It just wasn't safe—and the pilots knew it because of the map—to be anyplace but right on the beam when they were coming in at low level for landing.

Well, now, steady, steady on the beam; and the more sure word of prophecy and power will be yours.

Who are we anyway? Are we the ones who were born to be immune from any persecution or any penalties in connection with the gospel? Who are we anyway? Are we the one generation who was to be born with everything—popularity—everything else?

I think it's a marvelous time, a wonderfully marvelous time to live—when life becomes a challenge, when it becomes a test, a real test. And you have the opportunity—I envy your opportunity—to teach Latter-day Saint youth in the time of great spiritual peril.

Faces

There is one other thought that I would like to leave with you. It may be a little difficult to explain. President Berrett once talked about the faces that the institute teachers present—their face to the community, their face to the educational institution, their face to the local Church leaders, their face to the students—and then he mentioned one and underscored it as being the fundamental one—the face they present to God. And he made what I think is a marvelous statement. He said, "You probably will make mistakes." And he didn't seem to think that amounted to much—didn't need to be concerned about that as long as your desire was correct. You know, it's one thing to pull a boner when you didn't want to; and it's another thing to have an attitude which permits you to be pushing your ox in the mire during the week so you can pull it out on Sunday.

Why don't we have everyone here and all who belong here but who by appointment are still out teaching—that is, the whole body of seminary and institute people—why don't we accomplish something that's critical and vital that would bring monumental spiritual power into this group? Is there any reason why everyone of us, without exception, every single solitary soul, cannot be perfect in his desire to do that which is right?

Then it can be said one day when you're standing to be judged—either judged for your activities as a teacher of youth or judged for your ministry in life—that your desire was right. I suppose there are going to be some failures; I suppose I had some failures when I was teaching. I don't like to think about them. But there is one thing I have as protection. Beginning at a certain point in my life, any mistake I made I could truthfully say I didn't want to. I may have pulled a boner, but it was because of ignorance or something else—I didn't want to.

No Trespassing

I have the idea that many go through life with their minds something like a corner lot at a city intersection, just a lot on which there is no house. It's used for many things—children cross it to play, people cross it going here and there, sometimes a car will take a shortcut across it. Here is a mind, a vacant playing field; and anyone who comes by can crisscross it. I don't have that anymore. On my lot I have some signs that say No Trespassing, and then I list to whom that refers. I will not consent to contamination of the slightest single spot from a perverse source. I will not consent to it. If a thought like that enters my mind, it comes as a trespasser, an unwanted intruder. I do consent openly—without reservation, with hope, with anxiety—pleadingly with all invitation—for inspiration from the Lord.

Now I just ask you, do you have your No Trespassing signs up? Do you have your relationship with yourself and your relationship with the Lord established to the point that you have declared to whom you will listen and to whom you will not? Lots of influences come to the edge of the property, and they try to find a path that isn't marked. Once in a while they find a new one; and then I am busy making another sign to guard that one too, because I have my agency and I will not consent. I will not.

I will not consent to any influence from the adversary. I have come to know what power he has. I know all about that. But I also have come to know the power of truth and of righteousness and of good, and I want to be good. I'm not ashamed to say that—I want to be good. And I've found in my life that it has been critically important that this was established between me and the Lord so that I knew that He knew which way I had committed my agency. I went before Him and in essence said, "I'm not neutral, and You can do with me what You want. If You need my vote, it's there. I don't care what You do with me, and You don't have to take anything from me because I give it to You—everything, all I own, all I am." And that makes the difference.

Steady as She Goes

As the storms blow the issues become confused; and there will be many who present themselves to cross the pathway of your mind in order to reach the minds of your students. They will dress themselves in disguises, but you will know them soon enough if you have opened your mind to the light of inspiration and have committed your agency. So go on your quest to get this established individually, but let us agree that all of us together and each of us individually will desire to do what is right.

There is a mariner's command usually given by the captain to the helmsman which embodies what I have tried to say. It is a command that becomes an expression in the direction of reassurance, particularly when a vessel is set on course in difficult times. The expression is: "Steady as she goes."

Across the world there has been unrest, dissension, disorder, violence, insurrection, and the beginnings of a revolution. It has indeed been a period of storm and tension. Our voyage on the sea of life now heads into those troubled waters. During the school year we have already ridden out a squall or two. Storm clouds gather ominously ahead. Perhaps they will pass over, but perhaps we must face the storm and ride it out.

You are participants—more than witnesses—in the trying and important events in the history of the world and the history of the

Church in our day. Thank God that you are born in this era! Be grateful that you are alive and have the happy opportunity, the priceless opportunity, of teaching in this momentous, adventuresome time. I do not doubt that we are sailing into troubled waters. There are storms to ride out; there are reefs and shoals to negotiate ere we reach port; but we have been through them before and have found safe passage. Consider this verse of scripture: "The heavens shall be darkened, and a veil of darkness shall cover the earth; and the heavens shall shake, and also the earth; and great tribulation shall be among the children of men, but my people will I preserve." (Moses 7:61.)

Steady as she goes. Our craft has weathered the storm before. It is seaworthy. What a glorious time to be alive! What a marvelous age in which to live! Thank the Lord for the privilege of living in an adventuresome day of challenge. And now to you who teach there is a celestial radar—revelation from God guiding us and guiding you. There is an inspired captain—a prophet of God.

I bear witness to you that The Church of Jesus Christ of Latter-day Saints is just what you teach it to be—the only true and living church upon the face of the whole earth. I bear witness that Jesus is the Christ, and that the Church was formulated for strength in difficult times. Steady as she goes. Now I leave for your contemplation these words about another storm at another time:

> And there arose a great storm of wind, and the waves beat into the ship, so that it was now full.
> And they awake him, and say unto him [as many say in our day], Master, carest thou not that we perish?
> And he arose, and rebuked the wind, and said unto the sea, Peace, be still. And the wind ceased, and there was a great calm. (Mark 4:37-39.)

I bear to you my witness, now the special witness, that Jesus is the Christ. This I know. I invoke His blessings upon you as teachers in His seminary and institute program, praying that you will be sustained. In the name of Jesus Christ, amen.

28

The Arts and the Spirit of the Lord

I want to respond to a question that I face with some frequency. It has many variations, but the theme is this: Why do we not have more inspired and inspiring music in the Church? Or why do we have so few great paintings or sculptures depicting the Restoration? Why is it when we need a new painting for a bureau of information, or perhaps for a temple, frequently nonmember painters receive the commission? The same questions have an application to poetry, to drama, to dance, to creative writing, to all the fine arts.

Now, I'm sure there are those who will say, "Why does he presume to talk about that? He is uninformed. He is just out of his province." It may comfort them to know that I know that. My credentials to speak do not come from being a musician, for I'm not. I am not a composer nor a conductor, and certainly I am not a vocalist. I cannot, for example, play the piano. I would be very unwilling to do so. However, should I be pressed to it, I could without much difficulty, prove my point. I am not adequate as an artist nor as a sculptor, a poet, or a writer.

But then I do not intend to train you in any of those fields. My credentials, if I have any (some of them should be obvious), relate to spiritual things.

I hope for sufficient inspiration to comment on how the Spirit of the Lord influences or is influenced by the art forms that I have mentioned. Since I have been interested in these matters, I have, over the years, listened very carefully when they have been discussed by the Brethren. I have studied expressions of my Brethren and those who have led us in

---

Address given at a Brigham Young University twelve-stake fireside February 1, 1976.

times past in order to determine how those questions should be answered.

The reason why we have not yet produced a greater heritage in art and literature and music and drama is not, I am very certain, because we have not had talented people. For over the years we have had not only good ones but great ones. Some have reached great heights in their chosen fields. But few have captured the spirit of the gospel of Jesus Christ and the restoration of it in music, in art, in literature. They have not, therefore, even though they were gifted, made a lasting contribution to the on rolling of the Church and kingdom of God in the dispensation of the fulness of times. They have therefore missed doing what they might have done, and they have missed being what they might have become. I am reminded of the statement: "There are many who struggle and climb and finally reach the top of the ladder only to find that it is leaning against the wrong wall."

Concerns and Disappointments

I would like to express some concerns I have had over these matters and describe to you some disappointments I have heard expressed among the leaders of the Church.

Because I intend to be quite direct in my comments, I am a bit concerned. For I know when we touch this subject we talk of people who are very gifted. And people who are very gifted, it would seem tend to be temperamental. We were discussing some time ago the music and musicians of the Church when one of the Twelve pointed out that it may be difficult to get instruction across because some of our musicians, among others, have a tendency to be temperamental. "Yes," observed one of the senior members of our Quorum, "more temper than mental." That, I suppose, describes all of us at one time or another.

Before I continue, I want it clearly understood that we have in the Church tens of thousands of gifted people who not only have talent, but who are generous with it. Our gifted people are greatly needed in the Church. The work of the Lord has been moved by the members in the wards and stakes and branches who have been blessed with special gifts and who use them unselfishly. Because of what they do, we are able to feel and learn very quickly through music, through art, through

275

poetry some spiritual things that we would otherwise learn very slowly. All of us are indebted to them for their generous service. I am humbly grateful to those who render such service in the Church. But then it is only right that they should contribute.

Proper Use of Gifts

You who have such talents might well ask, "Whence comes this gift?" And gift it is. You may have cultivated it and developed it, but it was given to you. Most of us do not have it. You were not more deserving than we, but you are a good deal more responsible. If you use your gift properly, opportunities for service are opened that will be beneficial eternally for you and for others.

Has it ever occurred to you that you may leave this life without it? If the gift is yours because of the shape of your vocal cords, or the strength of your lungs, or because of the coordination of your hands, or because your eye registers form and color, you may leave the gift behind. You may have to be content with what you have become, because you possessed it while you were here. It has not been revealed just how this would be. I rather suspect that those gifts which we use properly will stay with us beyond the veil. And I repeat, you who are gifted may not be more deserving, but you are much more responsible than the rest of us.

Elder Orson F. Whitney said:

> We shall yet have Miltons and Shakespeares of our own. God's ammunition is not exhausted. His brightest spirits are held in reserve for the latter times. In God's name and by his help we will build up a literature whose top shall touch heaven, though its foundations may now be low in earth. ("Home Literature," Richard H. Cracroft and Neal E. Lambert, eds., *A Believing People: Literature of the Latter-day Saints* [Salt Lake City: Bookcraft, Inc., 1979], p. 132.)

We Move Slower Than Need Be

Since that statement was made in 1888, those foundations have been raised up very slowly. The greatest poems are not yet written, nor the paintings finished. The greatest hymns and anthems of the Restoration are yet to be composed. The sublimest renditions of them are yet to be conducted. We move forward much slower than need be, and I would like to underline some things that stand in our way.

276

The Arts and the Spirit of the Lord

You will quickly notice that I refer frequently to music. There is a reason for that. We use it more often. But the point that I shall make about the musician applies to all the arts: painting, poetry, drama, dance, and others.

For some reason it takes a constant vigilance on the part of priest-hood leaders—both general and local—to ensure that music presented in our worship and devotional services is music that is appropriate for worship and devotional services. I have heard presidents of the Church declare after a general conference, or after a temple dedication, words to this effect (and I am quoting verbatim from one such experience):

> I suppose we did not give enough attention to the music. It seems that our musicians must take such liberties. Something spiritual was lost from our meetings because the music was not what it should have been. Next time we must remember to give them more careful instructions.

Why is it that the president of the Church, or the president of the stake, or the bishop of the ward must be so attentive in arranging music for worship services and conference meetings? Why should the anxiety persist that if the musicians are left to do what they want to do, the result will not invite the Spirit of the Lord?

Invite the Spirit of the Lord

I have in the past made not altogether successful attempts to set a mood of devotion on a very sacred subject, having been invited to the pulpit immediately after a choir or choral number which was well performed but did nothing to inspire the spirit of devotion; or after a brass ensemble has rendered music that has nothing to do with spiritual inspiration.

The selections, which for other purposes might have been admirable, even impressive, failed in their inspiration simply because they were not appropriate. For some other gathering, some other time, some other place, yes—but they did not do what the hymns of the Restoration could have done. How sad when a gifted person has no real sense of propriety!

The Matter of Propriety

Let me illustrate this matter of propriety. Suppose you sponsor a pep rally in the stadium with the purpose of exciting the student body

277

to a high point of enthusiasm. Suppose you invite someone to present a musical number with the expectation that the music would contribute to your purpose. Imagine him playing a sonata on an organ in subdued tones that lulls everyone into a contemplative and reflective mood. However well composed the music, or however well performed, it would not be appropriate for the occasion.

This example, of course, is obvious. It makes me wonder, therefore, why we must be constantly alert to have appropriate music in our sacrament meetings, conference sessions, and other worship services. Music and art and dance and literature can be very appropriate in one place and in one setting and for one purpose and be very wrong in another. That can be true of instruments as well.

We have, in our instruction to the musicians of the Church, this suggestion:

> Organs and pianos are the standard musical instruments used in sacrament meetings. Other instruments, such as orchestral strings, may be used when appropriate, but the music presented must be in keeping with the reverence and spirituality of the meeting. Brass and percussion instruments are generally not appropriate. (*General Handbook of Instructions* [Salt Lake City: The Church of Jesus Christ of Latter-day Saints, 1976], p. 23.)

We are under resistance from some highly trained musicians who insist that they can get as much inspiration from brass instruments or a guitar solo as from a choir. I believe that an organ perhaps could be played at a pep rally in a way to incite great enthusiasm. And I think a brass section could play a hymn in such a way as to be reverent and fitting in a worship service. But if it should happen, it would have to be an exception. We cannot convey a sacred message in an art form that is not appropriate and have anything spiritual happen. But there is a constant attempt to do it.

Several years ago one of the organizations of the Church produced a filmstrip. The subject matter was very serious and the script was well written. The producer provided a story board. A story board is a series of loose, almost scribbled sketches, sometimes with a little color brushed across them, to roughly illustrate each frame of the filmstrip. Very little work is invested in a story board. It is merely to give an idea and is always subject to revision.

Some members of the committee were amused by the story board itself. It had a loose comical air about it. They decided to photograph the illustrations on the story board and use them in the filmstrip. They thought they would be quite amusing and entertaining.

When the filmstrip was reviewed by four members of the Council of the Twelve, it was rejected. It had to be made over again. Why? Because the art form used simply was not appropriate to the message. You just don't teach sacred, serious subjects with careless, scribbled illustrations.

Now, again to music. There have been a number of efforts to take sacred gospel themes and tie them to modern music in the hope of attracting our young people to the message. Few events in all of human history surpass the spiritual majesty of the First Vision. We would be ill advised to describe that event, the visit of Elohim and Jehovah, in company with rock music, even soft rock music, or to take equally sacred themes and set them to a modern beat. I do not know how that can be done and result in increased spirituality. I think it cannot be done.

There Is a Difference

When highly trained artists insist, as they occasionally do, that they receive spiritual experience in tying a sacred gospel theme to an inappropriate art form, I must conclude that they do not know, not really, the difference between when the Spirit of the Lord is present and when it is not.

Very frequently when our musicians, particularly the more highly trained among them, are left to do what they want to do, they perform in such a way as to call attention to themselves and their ability. They do this rather than give prayerful attention to what will inspire. I do not mean "inspire" as the music or art of the world can inspire. I mean *inspire!*

They are not content to use the hymns and anthems of the Restoration; for such a presentation, they feel, will not demonstrate their full capacities. When pressed to do so, they may grudgingly put a hymn on the program. But it is obvious that their heart isn't in it, for the numbers they select themselves seem to say, "Now let us show you what we really can do."

We instruct stake presidents that "preference should be given to the singing of well-known hymns" at stake conferences. (*1976 Stake Conference Program Schedules.*)

That All May Be Edified

I know there are those who think that our Church music is limited. Some with professional abilities evidently soon get very tired of it. They want to stray away from it and reach out into the world. They present the argument that many of the hymns in our hymnbook were not written for the Church or by members of the Church. I know that already. And some of them are not really as compelling as they might be. Their messages are not as specific as we could have if we produced our own. But by association they have taken on a meaning that reminds members of the Church, whenever they hear them, of the restoration of the gospel, of the Lord, and of His ministry.

The Sacred Message

Sometimes, to ensure that music will be appropriate, one of the hymns or anthems of the Restoration is specifically requested. "Oh, but they sang that last conference," our conductors will say. Indeed we did, and we preached the same gospel last conference also. The preaching of it over and over again gives it a familiar and warm feeling. We build it into our lives.

As speakers we are not trying to impress the world with how talented we are as preachers. We are simply trying to get across, by repetition if that's the only way, the sacred message that has been entrusted to us.

Those of us who lead the Church are not constantly seeking new doctrine to introduce. We simply teach over and over again that which was in the beginning. It is with great difficulty that we try to pass on to the next generation, in some form of purity, that which was given to us. We will lose it if we are not wise.

The musicians may say, "Do you really want us to take those few familiar hymns and present them over and over again with no introduction of anything new?" No, that is not what I would want, but it is close.

In Character with the Restoration

What I would desire would be to have the hymns of the Restoration *characteristic* of our worship services, with others added if they are appropriate. Many numbers can be used in our worship services with complete propriety.

Our hymns speak the truth as far as they go. They could speak more of it if we had more of them, specifically teaching the principles of the restored gospel of Jesus Christ.

If I had my way there would be many new hymns with lyrics near scriptural in their power, bonded to music that would inspire people to worship. Think how much we could be helped by an inspired anthem or hymn of the Restoration! Think how we could be helped by an inspired painting on a scriptural theme or on one which depicts our heritage. How much we could be aided by a graceful and modest dance, by a persuasive narrative, or poem, or drama! We could have the Spirit of the Lord more frequently and in almost unlimited intensity if we would.

For the most part, we do without because the conductor wants to win the acclaim of the world. He does not play to the Lord, but to other musicians. The composer and the arranger want to please the world. The painter wants to be in style. And so our resources of art and music grow ever so gradually. And we find that there have marched through this grand parade of mortality men and women who were sublimely gifted, but who spent all, or most, in the world and for the world. And I repeat that they may well one day come to learn that "many men struggle to reach the top of the ladder only to find that it is leaning against the wrong wall."

It is a mistake to assume that one can follow the ways of the world and then somehow, in a moment of intruded inspiration, compose a great anthem of the Restoration, or in a moment of singular inspiration paint the great painting. When it is done, it will be done by one who has yearned and tried and longed fervently to do it, not by one who has condescended to do it. It will take quite as much preparation and work as any masterpiece, and a different kind of inspiration.

There is a test you might apply if you are among the gifted. Ask yourself this question: When I am free to do what I really want to do, what will it be?

Our Humble Heritage in the Arts

If you find that you are ashamed of our humble heritage in the arts, that ought to be something of a signal to you. Often artists are not free to create what they most desire because the market demands other things of them. But what about when you are free? Do you have a

That All May Be Edified

desire to produce what the Church needs? Or do you desire to convince the Church that it needs to change style so the world will feel comfortable with it? Although our artistic heritage as yet is relatively small, we are losing some of what we have—through neglect!

At the recent rededication of the St. George Temple each session was closed, as is traditional in temple dedication, with the presentation of the "Hosanna Anthem." The audience, on the signal from the conductor, joins with the choir on that part of the anthem known widely through the Church as "The Spirit of God Like a Fire Is Burning." I sat through those sessions and carefully observed, with great sorrow, that fully 80 percent of those in the audience did not know the words.

We can lose our heritage. We have lost part of it. Let me cite an example in the field of poetry.

William Ernest Henley wrote "Invictus," a proud, almost defiant expression that concludes:

> I am the master of my fate,
> I am the captain of my soul.

The Answer to "Invictus"

Some years ago an answer to "Invictus" was given. Let me quote it to you:

> Art thou in truth?
> Then what of Him who bought thee with His blood?
> Who plunged into devouring seas
> And snatched thee from the flood,
>
> Who bore for all our fallen race
> What none but Him could bear—
> That God who died that man might live
> And endless glory share.
>
> Of what avail thy vaunted strength
> Apart from His vast might?
> Pray that His light may pierce the gloom
> That thou mayest see aright.
>
> Men are as bubbles on the wave,
> As leaves upon the tree,
> Thou, captain of thy soul! Forsooth,
> Who gave that place to thee?

The Arts and the Spirit of the Lord

Free will is thine—free agency,
To wield for right or wrong;
But thou must answer unto Him
To whom all souls belong.

Bend to the dust that "head unbowed,"
Small part of life's great whole,
And see in Him and Him alone,
The captain of thy soul.

(Orson F. Whitney, "The Soul's Captain," in Special Collections, Harold B. Lee Library, Brigham Young University.)

And who wrote that? Orson F. Whitney of the Council of the Twelve Apostles, a gifted and inspired poet whose work is virtually unknown in the Church.

Let me quote another of his poems:

There's a mountain named Stern Justice,
Tall and towering, gloomy, grand,
Frowning o'er a vale called Mercy,
Loveliest in all the land.

Great and mighty is the mountain,
But its snowy crags are cold,
And in vain the sunlight lingers
On the summit proud and bold.

There is warmth within the valley,
And I love to wander there,
'Mid the fountains and the flowers,
Breathing fragrance on the air.

Much I love the solemn mountain,
It doth meet my somber mood,
When, amid the muttering thunders,
O'er my soul the storm-clouds brood.

But when tears, like rain, have fallen
From the fountain of my woe,
And my soul has lost its fierceness,
Straight unto the vale I go;

Where the landscape, gently smiling,
O'er my heart pours healing balm,
And, as oil on troubled waters,
Brings from out its storm a calm.

That All May Be Edified

> Yes, I love both vale and mountain,
> Ne'er from either would I part;
> Each unto my life is needful,
> Both are dear unto my heart.
>
> For the smiling vale doth soften
> All the rugged steep makes sad,
> And from icy rocks meander
> Rills that make the valley glad.

(Orson F. Whitney, "The Mountain and the Vale," *Poetical Writings of Orson F. Whitney* [Salt Lake City: Juvenile Instructor Office, 1889], p. 183.)

Both of these poems are new to most of you. Why would that be? I think it more than a pity that work such as this remains unknown to most students and faculty—even to some of the faculty in the field of literature. It is sad when members of the faculty here would discard them in favor of assigning their students to read degenerate compositions that issue from the minds of perverted and wicked men.

Temptation to Replace Our Cultural Heritage

There is the temptation for college teachers, in the Church and outside of it, to exercise their authority to give assignments and thereby introduce their students to degradation under the argument that it is part of our culture. Teachers in the field of literature are particularly vulnerable.

I use the word *warning.* Such will not go unnoticed in the eternal scheme of things. Those who convey a degraded heritage to the next generation will reap disappointment by and by.

Teachers would do well to learn the difference between studying some things, as compared to studying *about* them. There is a great difference.

There is much to be said for a great effort to discover the humble and inspired contributions of gifted Saints of the past and thereby inspire the gifted in our day to produce works that will inspire those who come after us.

It is sad but true that, almost as a rule, our most gifted members are drawn to the world. They who are most capable to preserve our cultural heritage and to extend it, because of the enticements of the world, seek rather to replace it. That is so easy to do because for the most part they do not have that intent. They think that what they do is to improve

284

it. Unfortunately many of them will live to learn that indeed, "Many men struggle to climb to reach the top of the ladder only to find that it is leaning against the wrong wall."

There Is Yet Much to Do

I mentioned earlier that the greatest hymns and anthems have not been composed, nor have the greatest illustrations been set down, nor the poems written, nor the paintings finished. When they are produced, who will produce them? Will it be the most talented and the most highly trained among us? I rather think it will not. They will be produced by those who are the most inspired among us. Inspiration can come to those whose talents are barely adequate, and their contribution will be felt for generations; and the Church and kingdom of God will move forward just a little more easily because they have been here.

Some of our most gifted people struggle to produce a work of art, hoping that it will be described by the world as masterpiece! monumental! epic! when in truth the simple, compelling theme of "I Am a Child of God" has moved and will move more souls to salvation than would such a work were they to succeed.

Some years ago I was chairman of a committee of seminary men responsible to produce a filmstrip on Church history. One of the group, Trevor Christensen, remembered that down in Sanpete County was a large canvas roll of paintings. They had been painted by one of his progenitors, C. A. A. Christensen, who traveled through the settlements giving a lecture on Church history as each painting was unrolled and displayed by lamplight. The roll of paintings had been stored away for generations. We sent a truck for them and I shall not forget the day we unrolled them.

Brother Christensen was not masterful in his painting, but our heritage was there. Some said it was not great art, but what it lacked in technique was more than compensated in feeling. His work has been shown more widely and published more broadly and received more attention than that of a thousand and one others who missed that point.

I do not think Brother Christensen was a great painter, some would say not even a good one. I think his paintings are masterful. Why? Because the simple, reverent feeling he had for his spiritual heritage is captured in them. I do not think it strange that the world would honor a man who could not paint very well.

285

That All May Be Edified

Willingness to Sacrifice

The ideal, of course, is for one with a gift to train and develop it to the highest possibility, including a sense of spiritual propriety. No artist in the Church who desires unselfishly to extend our heritage need sacrifice his career or an avocation, nor need he neglect his gift as only a hobby. He can meet the world and "best" it, and not be the loser. In the end, what appears to be such sacrifice will have been but a test.

Abraham did not have to kill Isaac, you know. He only had to be willing to. Once that was known, that he would sacrifice his only begotten, he was known to be godlike and the blessings poured out upon him.

A few years ago Sister Packer and I were in Washington, D.C., to represent the Church at an awards banquet held in the reception hall of the Department of State. The elegant and stately surroundings, with a priceless collection of antiques and memorabilia, were impressive. Here, for instance, hangs the painting of George Washington by Gilbert Stuart and other priceless works of art. Both the occasion and the setting were ideal to make reference to the spiritual heritage of our country. And what was the program? A large brass section from one of the service bands played at great length, and with deafening volume, music from *Jesus Christ, Superstar.*

I sat next to a lovely, dignified woman, the wife of an officer of the government. When the crescendo weakened for a moment I was able to ask, by raising my voice a bit, if she was able to hear them all right. Her obvious amusement at the question soon changed to serious disappointment as she asked in return, "What would Jesus think?"

What Would Jesus Think?

That is well worth keeping in our minds if we have the talent to compose music or poetry, to illustrate or paint, or sculpt or act or sing or play or conduct.

What do I think He would think? I think He would rejoice at the playing of militant martial music as men marched to defend a righteous cause. I think that He would think there are times when illustrations should be vigorous, with bold and exciting colors. I think He would chuckle with approval when at times of recreation the music is comical or melodramatic or exciting. Or at times when a carnival air is in order that decorations be bright and flashy, even garish.

I think at times of entertainment He would think it quite in order for poetry that would make one laugh or cry—perhaps both at once. I think that He would think it would be in righteous order on many occasions to perform with great dignity symphonies and operas and ballets. I think that He would think that soloists should develop an extensive repertoire, each number to be performed at a time and in a place that is appropriate.

A Place for All Art Forms

I would think that He would think there is a place for art work of every kind—from the scribbled cartoon to the masterpiece in the hand-carved gold-leaf frame.

But I am sure He would be offended at immodesty and irreverence in music, in art, in poetry, in writing, in sculpture, in dance, or in drama. I know what He would think about music or art or literature or poetry that is purely secular being introduced into our worship services. And how do I know that? Because He has told His servants that. In what ways has He told them? He has told them by either withholding, or on occasions withdrawing His Spirit when it is done.

I have sometimes struggled without much success to teach sacred things which have been preceded by music that is secular or uninspired. Let me mention the other side of it.

I have been in places where I have felt insecure and unprepared. I have yearned inwardly in great agony for some power to pave the way or loosen my tongue, that an opportunity would not be lost because of my weakness and inadequacy. On more than a few occasions my prayers have been answered by the power of inspired music. I have been lifted above myself and beyond myself when the Spirit of the Lord has poured in upon the meeting, drawn there by beautiful, appropriate music. I stand indebted to the gifted among us who have that unusual sense of spiritual propriety.

Bless Others with Your Gift

Go to, then you who are gifted; cultivate your gift. Develop it in any of the arts and in every worthy example of them. If you have the ability and the desire, seek a career or employ your talent as an avocation or cultivate it as a hobby. But in all ways bless others with it. Set a standard of excellence. Employ it in the secular sense to every worthy advantage, but never use it profanely. Never express your gift unworthily. Increase our spiritual heritage in music, in art, in literature, in dance, in drama.

When we have done it, our activities will be a standard to the world. And our worship and devotion will remain as unique from the world as the Church is different from the world. Let the use of your gift be an expression of your devotion to Him who has given it to you. We who do not share in it will set a high standard of expectation: "For of him unto whom much is given much is required." (D&C 82:3.)

Now, in conclusion, may I remind you what I said at the beginning. My credential to speak does not come from personal mastery of the arts. I repeat my confession. I am not gifted as a musician or as a poet, nor adequate as an artist, nor accomplished in the field of dance or writing or drama. I have a calling, one which not only permits but even requires that we stay close to Him and to His Spirit.

If we know nothing of the arts, we know something of the Spirit. We know that it can be drawn upon meagerly or almost to the consuming of an individual.

Draw Near Unto Me

In 1832 the Prophet Joseph Smith received a revelation which now stands as Section 88 of the Doctrine and Covenants and was designated by the Prophet as "The Olive Leaf." I quote a few verses:

> Draw near unto me and I will draw near unto you; seek me diligently and ye shall find me; ask, and ye shall receive; knock, and it shall be opened unto you.
>
> Whatsoever ye ask the Father in my name it shall be given unto you, that is expedient for you;
>
> And if ye ask anything that is not expedient for you, it shall turn unto your condemnation.
>
> Behold, that which you hear is as the voice of one crying in the wilderness—in the wilderness, because you cannot see him—my voice, because my voice is Spirit; my Spirit is truth; truth abideth and hath no end; and if it be in you it shall abound.
>
> And if your eye be single to my glory, your whole bodies shall be filled with light, and there shall be no darkness in you; and that body which is filled with light comprehendeth all things.

288

The Arts and the Spirit of the Lord

Therefore, sanctify yourselves that your minds become single to God, and the days will come that you shall see him; for he will unveil his face unto you, and it shall be in his own time, and in his own way, and according to his own will. (D&C 88:63-68.)

The Spirit of the Lord can be present on His terms only. God grant that we may learn, each of us, particularly those who are gifted, how to extend that invitation.

He lives. Of Him I bear witness. Jesus is the Christ, the Son of God, the Only Begotten of the Father. Spencer W. Kimball is a prophet of God. We have on our shoulders in this generation the Church and kingdom of God to bear away. God grant that those among us who are the most gifted will devote themselves in order that our task may be easier, I pray in the name of Jesus Christ, amen.

29

Marriage

The prophet Jacob foretold the destruction of a people because they were blind to ordinary things, "which blindness," he said, "came by looking beyond the mark." (Jacob 4:14.)

We often seek for things we cannot seem to find when they are within easy reach—ordinary, obvious things.

I wish to talk about an ordinary word. I have tried for months—really tried—to find some way to hold this word up in such a way that you would be very impressed with what it means.

The word is *marriage*.

It Is Priceless

I have wished that I could set before you a finely carved chest, placing it where the light is just right. I would carefully unlatch it and reverently uncover the word—*marriage*.

Perhaps then you would see that it is priceless!

I cannot show it to you that way, so I will do the best I can using other ordinary words.

It is my purpose to endorse and to favor, to encourage and defend marriage.

Many regard it nowadays as being, at best, semiprecious, and by some it is thought to be worth nothing at all.

I have seen and heard, as you have seen and heard, the signals all about us, carefully orchestrated to convince us that marriage is out of date and in the way.

There is a practice, now quite prevalent, for unmarried couples to live together, a counterfeit of marriage. They suppose that they shall

Address given at general conference April 1981.

have all that marriage can offer without the obligations connected with it. They are wrong.

However much they hope to find in a relationship of that kind, they will lose more. Living together without marriage destroys something inside all who participate. Virtue, self-esteem, and refinement of character wither away.

Claiming that it will not happen does not prevent the loss; and these virtues, once lost, are not easily reclaimed.

To suppose that one day they may nonchalantly change their habits and immediately claim all that might have been theirs had they not made a mockery of marriage is to suppose something that will not be.

One day, when they come to themselves, they will reap disappointment.

One Cannot Degrade Marriage

One cannot degrade marriage without tarnishing other words as well, such words as *boy, girl, manhood, womanhood, husband, wife, father, mother, baby, children, family, home.*

Such words as *unselfishness* and *sacrifice* will then be tossed aside. Then self-respect will fade, and love itself will not want to stay.

If you have been tempted to enter such a relationship or if you now live with another without marriage, leave. Withdraw from it. Run away from it. Do not continue with it. Or, if you can, make a marriage out of it.

Even a rickety marriage will serve good purpose as long as two people struggle to keep it from falling down around them.

And now a word of warning: One who destroys a marriage takes upon himself a very great responsibility indeed. Marriage is sacred.

To willfully destroy a marriage, either your own or that of another couple, is to offend our God. Such a thing will not be lightly considered in the judgments of the Almighty and in the eternal scheme of things will not easily be forgiven.

Do not threaten nor break up a marriage. Do not translate some disenchantment with your own marriage partner or an attraction for someone else into justification for any conduct that would destroy a marriage.

This monumental transgression frequently places heavy burdens upon little children. They do not understand the selfish yearnings of unhappy adults who are willing to buy their own satisfaction at the expense of the innocent.

God Himself decreed that the physical expression of love, that union of male and female which has power to generate life, is authorized only in marriage.

Marriage Is a Shelter

Marriage is the shelter where families are created. That society which puts low value on marriage sows the wind and, in time, will reap the whirlwind—and thereafter, unless they repent, bring upon themselves a holocaust.

Some think that every marriage must expect to end in unhappiness and divorce, and with the hopes and dreams predestined to end in a broken, sad wreck of things.

Some marriages do bend, and some will break; but we must not, because of this, lose faith in marriage nor become afraid of it.

Broken marriages are not typical.

Remember that trouble attracts attention. We travel the highways with thousands of cars moving in either direction without paying much attention to any of them. But should an accident occur, we notice immediately.

If it happens again, we get the false impression that no one can go safely down the road.

One accident may make the front page, while a hundred million cars that safely pass are not regarded as worth mentioning.

Writers think that a happy, stable marriage does not have the dramatic appeal, the conflict worth featuring in a book or a play or a film. Therefore, we constantly hear about the ruined ones and we lose our perspective.

I believe in marriage. I believe it to be the ideal pattern for human living. I know it to be ordained of God. The restraints relating to it were designed to protect our happiness.

I do not know of any better time in all of the history of the world for a young couple who are of age and prepared and who are in love to think of marriage. There is no better time because it is *your* future.

I know that these are very troubled times. Troubles like we have now are very hard on marriages.

Do Not Lose Faith in Marriage

Do not lose faith in marriage. Not even if you have been through the unhappiness of a divorce and are surrounded with pieces of a marriage that has fallen apart.

If you have honored your vows and your partner did not do so, remember God is watching over us. One day, after all of the tomorrows have passed, there will be recompense. Those who have been moral and faithful to their covenants will be happy and those who have not will be otherwise.

Some marriages have broken up in spite of all that one partner could do to hold the marriage together. While there may be faults on both sides, I do not condemn the innocent one who suffers in spite of all that was desired and done to save the marriage.

And to you I say, do not lose faith in marriage itself. Do not let your disappointment leave you bitter or cynical or justify any conduct that is unworthy.

If you have had no opportunity for marriage or if you have lost your companion in death, keep your faith in marriage.

Some years ago an associate of mine lost his beloved wife. She died after a lingering illness, and he watched in helpless agony as the doctors withdrew all hope.

One day near the end she told him that when she was gone she wanted him to marry again and he was not to wait too long a time. He protested. The children were nearly grown and he would go the rest of the way alone.

She turned away and wept and said, "Have I been such a failure that after all our years together you would rather go unmarried? Have I been such a failure?"

In due time there came another, and their life together has reaffirmed his faith in marriage. And I have the feeling that his first beloved wife is deeply grateful to the second one who filled the place that she could not keep.

Marriage Is Yet Safe

Marriage is yet safe, with all its sweet fulfillment, with all its joy and love. In marriage all of the worthy yearnings of the human soul, all that is physical and emotional and spiritual, can be fulfilled.

That All May Be Edified

Marriage is not without trials of many kinds. These tests forge virtue and strength. The tempering that comes in marriage and family life produces men and women who will someday be exalted.

God has ordained that life should have its beginning within the protecting shelter of marriage, conceived in a consummate expression of love and nutured and fostered with that deeper love which is accompanied always by sacrifice.

Marriage offers fulfillment all the way through life—in youth and young love, the wedding and on the honeymoon, with the coming of little children and the nurturing of them. Then come the golden years when young ones leave the nest to build one of their own. The cycle then repeats itself, as God has decreed it should.

There is another dimension to marriage that we know of in the Church. It came by revelation. This glorious, supernal truth teaches us that marriage is meant to be eternal.

There are covenants we can make if we are willing and bounds we can seal if we are worthy that will keep marriage safe and intact beyond the veil of death.

The Lord has declared, "For behold, this is my work and my glory —to bring to pass the immortality and eternal life of man." (Moses 1:39.)

The Home and the Family

The ultimate end of all activity in the Church is that a man and his wife and their children can be happy at home and that the family continue through eternity. All Christian doctrine is formulated to protect the individual, the home, and the family.

These lines I wrote express something of the place of marriage in the eternal progress of man:

> We have within a burning flame,
> A light to kindle lights,
> The sacred fire of life itself,
> Which if misused ignites
> A smold'ring, suffocating cloud
> Of sorrow and distress.
> When used by law this power brings forth
> A life, a family, happiness.
>
> Tempters from the darkest realm
> Seek to pervert this power

Marriage

In acts of wickedness and waste
Until there comes the hour
Of judgment and of recompense,
When bitter tears are shed
O'er power once held to foster life
That now is gone and dead.

I know this power to be a key,
A very key to God's own plan
Which brings to pass eternal life
And immortality for man.
And marriage is the crucible
Where elements of life combine,
Where mortal temples are conceived
Within that plan divine.

Then spirit offspring of our God
Can come through mortal birth
To have a choice, to face the test—
The purpose of our stay on earth.
Here good and evil stand alike
Before decision's sovereign nod.
Those who elect the righteous path
Will part the veil, return to God.

A gift from God, the plan provides
That mortal beings in humble strait
Be given power, supernal power,
To share their love and help create
A living child, a living soul,
Image of man, and of Deity.
How we regard this sacred gift
Will fix our course, our destiny!

Eternal love, eternal marriage, eternal increase. This ideal, which is new to many, when thoughtfully considered, can keep a marriage strong and safe. No relationship has more potential to exalt a man and a woman than the marriage covenant. No obligation in society or in the Church supersedes it in importance.

I thank God for marriage. I thank God for temples. I thank God for the glorious sealing power, that power which transcends all that we have been given, through which our marriages may become eternal. May we be worthy of this sacred gift, I pray in the name of Jesus Christ, amen.

295

30

Someone Up There Loves You

There somehow seems to be the feeling that genealogical work is an all-or-nothing responsibility. Genealogical work is *another* responsibility for every Latter-day Saint. And we may do it successfully along with all the other callings and responsibilities that rest upon us.

The bishop can do it without neglecting his flock. A stake missionary can do it without abandoning his mission. A Sunday School teacher can accomplish it without forgetting his lesson. A Relief Society president can do it without forsaking her sisters.

You can fulfill your obligation to your kindred dead and to the Lord without forsaking your other Church callings. You can do it without abandoning your family responsibilities. You can do this work. You can do it without becoming a so-called "expert" in it.

Many members live far from a temple. Some are not able to attend ever, and others only rarely. And yet Latter-day Saints have a feeling for the word *temple* and are drawn to it. Somehow temples and temple work are such a part of us that we find very few, if any, who object to the work, who resist it, or who are against it.

It is not likely that you need to be converted to genealogical work. There are very few in the Church who need to be converted to it. Most of us really don't understand the procedures, but somehow we sense that it is an inspired, spiritual work.

An Inspired and Spiritual Work

We may never have done any and may not really know how to get started. We just don't quite know how to take hold of it, or where to begin. Those who have become experts in it sometimes are not wise in the way they introduce this work to the beginners.

Article published in the *Ensign* January 1977.

Many a beginner has gone to a class with the feeling that he wants to start in this work. There he has been confronted with a pedigree extending across the blackboard or taped to the wall, and stacks of forms with blanks and numbers and spaces, lists of procedures and regulations. He has been overwhelmed. *Surely this is too difficult for me,* he decides. *I could never be expert at that.*

Genealogical work has, I fear, sometimes been made to appear too difficult, too involved, and too time consuming to really be inviting to the average Church member. Elder John A. Widtsoe said on one occasion:

> In many a science, the beginning courses are so taught as if the whole class were intending to become candidates for the Ph.D. degree in that subject. Students fall out in despair.
>
> ...the beginning courses...are crowded with difficult, remote problems...until the freshman loses interest in the whole subject.
>
> It took some time to make them understand that a good teacher does such work as to enable his students to pass, with ordinary diligence. (John A. Widtsoe, *In a Sunlit Land,* pp. 150, 90.)

It is so very easy for one teaching a subject as involved as genealogy to assume that because he understands it, everyone else understands it. There is the tendency to want everybody to know everything all at once. But the beginner sometimes doesn't see it. As the little girl said, it becomes complicateder and complicateder.

There Is a Place to Begin

There is a way that it can be done. And there is a place to begin. You don't need to begin with the pedigree charts or the stacks of forms, or the blank spaces, or the numbers, the procedures, or the regulations. You can begin with *you,* with who you are and with what you have right now.

It is a matter of getting started. You may come to know the principle that Nephi knew when he said, "And I was led by the Spirit, not knowing beforehand the things which I should do." (1 Nephi 4:6.)

If you don't know where to start, start with *yourself.* If you don't know what records to get, and how to get them, start with what *you've* got.

If you can start with what you've got and with what you know, it's a little hard to refuse to begin genealogical work. And it may be spiritually dangerous to delay it too long.

During the first part of 1976 all of the General Authorities attending stake quarterly conferences carried with them the message that all Latter-day Saints were to prepare a life history and to make a record of events which had transpired in their lives. The responsibility to lead out in this work was placed on the high priests. They are to do it first to set an example, then see that all others are encouraged and helped with this assignment.

There are two very simple instructions. Here's what you are to do:

Get a Cardboard Box

Get a cardboard box. Any kind of a box will do. Put it some place where it is in the way, perhaps on the couch or on the counter in the kitchen—anywhere where it cannot go unnoticed. Then, over a period of a few weeks, collect and put into the box every record of your life: your birth certificate, your certificates of blessing, of baptism, of ordination, of graduation. Collect diplomas, all of your photographs, honors, or awards, a diary, if you have kept one, everything that you can find pertaining to *your* life—anything that is written or registered or recorded that testifies that you are alive and what you have done.

Don't try to do this in a day. Take your time with it. Most of us have these things scattered around here and there. Some of them are in a box in the garage under that stack of newspapers; others are stored away in drawers or in the attic or one place or another. Perhaps some have been tucked in the leaves of the Bible or elsewhere.

Gather all of these things together; put them in the box. Keep it there until you have collected everything you think you have. Then make some space on a table or even on the floor and sort out all that you have collected. Divide your life into three periods. The Church does it that way. All of our programming in the Church is divided into three general categories—children, youth, and adult.

Start with the childhood section and begin with your birth certificate. Put together every record in chronological order—the pictures, the record of your baptism, etc., up until the time you were twelve years of age.

Next assemble all that which pertains to your youth, from twelve to eighteen, or up until the time you were married. Put all of that together in chronological order. Line up the records—the certificates, the photographs—and put them in another box or envelope.

Do the same with the records on the rest of your life.

Once you have that accomplished you have what is necessary to complete your life story. Simply take out your birth certificate and begin writing: "I was born September 10, 1924, the son of Ira W. Packer and Emma Jensen Packer, at Brigham City, Utah. I was the tenth child and the fifth son in the family." Etc., etc., etc.

It really won't take you long to write, or dictate into a tape recorder, the account of your life, and it will have an accuracy because you have collected those records.

Now don't say that you can't collect them. All you are asked to do is to collect what information you have and what you know. It is your obligation.

What then? After you've made the outline of your life history up to date, what do you do with all of the materials you have collected?

Your Book of Remembrance

That, of course, brings you to your book of remembrance. Simply paste those records of lasting importance lightly on the pages so that they can be taken out, if necessary, from time to time. You then have your book of remembrance. Keep only important documents.

Once you begin this project, very interesting and inspiring things will happen. You cannot do this much without getting something of the spirit of it and without talking about it, at least in your family circle. Some very interesting things will start to happen once you show some interest in your own genealogical work. It is a very real principle. There are many, many testimonies about it. It will happen to you.

Aunt Clara will tell you that she has a picture of you with your great-grandfather. You know that cannot be so, because he died the year before you were born. But Aunt Clara produces the picture. There is your great-grandfather holding you as a tiny baby. As you check through the records, you find that he died the year *after* you were born, an important detail in your family history.

That accurate date means something. The middle name written·on the back of the picture means something too. You may not know it at the moment, but it is a key, the beginning of ordinance work in the temple for some of your ancestors.

299

Belief in the Resurrection

You believe in the Resurrection. You must know that baptism for someone who is dead is quite as essential as baptism for someone who is living. There is no difference in the importance of it. One by one it must happen. They must do it here, or it must be done *for* them here.

The whole New Testament centers on the resurrection of the Lord. The message is that *all* are resurrected. Every scripture and every motivation that applies to missionary work has its application to ordinance work for the dead.

Now you have your own family history written, you have your book of remembrance assembled. It sounds too easy—well it is, almost. But it does mean that you have to get started. Like Nephi, you will be "led by the Spirit, not knowing beforehand the things which [you] should do." (1 Nephi 4:6.)

Getting Our Records in Order

Several years ago Sister Packer and I determined that we should get our records in order. However, under the pressure of Church responsibilities with my travels about the world and the obligations with our large family and a home to keep up both indoors and outdoors, there just was not enough time. We were restless and finally determined that we would have to make more time in the day.

So during the Christmas holidays, when we had a little extra time, we started. Then as we moved back to a regular schedule after the holidays, we adopted the practice of getting up an hour or two earlier each day.

We gathered everything we had together and in the course of a few weeks we were amazed at what we were able to accomplish. The thing that was most impressive, however, was the fact that we began to have experiences that told us somehow that we were being guided, that there were those beyond the veil who were interested in what we were doing. Things began to fall into place.

As we have traveled about the Church and paid particular attention to this subject, many testimonies have come to light. Others who assemble their records together are having similar experiences. It was as though the Lord was waiting for us to begin.

We found things we had wondered about for a long time. It seemed as though they came to us almost too easily. More than this, things that we never dreamed existed began to show up. We began to learn by personal experience that this research into our families is an inspired work. We came to know that an inspiration will follow those who move into it. It is just a matter of getting started.

There is an old Chinese proverb which states, "Man who sit with legs crossed and mouth open, waiting for roast duck to fly in, have long hunger."

Doing Increases Inspiration

Once we started, we found the time. Somehow we were able to carry on all of the other responsibilities. There seemed to be an increased inspiration in our lives because of this work.

But we must decide, and the Lord will not tamper with our agency. If we want a testimony of genealogical and temple work, we must go about doing something about it.

Someone paraphrased the proverb this way, Wisdom is the principal thing; therefore get wisdom. But with all thy getting, get *going!* Here is an example of what happens when you do.

In January of this year I attended conference in the Hartford Connecticut Stake. The assignment had been made the previous September to all members of the stake presidencies who were to speak on this subject. Brother Lawrence Marostica, who had been a counselor in the stake presidency but became stake patriarch at that conference, told this interesting incident.

He had not been able to get started in genealogical work, although he was "converted" to it. He just didn't know where to start. When he received the assignment to prepare a life history from his own records, he was unable to find anything about his childhood and youth, except his birth certificate. He was one of eleven children born to Italian immigrants. He is the only member of his family in the Church.

He tried to put together everything he could find on his life, in answer to the assignment. At least he was started, but there just didn't seem to be anywhere to go. He could get his own life story put together from his own memory and from what few records he had.

Then a very interesting thing happened. His aged mother, who was in a rest home, had a great yearning to return once more to her homeland in Italy. Finally, because she was obsessed with this desire, the doctors felt nothing would be gained by denying her this request, and the family decided to grant their mother her dying wish. And for some reason they all decided that Brother Marostica (the only member of the family in the Church) should be the one to accompany his mother to Italy.

A Door Was Opened

All at once, then, he found himself returning to the ancestral home. A door was opening. While in Italy he visited the parish church where his mother was baptized, and also the parish church were his father was baptized. He met many relatives. He learned that the records in the parish go back for 500 years. He visited the town hall to look into the records and found the people very cooperative there. The town clerk told him that the previous summer a seminarian and a nun had been there together looking for records of the Marostica family, and said that they were collecting the genealogy of the family. He was given the name of the city where they lived and now can follow that lead. He learned also that there is a city of Marostica in Italy.

But this is not all. When he came to general conference in April he returned by way of Colorado, where many of his family live. There, with very little persuasion, a family organization was effected and a family reunion was planned that has now been held.

And then, as always happens, some of his relatives, his aunts and uncles, his brothers and sisters, began to provide pictures and information about *his* life that he never knew existed. And, as always happens, he learned that this is a work of inspiration.

The Lord Will Bless You

The Lord will bless you once you begin this work. This has been very evident to us. Since the time we decided that we would start where we were, with what we had, many things have opened to us.

Several months ago I took to the Genealogical Society eight large volumes, manuscript genealogical work, consisting of 6,000 family group sheets of very professional genealogical work, all on the Packer family. All of it was compiled by Warren Packer, originally from Ohio, a school teacher, a Lutheran. He has spent thirty years doing this work, not really knowing why. There are two more volumes that he has yet to finish. He senses now why he has been involved in this work over the years and very much has the spirit of the work.

We have had the opportunity too of locating and visiting the ancestral Packer home in England. Many of the large manor houses in England in recent years have been opened to the public. This one is not. It is about a fifteen-minute drive from the London Temple and is built on the site of an ancient castle with a moat around it. It stands just as it was finished in the early 1600s. The portraits of our ancestors are hanging where they were placed nearly three hundred years ago. On the estate is a little chapel. In it is a stained glass window with the Packer coat of arms put there in 1625.

Things began to emerge once we got to work. We still are not, by any means, experts in genealogical research. We are, however, dedicated to our family. And it is my testimony that if we start where we are, each of us with ourselves, with such records as we have, and begin putting those in order, things will fall into place as they should.

Get Started Now!

So, go get started now! Find a cardboard box and put it in the way and begin to put things in it, and as the things unfold you will sense something spiritual happening and not be too surprised.

There is an expression common among nonmembers of the Church when some unusual good fortune befalls a person. They respond with, "Someone up there likes me," and credit to some divine providence the good thing that has come into their lives.

You won't get very far in putting together your own records and writing your own history until you find things put in your way that could not have been put there by accident, and you are compelled to say, generally to yourself, *Someone over there wants this work done and he is helping me.*

"Brethren, shall we not go on in so great a cause? Go forward and not backward. Courage, brethren; and on, on to the victory! Let your hearts rejoice, and be exceedingly glad. Let the earth break forth into singing. Let the dead speak forth anthems of eternal praise to the King

Immanuel, who hath ordained, before the world was, that which would enable us to redeem them out of their prison; for the prisoners shall go free.

"Let the mountains shout for joy, and all ye valleys cry aloud; and all ye seas and dry lands tell the wonders of your Eternal King! And ye rivers, and brooks, and rills, flow down with gladness. Let the woods and all the trees of the field praise the Lord; and ye solid rocks weep for joy! And let the sun, moon, and the morning stars sing together, and let all the sons of God shout for joy!...

"...Let us, therefore, as a church and a people, and as Latter-day Saints, offer unto the Lord an offering in righteousness; and let us present in his holy temple...a book containing the records of our dead, which shall be worthy of all acceptation." (D&C 128:22-23, 24.)

Pure witness *becomes the steeple, the capstone, the pinnacle.*

Witness

"The gospel is true, and it is exactly and precisely like you should hope it to be. The president of the Church is a prophet. The Twelve are Apostles and they are witnesses of the Lord Jesus Christ. The Church and kingdom of God has been established, and the Lord does direct it. The kingdom will roll forth. It will fill the whole earth. The Resurrection is a reality. There is a tremendous work of responsibility upon the Church and the kingdom of God." (From an address given at the Ogden Division Midyear Convention, February 6, 1976.)

That All May Be Edified

Aprerequisite to the call of an Apostle of the Lord Jesus Christ is total commitment to Him and to His work. As members of the Church it is the responsibility of every one of us to bear bold and powerful testimony whenever or wherever it is appropriate to do so. I have come to know the power of truth, of righteousness, and of *good,* and I want to be good. I am not ashamed to say that: I want to be good! It has been critically important that an understanding of this was established between me and the Lord. It is very important that I know that He knows which way I committed my agency.

Each of us may go before Him and tell Him that we are not neutral, that He can do with us as He will. If He needs our vote, it is there. For myself, I do not care what He does with me. He does not have to take anything from me because I give it to Him—everything, all I own, all I am I will consecrate unto Him and His work.

Many Church members, not yet totally sure or not yet totally committed, hesitate to say, "I know."

To them I would say: "While a testimony may be sparked from hearing another bear witness, I am convinced that it comes more surely when the Spirit of the Lord falls upon a man or woman as he or she is personally bearing testimony. Can't you see where it is hidden? It isn't seeing is believing; it is believing is seeing. The skeptic, the sophisticate, the insincere, will never take that step; so the true witness is pefectly protected from the unworthy."

It is this "one-to-oneness," this inner "knowing" that makes the difference. Occasionally a missionary is slow to catch the vision—like the one who after two months' service, took it upon himself to leave his field of labor. As his mission president talked to him, the missionary said, "I don't like this mission."

"Does that matter?" his president asked.

"To me it does," was the answer.

The president was not through. "Once you were set apart, it wasn't your mission anymore; it was the Lord's mission. It doesn't matter whether you like it or don't, or whether it is convenient or easy or hard. It is your obligation to the Lord to fill this mission."

This line of reasoning made sense to the young man. It touched his basic, though weak, testimony. He returned to his work renewed and resolved to fill his commitment.

That All May Be Edified

When an individual comes to accept the principles of consecration and of commitment, the doors to that sanctuary as spoken of in the introduction of the book are set ajar. There comes a witness. In due time, there may come *the* witness. Then we are edified, built up, and inspired beyond all we had hoped to achieve in this life. It was to this part of our building that the talks in this section on witness were addressed.

(31) I was called as a member of the Quorum of the Twelve Apostles in the closing session of the 140th annual conference of the Church. It was a solemn assembly at which President Joseph Fielding Smith was sustained as President of the Church. I was called to fill the vacancy in the Quorum when he succeeded President David O. McKay, who had died the previous January. I had already spoken in the priesthood session of that conference on Saturday evening and therefore was not called upon to respond as a member of the Quorum of the Twelve. It was not until the following October conference that I spoke first in that capacity. During those six months I felt the burden weighing heavily on me. Occasionally some thoughtless person asking about the witness that comes to the Apostles would inquire, "Have you seen Him?" They did not realize that they touched upon the most sacred of all relationships with the Lord. Finally, I determined to answer their question to the limit I felt free to answer it in my conference address. Following the session, President Harold B. Lee, then first counselor in the First Presidency, made a comment to me that let me know he approved of what I had said. Even now, when another asks that question, I refer them to this talk with the suggestion that that is as much of an answer as I am free to give.

(32) When I began as a seminary teacher in 1949, the Book of Mormon course was not a part of the curriculum because of credit problems. The three courses were Old Testament, New Testament, and Church History. We began (and this was an innovation at the time) a course in the Book of Mormon for those still in high school who had graduated from seminary. We held it at seven in the morning before the regular classes or activities began for the day. Since there was no text beyond the scriptures, as there was for the other courses, I worked out an approach to teaching the Book of Mormon to high school

students. I determined that we would not touch upon the archaeology of the book, the military aspects, or the many other things people seem to find so interesting. Rather we would work our way through the Book of Mormon, seeking the answer to the questions: Who is speaking to us through these pages? What is it He is trying to tell us? I remember finding, particularly in Alma, the references to and sermons on the subject of mercy and justice. These two seemed to contradict one another. It was most difficult to explain to young minds or to old ones. I invented a sort of parable depicting a boy who had broken a window and how he was able to escape the full penalties. It helped, but was not fully satisfying to me. I felt there was a way to teach that great principle clearly to the young minds. Over the years I worked upon it; occasionally spoke of it. Then, when I was ready (and it took that many years) I decided to speak of it in conference. The talk "The Mediator" is the result of that long period of preparation.

(33) "Do I Have To?" adds a new dimension to this collection of talks, for it inserts the voice of my gifted and devoted wife, Donna Smith Packer, as she bears testimony. Her gratitude for and certainty of gospel truth and its way of life speak eloquently of her support, her great contribution to my sacred call. Words could never express the depth and the breadth and the power of inspiration she has brought to the work we share.

(34) The "Redemption of the Dead" indicates the almost incomprehensible task before the relative handful of Church members in filling their assignment for all the dead who ever lived upon the earth. A confident answer and witness to the challenge is: "Impossible? Perhaps. But we shall do it anyway!"

(35) When assignments were changed and I was appointed vice-chairman of the Missionary Executive Committee under the direction of President Gordon B. Hinckley, I was greatly concerned about the seminar for new mission presidents and their wives. I knew I would have a prominent place among the speakers and wondered what counsel I should give that would in a very material way benefit missionary work. I knew it would not be in the field of administration, for others were more experienced and much more competent to counsel them on that subject. Finally I determined that the thing that would help the most was that which would increase the testimony and

spirituality of the missionaries across the world. Therefore, I determined that I would not talk to the mission presidents and their wives, but I would talk through them to the missionaries. "The Candle of the Lord" is that message.

31

The Spirit Beareth Record

I t was one year ago today, in a solemn assembly, that we had the privilege of raising our hands to sustain the authorities of the Church, much as we have done this morning. It was on that April morning that I heard my name read as one presented for your sustaining vote as a member of the Quorum of the Twelve Apostles. It became my obligation to stand with those other living men who have been called as special witnesses of the Lord Jesus Christ upon the earth.

You must have wondered, as I did, why this call should come to me. It seemed accidental at times, that I was preserved in worthiness, yet there was always the constant, quiet, lingering feeling about being guided and being prepared.

A Powerful Witness

Some weeks before the meeting of last April, I left the office one Friday afternoon thinking of the weekend conference assignment. I waited for the elevator to come down from the fifth floor.

As the elevator doors quietly opened, there stood President Joseph Fielding Smith. There was a moment of surprise in seeing him, since his office is on a lower floor.

As I saw him framed in the doorway, there fell upon me a powerful witness—there stands the prophet of God. That sweet voice of Spirit that is akin to light, that has something to do with pure intelligence, affirmed to me that this was the prophet of God.

I need not try to define that experience to Latter-day Saints. That kind of witness is characteristic of this church. It is not something reserved to those in high office. It is a witness, not only available but vital, to every member.

Address given at general conference April 1971.

That All May Be Edified

As it is with the President, so it is with his counselors.

North of us in the Wasatch range stand three mountain peaks. The poet would describe them as mighty pyramids of stone. The center one, the highest of the three, the map would tell you is Willard Peak. But the pioneers called them "The Presidency." If you should go to Willard, look to the east, and up, way up, there stands "The Presidency."

Their Call Is to Please God

Thank God for the presidency! Like those peaks, they stand with nothing above them but the heavens. They need our sustaining vote. It is sometimes lonely in those lofty callings of leadership—for their calling is not to please man, but to please the Lord. God bless these three great and good men.

Occasionally during the past year I have been asked a question. Usually it comes as a curious, almost an idle question about the qualifications to stand as a witness for Christ. The question they ask is, "Have you seen Him?"

That is a question that I have never asked of another. I have not asked that question of my Brethren in the Quorum, thinking that it would be so sacred and so personal that one would have to have some special inspiration, indeed, some authorization, even to ask it.

There are some things just too sacred to discuss. We know that as it relates to the temples. In our temples sacred ordinances are performed; sacred experiences are enjoyed. And yet we do not, because of the nature of them, discuss them outside those sacred walls.

The Greater Portion of the Word

It is not that they are secret, but they are sacred; not to be discussed, but to be harbored and to be protected and regarded with the deepest of reverence.

I have come to know what the prophet Alma meant:

> It is given unto many to know the mysteries of God; nevertheless they are laid under a strict command that they shall not impart only according to the portion of his word which he doth grant unto the children of men, according to the heed and diligence which they give unto him.

312

And therefore, he that will harden his heart, the same receiveth the lesser portion of the word; and he that will not harden his heart, to him is given the greater portion of the word, until it is given unto him to know the mysteries of God until he know them in full. (Alma 12:9-10.)

There are those who hear testimonies borne in the Church by those in high station and by members in the wards and branches, all using the same words—"I know that God lives; I know that Jesus is the Christ," and come to question, "Why cannot it be said in plainer words? Why aren't they more explicit and more descriptive? Cannot the Apostles say more?"

How like the sacred experience in the temple becomes our personal testimony! It is sacred, and when we are wont to put it into words, we say it in the same way—all using the same words. The Apostles declare it in the same phrases with the little Primary or Sunday School youngster. "I know that God lives and I know that Jesus is the Christ."

We would do well not to disregard the testimonies of the prophets or of the children, for "he imparteth his words by angels unto men, yea, not only men but women also. Now this is not all; little children do have words given unto them many times, which confound the wise and the learned." (Alma 32:23.)

Some seek for a witness to be given in some new and dramatic and different way.

The Bearing of a Testimony

The bearing of a testimony is akin to a declaration of love. The romantics and poets and couples in love, from the beginning of time, have sought more impressive ways of saying it or singing it or writing it. They have used all of the adjectives, all of the superlatives, all manner of poetic expression. And when all is said and done, the declaration which is most powerful is the simple, three-word variety.

To one who is honestly seeking, the testimony borne in these simple phrases is enough, for it is the Spirit that beareth record, not the words.

There is a power of communication as real and tangible as electricity. Man has devised the means to send images and sound through the air to be caught on an antenna and reproduced and heard and seen. This other communication may be likened to that, save it be a million times more powerful, and the witness it brings is always the truth.

313

That All May Be Edified

There is a process by which pure intelligence can flow, by which we can come to know of a surety, nothing doubting.

I said there was a question that could not be taken lightly nor answered at all without the prompting of the Spirit. I have not asked that question of others, but I have heard them answer it—but not when they were asked. They have answered it under the prompting of the Spirit, on sacred occasions, when "the Spirit beareth record." (D&C 1:39.)

The Spirit Beareth Record

I have heard one of my Brethren declare: "I know from experiences, too sacred to relate, that Jesus is the Christ."

I have heard another testify: "I know that God lives; I know that the Lord lives. And more than that, I know the Lord."

It was not their words that held the meaning or the power. It was the Spirit. "For when a man speaketh by the power of the Holy Ghost the power of the Holy Ghost carrieth it unto the hearts of the children of men." (2 Nephi 33:1.)

I speak upon this subject in humility, with the constant feeling that I am the least in every way of those who are called to this holy office.

I have come to know that the witness does not come by seeking after signs. It comes through fasting and prayer, through activity and testing and obedience. It comes through sustaining the servants of the Lord and following them.

Karl G. Maeser was taking a group of missionaries across the Alps. As they reached a summit, he stopped. Gesturing back down the trail to some poles set in the snow to mark the way across the glacier, he said, "Brethren, there stands the Priesthood. They are just common sticks like the rest of us ... but the position they hold makes them what they are to us. If we step aside from the path they mark, we are lost." (Alma P. Burton, *Karl G. Maeser, Mormon Educator* [Salt Lake City: Deseret Book Co., 1953], p. 22.)

The witness depends upon sustaining his servants, as we have done here in sign and as we should do in action.

I Have That Witness

Now, I wonder with you why one such as I should be called to the holy apostleship. There are so many qualifications that I lack. There is so much in my effort to serve that is wanting. As I have pondered on it, I have come to only one single thing, one qualification in which there may be cause, and that is, I have *that* witness.

I declare to you that I know that Jesus is the Christ. I know that He lives. He was born in the meridian of time. He taught His gospel, was tried, was crucified. He rose on the third day. He was the first fruits of the Resurrection. He has a body of flesh and bone. Of this I bear testimony. Of Him I am a witness. In the name of Jesus Christ, amen.

32

The Mediator

What I shall say I could say much better if we were alone, just the two of us. It would be easier also if we had come to know one another and had that kind of trust which makes it possible to talk of serious, even sacred things.

If we were that close, because of the nature of what I shall say, I would study you carefully as I spoke. If there should be the slightest disinterest or distraction, the subject would quickly be changed to more ordinary things.

I have not, to my knowledge, in my ministry said anything more important. I intend to talk about the Lord Jesus Christ, about what He really did—and why it matters now.

One may ask, "Aside from the influence He has had on society, what effect can He have on me individually?"

To answer that question I ask, "Have you ever been hard-pressed financially? Have you ever been confronted with an unexpected expense, a mortgage coming due, with really no idea how to pay it?"

Such an experience, however unpleasant, can be, in the eternal scheme of things, very, very useful. If you miss that lesson you may have to make it up before you are spiritually mature, like a course that was missed or a test that was failed.

That may be what the Lord had in mind when He said, "It is easier for a camel to go through the eye of a needle, than for a rich man to enter into the kingdom of God." (Matthew 19:24.)

Those who have faced a foreclosure know that one looks helplessly around, hoping for someone, anyone to come to the rescue.

There Is a Spiritual Account

This lesson is so valuable because there is a spiritual account, with a balance kept and a statement due, that no one of us will escape.

Address given at general conference April 1977.

To understand this spiritual debt, we must speak of such intangibles as love, faith, mercy, justice.

Although these virtues are both silent and invisible, surely I do not need to persuade you that they are real. We learn of them by processes that are often silent and invisible as well.

We become so accustomed to learning through our physical senses —by sight and sound and smell, by taste and touch—that some of us seem to learn in no other way.

But there are spiritual things that are not registered that way at all. Some things we simply feel, not as we feel something we touch, but as we feel something we *feel.*

There are things, spiritual things, that are registered in our minds and recorded in our memories as pure knowledge. A knowledge of "things which have been, things which are, things which must shortly come to pass." (D&C 88:79; see also D&C 93:24 and Jacob 4:13.)

As surely as we know about material things, we can come to know of spiritual things.

Each of us, without exception, one day will settle that spiritual account. We will, that day, face a judgment for our doings in mortal life and face a foreclosure of sorts.

One thing I know: We will be justly dealt with. Justice, the eternal law of justice, will be the measure against which we settle this account.

Justice is usually pictured holding a set of scales and blindfolded against the possibility that she may be partial or become sympathetic. There is no sympathy in justice alone—only justice. Our lives will be weighed on the scales of justice.

The Prophet Alma declared: "Justice claimeth the creature and executeth the law, and the law inflicteth the punishment; if not so, the works of justice would be destroyed, and God would cease to be God." (Alma 42:22.)

I commend to you the reading of the forty-second chapter of Alma. It reveals the place of justice and should confirm that the poet spoke the truth when he said, "In the course of justice [only], none of us should see salvation." (Shakespeare, *The Merchant of Venice,* IV. i. 199-200.)

Justice and Mercy—A Parable

Let me tell you a story—a parable.

317

That All May Be Edified

There once was a man who wanted something very much. It seemed more important than anything else in his life. In order for him to have his desire, he incurred a great debt.

He had been warned about going into that much debt, and particularly about his creditor. But it seemed so important for him to do what he wanted to do and to have what he wanted right now. He was sure he could pay for it later.

So he signed a contract. He would pay it off sometime along the way. He didn't worry too much about it, for the due date seemed such a long time away. He had what he wanted now, and that was what seemed important.

The creditor was always somewhere in the back of his mind, and he made token payments now and again, thinking somehow that the day of reckoning really would never come.

But as it always does, the day came, and the contract fell due. The debt had not been fully paid. His creditor appeared and demanded payment in full.

Only then did he realize that his creditor not only had the power to repossess all that he owned, but the power to cast him into prison as well.

"I cannot pay you, for I have not the power to do so," he confessed.

"Then," said the creditor, "we will exercise the contract, take your possessions, and you shall go to prison. You agreed to that. It was your choice. You signed the contract, and now it must be enforced."

"Can you not extend the time or forgive the debt?" the debtor begged. "Arrange some way for me to keep what I have and not go to prison. Surely you believe in mercy? Will you not show mercy?"

The creditor replied, "Mercy is always so one sided. It would serve only you. If I show mercy to you, it will leave me unpaid. It is justice I demand. Do you believe in justice?"

"I believed in justice when I signed the contract," the debtor said. "It was on my side then, for I thought it would protect me. I did not need mercy then, nor think I should need it ever. Justice, I thought, would serve both of us equally as well."

"It is justice that demands that you pay the contract or suffer the penalty," the creditor replied. "That is the law. You have agreed to it and that is the way it must be. Mercy cannot rob justice."

There they were: One meting out justice, the other pleading for mercy. Neither could prevail except at the expense of the other.

"If you do not forgive the debt there will be no mercy," the debtor pleaded.

"If I do, there will be no justice," was the reply.

Both laws, it seemed, could not be served. They are two eternal ideals that appear to contradict one another. Is there no way for justice to be fully served, and mercy also?

There is a way! The law of justice *can* be fully satisfied and mercy *can* be fully extended—but it takes someone else. And so it happened this time.

The debtor had a friend. He came to help. He knew the debtor well. He knew him to be shortsighted. He thought him foolish to have gotten himself into such a predicament. Nevertheless, he wanted to help because he loved him. He stepped between them, faced the creditor, and made this offer.

"I will pay the debt if you will free the debtor from his contract so that he may keep his possessions and not go to prison."

As the creditor was pondering the offer, the mediator added, "You demanded justice. Though he cannot pay you, I will do so. You will have been justly dealt with and can ask no more. It would not be just."

And so the creditor agreed.

The mediator turned then to the debtor. "If I pay your debt, will you accept me as your creditor?"

"Oh yes, yes," cried the debtor. "You save me from prison and show mercy to me."

"Then," said the benefactor, "you will pay the debt to me and I will set the terms. It will not be easy, but it will be possible. I will provide a way. You need not go to prison."

And so it was that the creditor was paid in full. He had been justly dealt with. No contract had been broken.

The debtor, in turn, had been extended mercy. Both laws stood fulfilled. Because there was a mediator, justice had claimed its full share, and mercy was fully satisfied.

Each Lives on Spiritual Credit

Each of us lives on a kind of spiritual credit. One day the account will be closed, a settlement demanded. However casually we may view it now, when that day comes and the foreclosure is imminent, we will look around in restless agony for someone, anyone, to help us.

And, by eternal law, mercy cannot be extended save there be one who is both willing and able to assume our debt and pay the price and arrange the terms for our redemption.

Unless there is a mediator, unless we have a friend, the full weight of justice untempered, unsympathetic, must, positively must, fall on us. The full recompense for every transgression, however minor or however deep, will be exacted from us to the uttermost farthing.

But know this: Truth, glorious truth, proclaims there is such a mediator.

"For there is one God, and one mediator between God and men, the man Christ Jesus." (1 Timothy 2:5.)

Through Him mercy can be fully extended to each of us without offending the eternal law of justice.

This truth is the very root of Christian doctrine. You may know much about the gospel as it branches out from there, but if you only know the branches and those branches do not touch that root, if they have been cut free from that truth, there will be no life nor substance nor redemption in them.

Mercy Is Not Automatic

The extension of mercy will not be automatic. It will be through covenants with Him. It will be on His terms, His generous terms, which include, as an absolute essential, baptism by immersion for the remission of sins.

All mankind can be protected by the law of justice, and at once each of us individually may be extended the redeeming and healing blessing of mercy.

A knowledge of what I am talking about is of a very practical value. It is very useful and very helpful personally; it opens the way for each of us to keep his spiritual accounts paid up.

You, perhaps, are among those troubled people. When you come face to face with yourself in those moments of quiet contemplation— that many of us try to avoid—are there some unsettled things that bother you?

320

Do you have something on your conscience? Are you still, to one degree or another, guilty of anything small or large?

We often try to solve guilt problems by telling one another that they don't matter. But somehow, deep inside, we don't believe one another. Nor do we believe ourselves if we say it. We know better. They do matter!

Our transgressions are all added to our account, and one day if it is not properly settled, each of us, like Belshazzar of Babylon, will be weighed in the balance and found wanting.

There Is a Redeemer

There is a Redeemer, a Mediator, who stands both willing and able to appease the demands of justice and extend mercy to those who are penitent, for "He offereth himself a sacrifice for sin, to answer the ends of the law, unto all those who have a broken heart and a contrite spirit; and unto none else can the ends of the law be answered." (2 Nephi 2:7.)

Already He has accomplished the redemption of all mankind from mortal death; resurrection is extended to all without condition.

He also makes possible redemption from the second death, which is the spiritual death, which is separation from the presence of our Heavenly Father. This redemption can come only to those who are clean, for no unclean thing can dwell in the presence of God.

If justice decrees that we are not eligible because of our transgression, mercy provides a probation, a penitence, a preparation to enter in.

I have carried with me a great desire to bear testimony of the Lord Jesus Christ. I have yearned to tell you in as simple terms as I can, what He did, and who He is.

Although I know how poor mere words can be, I know also that such feelings are often carried by the Spirit, even without words.

I Know That He Lives

At times I struggle under the burden of imperfections. Nevertheless, because I know that He lives, there is a supreme recurring happiness and joy.

There is one place where I am particularly vulnerable—when I know that I have abused someone, or caused them hurt, or offended them. It is then I know what agony is.

How sweet it is, on those occasions, to be reassured that He lives and to have my witness reaffirmed! I want, with fervent desire, to show you how our burdens of disappointment, sin, and guilt can be laid before Him, and on His generous terms have each item on the account marked: "Paid in full."

I claim with my Brethren of the Twelve to be a special witness of Him. My witness and theirs are true. I love the Lord, and I love the Father who sent Him.

Eliza R. Snow, with deep spiritual inspiration, wrote these words, with which I close.

> How great the wisdom and the love
> That filled the courts on high
> And sent the Savior from above
> To suffer, bleed, and die!
>
> His precious blood he freely spilt;
> His life he freely gave,
> A sinless sacrifice for guilt,
> A dying world to save.
>
> How great, how glorious, how complete,
> Redemption's grand design,
> Where justice, love, and mercy meet
> In harmony divine!
> ("How Great the Wisdom and the Love," *Hymns,* no. 68.)

In the name of Jesus Christ, amen.

33

Do I Have To?

Do I *have* to?" pleaded two Guide Patrol boys at the church door yesterday afternoon. They had a ball in their hands, and for our winter pre-Primary program we had given them the privilege of playing in the cultural hall. But yesterday was a beautiful spring day and we were initiating our new spring pre-Primary. They looked at their Primary president and pled again, "Do we *have* to?" I smiled and said, "You don't *have* to—you *get* to!"

Every once in a while I hear that same type of pleading. Sometimes a seven-year-old will say, "Do I *have* to go to sacrament meeting? It's *so* long!" Sometimes a priesthood boy who is thirteen makes the comment, "It's stake priesthood meeting tonight, do I *have* to go?"

An Opportunity

Maybe it's an opportunity to give a two-and-a-half-minute talk, or to participate in a family home evening. "Do I *have* to?" And always the answer is just the same: "You don't *have* to—you *get* to." You get to because our Heavenly Father loves us and He has given us the opportunity to choose. We have our free agency. You Guide Patrol boys, you don't *have* to do what Sister Packer says: you *get* to. You *get* to be obedient to authority.

If I could choose, and I did get the opportunity to choose, I would come to earth. And if I could choose, I'd want to be a girl spirit. Coming into that same special home of goodly parents. In my childhood home there radiated a special spirit. A spirit of calmness, of sympathy, of sweetness, of hope, a spirit of loyalty, of sharing, of happiness. Yes, I would choose to go to that very same home.

Address given by Donna Packer in the Tabernacle to the Latter-day Saint Student Association of the University of Utah March 4, 1970.

That All May Be Edified

I Would Choose to Be a Woman

I would choose to be a woman. A woman to stand as a helpmate to a noble son of our Heavenly Father. I would know that I share in the blessings of the priesthood. And I know that if we would work together, pull together, then we would have eternal life together.

Yes, I would choose to be a mother, a mother of spirit children of our Father in Heaven. I would fill my days with useful activities that would give life, spirit, and beauty to our home, realizing that my family's salvation depends to a great degree on my skills as a wife and a homemaker. I would labor diligently that the Spirit of the Lord could always walk with me.

The priesthood is in my home, and I would lean heavily on it for guidance and direction.

Yes, I would choose to be right here, right now. To be here in your presence, to feel your power—your power because of righteous living. I would choose to be in the presence of the priesthood. I know that Elder Brown, Elder Packer, and the other Brethren hold the priesthood of God. That the gospel of Jesus Christ has been restored to the earth. I know that the messages that Elder Brown and Elder Packer will give to you tonight shall be the truth. They will lift your soul, and if you live the things they share with you tonight, you shall have happiness and true joy.

I Bear You My Witness

If I could choose, I would choose to bear you my witness that Jesus is the Christ. That there is a God in the heavens who is mindful and concerned with each one of you.

I know that we do not find happiness. We choose happiness by making righteous decisions. We don't *have* to be happy. We *get* to be happy. We have our free agency, and we get to choose.

The gospel of Jesus Christ is true. Jesus is the Christ, the Savior of mankind. Joseph Smith is a prophet of God. Joseph Fielding Smith, recently sustained, is a prophet. I'm grateful to be a member of The Church of Jesus Christ of Latter-day Saints. To be a part of our Heavenly Father's family and have the right to choose happiness.

In the name of Jesus Christ, amen.

34

The Redemption of the Dead

W hen the Lord was upon the earth He made it very clear that there was one way, and one way only, by which man may be saved. "I am the way, the truth, and the life: no man cometh unto the Father, but by me." (John 14:6.) To proceed on that way, these two things emerge as being very fixed. First, in His name rests the authority to secure the salvation of mankind. "For there is none other name under heaven given . . . whereby we must be saved." (Acts 4:12.) And next, there is an essential ordinance—baptism—standing as a gate through which every soul must pass to obtain eternal life.

The Lord was neither hesitant nor was He apologetic in proclaiming exclusive authority over those processes, all of them in total, by which we may return to the presence of our Heavenly Father. This ideal was clear in the minds of His Apostles also, and their preaching provided for one way, and one way only, for men to save themselves.

Over the centuries men saw that many, indeed most, never found that way. This became very hard to explain. Perhaps they thought it to be generous to admit that there are other ways. So they tempered or tampered with the doctrine.

One Lord, One Baptism

This rigid emphasis on "one Lord and one baptism" was thought to be too restrictive, and too exclusive, even though the Lord Himself had described it as being narrow, for, "Strait is the gate, and narrow is the way, which leadeth unto life." (Matthew 7:14.)

Since baptism is essential, there must be an urgent concern to carry the message of the gospel of Jesus Christ to every nation, kindred, tongue, and people. That came as a commandment from Him.

Address given at general conference October 1975.

His true servants will be out to convert all who will adhere to the principles of the gospel and they will offer them that one baptism which He proclaimed as essential. The preaching of the gospel is evident to one degree or another in most Christian churches. Most, however, are content to enjoy whatever they can gain from membership in their church without any real effort to see that others hear about it.

The Missionary Spirit

The powerful missionary spirit and the vigorous missionary activity in The Church of Jesus Christ of Latter-day Saints become a very significant witness that the true gospel and that the authority are possessed here in the Church. We accept the responsibility to preach the gospel to every person on earth. And if the question is asked, "You mean you are out to convert the entire world?" the answer is, "Yes. We will try to reach every living soul."

Some who measure that challenge quickly say, "Why, that's impossible! It cannot be done!"

To that we simply say, "Perhaps, but we shall do it anyway."

Against the insinuation that it cannot be done, we are willing to commit every resource that can be righteously accumulated to this work. Now, while our effort may seem modest when measured against the challenge, it is hard to ignore when measured against what is being accomplished or even what is being attempted elsewhere.

Presently we have over twenty-one thousand missionaries serving in the field—and paying for the privilege. And that's only part of the effort. Now, I do not suggest that the number should be impressive, for we do not feel we are doing nearly as well as we should be. And more important than that, any one of them would be evidence enough if we knew the source of the individual conviction that each carries.

We ask no relief of the assignment to seek out every living soul, teach them the gospel, and offer them baptism. And we're not discouraged, for there is a great power in this work and that can be verified by anyone who is sincerely inquiring.

Baptism for the Dead

There is another characteristic that identifies His Church and also has to do with baptism. There is a very provoking and a very disturbing question about those who died without baptism. What about them? If there is none other name given under heaven whereby man must be saved (and that is true), and they have lived and died without even hearing that name, and if baptism is essential (and it is), and they died without even the invitation to accept it, where are they now?

That is hard to explain. It describes most of the human family.

There are several religions larger than most Christian denominations, and together they are larger than all of them combined. Their adherents for centuries have lived and died and never heard the word baptism. What is the answer for them?

That is a most disturbing question. What power would establish one Lord and one baptism, and then allow it to be that most of the human family never comes within its influence? With that question unanswered, the vast majority of the human family must be admitted to be lost, and against any reasonable application of the law of justice or of mercy, either. How could Christianity itself be sustained?

When you find the true church you will find the answer to that disturbing question.

If a church has no answer for that, how can it lay claim to be His church? He is not willing to write off the majority of the human family who were never baptized.

Those who admit in puzzled frustration that they have no answer to this cannot lay claim to authority to administer to the affairs of the Lord on the earth, or to oversee the work by which all mankind must be saved.

Since they had no answer concerning the fate of those who had not been baptized, Christians came to believe that baptism itself was not critical in importance, and that the name of Christ may not be all that essential. There must, they supposed, be other names whereby man could be saved.

Revelation Characteristic of His Church

The answer to that puzzling challenge could not be invented by men, but was *revealed.* I emphasize the word *revealed.* Revelation too is an essential characteristic of His church. Communication with Him through revelation was established when the Church was established. It has not ceased and it is constant in the Church today.

As I address myself to the question of those who died without baptism, I do so with the deepest reverence, for it touches on a sacred work. Little known to the world, we move obediently forward in a work that is so marvelous in its prospects, transcendent above what man might have dreamed of, supernal, inspired, and true. In it lies the answer.

In the earliest days of the Church, the Prophet was given direction through revelation that work should commence on the building of a temple, akin to the temples that had been constructed anciently. There was revealed ordinance work to be performed there for the salvation of mankind.

Then another ancient scripture, ignored or overlooked by the Christian world in general, was understood and moved into significant prominence: "Else what shall they do which are baptized for the dead, if the dead rise not at all? why are they then baptized for the dead?" (1 Corinthians 15:29.)

With Proper Authority

Here then, was the answer. With proper authority an individual could be baptized for and in behalf of someone who had never had the opportunity. That individual would then accept or reject the baptism according to his own desire.

This work came as a great reaffirmation of something very basic that the Christian world now only partly believes: and that is that there is life after death. Mortal death is no more an ending than birth was a beginning. The great work of redemption goes on beyond the veil as well as here in mortality.

The Lord said, "Verily, verily, I say unto you, The hour is coming, and now is, when the dead shall hear the voice of the Son of God: and they that hear shall live." (John 5:25.)

On October 3, 1918, President Joseph F. Smith was pondering on the scriptures, including this one from Peter: "For for this cause was the gospel preached also to them that are dead, that they might be judged according to men in the flesh, but live according to God in the spirit." (1 Peter 4:6.)

A Marvelous Vision

There was opened to him a marvelous vision. In it he saw the concourses of the righteous. And he saw Christ ministering among them. Then he saw those who had not had the opportunity and those who had not been valiant. And he saw the work for their redemption. And I quote his record of this vision:

> I perceived that the Lord went not in person among the wicked and the disobedient who had rejected the truth, to teach them.
> But behold, from among the righteous he organized his forces and appointed messengers, clothed with power and authority, and commissioned them to go forth and carry the light of the gospel to them that were in darkness, even to all the spirits of men; And thus was the gospel preached to the dead. (D&C 138:29-30.)

We have been authorized to perform baptisms vicariously so that when they hear the gospel preached and desire to accept it, that essential ordinance will have been performed. They need not ask for any exemption from that essential ordinance. Indeed, the Lord Himself was not exempted from it.

Here and now then, we move to accomplish the work to which we are assigned. We are busily engaged in that kind of baptism. We gather the records of our kindred dead, indeed, the records of the entire human family; and in sacred temples in baptismal fonts designed as those were anciently, we perform these sacred ordinances.

"Strange," one may say. It *is* passing strange. It is transcendent and supernal. The very nature of the work testifies that He is our Lord, that baptism is essential, that He taught the truth.

We Have Been Commanded

And so the question may be asked, "You mean you are out to provide baptism for all who have ever lived?"

And the answer is simply, yes. For we have been commanded to do so.

"You mean for the entire human family? Why, that is impossible. If the preaching of the gospel to all who are living is a formidable

329

challenge, then the vicarious work for all who have ever lived is impossible indeed."

To that we say, "Perhaps, but we shall do it anyway."

And once again we certify that we are not discouraged. We ask no relief of the assignment, no excuse from fulfilling it. Our effort today is modest indeed when viewed against the challenge. But since nothing is being done for them elsewhere, our accomplishments, we have come to know, have been pleasing to the Lord.

Already we have collected hundreds of millions of names, and the work goes forward in the temples and will go on in other temples that will be built. The size of the effort we do not suggest should be impressive, for we are not doing nearly as well as we should be.

Those who thoughtfully consider the work inquire about those names that cannot be collected. "What about those for whom no record was ever kept? Surely you will fail there. There is no way you can search out those names."

There Is a Way

To this I simply observe, "You have forgotten revelation." Already we have been directed to many records through that process. Revelation comes to individual members as they are led to discover their family records in ways that are miraculous indeed. And there is a feeling of inspiration attending this work that can be found in no other. When we have done all that we can do, we shall be given the rest. The way will be opened up.

Every Latter-day Saint is responsible for this work. Without this work, the saving ordinances of the gospel would apply to so few who have ever lived that it could not be claimed to be true.

There is another benefit from this work that relates to the living. It has to do with family life and the eternal preservation of it. It has to do with that which we hold most sacred and dear—the association with our loved ones in our own family circle.

Something of the spirit of this can be sensed as I quote from a letter dated January the 17th, 1889, Safford, Graham County, Arizona, from my own family records. It concerns my great-grandfather, who was the first of our line in the Church, and who died a few days later, Jonathan Taylor Packer. This letter was written by a daughter-in-law to the family.

After describing the distress and difficulty he had suffered for several weeks, she wrote:

> But I will do all I can for him, for I consider it my duty. I will do for him as I would like someone to do for my dear mother, for I am afraid I shall never see her again in this world.
>
> Your father says for you all to be faithful to the principles of the gospel and asks the blessings of Abraham, Isaac, and Jacob upon you all, and bids you all good-bye until he meets you in the morning of the resurrection.
>
> Well, Martha, I can't hardly see the lines for tears, so I will stop writing. From your loving sister, Mary Ann Packer.

I Shall See Them

I know that I shall see this great-grandfather beyond the veil, and also my grandfather and my father. And I know that I shall there also meet those of my ancestors who lived when the fulness of the gospel was not upon the earth; those who lived and died without ever hearing His name, nor having the invitation to be baptized.

I say that no point of doctrine sets this Church apart from the other claimants as this one does. Save for it, we would, with all of the others, have to accept the clarity with which the New Testament declares baptism to be essential and then admit that most of the human family could never have it.

But we have the revelations. We have those sacred ordinances. The revelation that places upon us the obligation for this baptism for the dead is section 128 of the Doctrine and Covenants. And I should like to read two or three of the closing verses of that section.

> Brethren, shall we not go on in so great a cause? Go forward and not backward. Courage, brethren; and on, on to the victory! Let your hearts rejoice, and be exceedingly glad. Let the earth break forth into singing. Let the dead speak forth anthems of eternal praise to the King Immanuel, who hath ordained, before the world was, that which would enable us to redeem them out of their prison.
>
> Let the mountains shout for joy, and all ye valleys cry aloud; and all ye seas and dry lands tell the wonders of your Eternal King! And ye rivers, and brooks, and rills, flow down with gladness. Let the woods and all the trees of the field praise the Lord; and ye solid rocks weep for joy!
>
> ...Let us, therefore, as a church and a people, and as Latter-day Saints, offer unto the Lord an offering in righteousness; and let us present in his holy temple...a book containing the records of our dead, which shall be worthy of all acceptation. (D&C 128:22-24.)

331

That All May Be Edified

I bear witness that this work is true, that God lives, that Jesus is the Christ, that there is on this earth today a prophet of God to lead modern Israel in this great obligation. I know that the Lord lives and that He broods anxiously over the work for the redemption of the dead, in the name of Jesus Christ, amen.

35

The Candle of the Lord

We do not learn spiritual things in exactly the same way we learn other things that we know, even though such things as reading, listening, and pondering may be used.

I have learned that it requires a special attitude both to teach and to learn spiritual things. There are some things you know, or may come to know, that you will find quite difficult to explain to others. I am very certain that it was meant to be that way.

I Know There Is a God

I will tell you of an experience I had (before I was a General Authority) which affected me profoundly. I sat on a plane next to a professed atheist who pressed his disbelief in God so urgently that I bore my testimony to him. "You are wrong," I said, "there is a God. I *know* He lives!"

He protested, "You don't *know*. Nobody *knows* that. You can't *know* it." When I would not yield, the atheist, who was an attorney, asked perhaps the ultimate question on the subject of testimony. "All right," he said in a sneering, condescending way, "you say you know." Then (inferring, if you're so smart), "Tell me *how* you know."

When I attempted to answer, even though I held advanced academic degrees, I was helpless to communicate.

Sometimes our youth, you young missionaries, are embarrassed when the cynic, the skeptic, treat you with contempt because you do not have ready answers for everything. Before such ridicule some turn away in shame. (Remember the iron rod, the spacious building, and the mocking; see 1 Nephi 8:28.)

Address given at a seminar for new mission presidents June 25, 1982.

<hr>

That All May Be Edified

When I used the words *spirit* and *witness* the atheist responded, "I don't know what you are talking about." The words *prayer, discernment,* and *faith* were meaningless to him also.

"You see," he said, "you don't really know. If you did, you would be able to tell me *how you know.*"

I felt, perhaps, that I had borne my testimony to him unwisely and was at a loss as to what to do. Then came the experience. Something came into my mind. And, I mention here a statement of the Prophet Joseph Smith.

> A person may profit by noticing the first intimation of the spirit of revelation; for instance, when you feel pure intelligence flowing into you, it may give you sudden strokes of ideas. . . . And thus by learning the Spirit of God and understanding it, you may grow into the principle of revelation, until you become perfect in Christ Jesus. (*Teachings of the Prophet Joseph Smith,* pp. 151.)

The Taste of Salt

Such an idea came into my mind, and I said to the atheist, "Let me ask if you know what salt tastes like?"

"Of course I do," was his reply.

"When did you taste salt last?"

"I just had dinner on the plane."

"You just think you know what salt tastes like," I said.

He insisted, "I know what salt tastes like as well as I know anything."

"If I gave you a cup of salt and a cup of sugar and let you taste them both, could you tell the salt from the sugar?"

"Now you are getting juvenile," was his reply. "Of course I could tell the difference. I know what salt tastes like. It is an everyday experience. I know it as well as I know anything."

"Then," I said, "assuming that I have never tasted salt, explain to me just what it tastes like."

After some thought, he ventured, "Well—I—uh, it is not sweet, and it is not sour."

"You've told me what it isn't, not what it is."

After several attempts, of course, he could not do it. He could not convey, in words alone, so ordinary an experience as tasting salt. I bore testimony to him once again and said, "I know there is a God. You ridiculed that testimony and said that if I *did* know, I would be able to tell you exactly *how* I know. My friend, spiritually speaking, I have tasted salt. I am no more able to convey to you in words how this knowledge has come than you are to tell me what salt tastes like. But I say to you again, there is a God! He does live! And just because you don't know, don't try to tell me that I don't know, for I do!"

As we parted, I heard him mutter, "I don't need your religion for a crutch. I don't need it."

From that experience forward, I have never been embarrassed or ashamed that I could not explain in words alone everything I know spiritually, or tell how I received it.

The Apostle Paul said it this way:

> We speak, not in the words which man's wisdom teacheth, but which the Holy Ghost teacheth; comparing spiritual things with spiritual.
>
> But the natural man receiveth not the things of the Spirit of God: for they are foolishness unto him: neither can he know them, because they are spiritually discerned. (1 Corinthians 2:13-14.)

How to Prepare

We cannot express spiritual knowledge in words alone. We can, however, with words, show another how to prepare for the reception of the Spirit.

The Spirit of itself will help. "For when a man speaketh by the power of the Holy Ghost the power of the Holy Ghost carrieth it unto the hearts of the children of men." (2 Nephi 3:1.)

Then when they have a spiritual communication, they say within themselves, *This is it. This is what is meant by those words in the revelation.* Thereafter, if they are carefully chosen, words are adequate for teaching about spiritual things.

We do not have the words (even the scriptures do not have words) which perfectly describe the Spirit. The scriptures generally use the word voice, which does not exactly fit.

The Voice One Can Feel

These delicate, refined spiritual communications are not seen with our eyes nor heard with our ears. And even though it is described as a voice, it is a voice that one feels more than one hears.

335

Once I came to understand this, one verse in the Book of Mormon took on a profound meaning and my testimony of the book increased immeasurably. It had to do with Laman and Lemuel, who rebelled against Nephi. Nephi rebuked them and said, "Ye have seen an angel, and he spake unto you; yea, ye have heard his voice from time to time; and he hath spoken unto you in a still small voice, but ye were past *feeling,* that ye could not *feel* his words." (1 Nephi 17:45; italics added.)

Nephi, in a great, profound sermon of instruction, explained that "angels speak by the power of the Holy Ghost; wherefore, they speak the words of Christ. Wherefore, I said unto you, feast upon the words of Christ; for behold, the words of Christ will tell you all things what ye should do." (2 Nephi 32:3.)

Should an angel appear and converse with you, neither you, nor he would be confined to corporeal sight or sound in order to communicate. For there *is* that spiritual process, described by the Prophet Joseph Smith, by which pure intelligence *can* flow into our minds and we can know what we need to know without either the drudgery of study or the passage of time, for it is revelation.

And the Prophet said further:

> All things whatsoever God in his infinite wisdom has seen fit and proper to reveal to us, while we are dwelling in mortality, in regard to our mortal bodies, are revealed to us in the abstract...revealed to our spirits precisely as though we had no mortal bodies at all; and those revelations which will save our spirits will save our bodies. (*Teachings of the Prophet Joseph Smith,* p. 355.)

The Still Small Voice

The voice of the Spirit is described in the scripture as being neither loud, nor harsh. (See 3 Nephi 11:3.) "Not a voice of thunder, neither...a voice of a great tumultuous noise." But rather, still and small, "of perfect mildness, as if it had been a whisper," and it can "pierce even to the very soul" (Helaman 5:30) and cause the heart to burn. (See 3 Nephi 11:3; D&C 85:6-7.) Remember Elijah found the voice of the Lord was not in the wind, nor the earthquake, nor the fire, but was a "still small voice." (1 Kings 19:12.)

The Spirit does not get our attention by shouting or shaking us with a heavy hand. Rather it whispers. It caresses so gently that if we are preoccupied we may not feel it at all.

(No wonder that the Word of Wisdom was revealed to us, for how could the drunkard or the addict feel such a voice?)

Occasionally it will press just firmly enough for us to pay heed. But most of the time, if we do not heed the gentle feeling, the Spirit will withdraw and wait until we come seeking and listening and say in our manner and expression, like Samuel of ancient times, "Speak, for thy servant heareth." (1 Samuel 3:10.)

I have learned that strong, impressive spiritual experiences do not come to us very frequently. And when they do, they are generally for our own edification, instruction, or correction. Unless we are called by proper authority to do so, they do not position us to counsel or to correct others.

Spiritual Things Must be Guarded

I have come to believe also that it is not wise to continually talk of unusual spiritual experiences. They are to be guarded with care and shared only when the Spirit itself prompts us to use them to the blessing of others.

I am ever mindful of Alma's words:

> It is given unto many to know the mysteries of God; nevertheless they are laid under a strict command that they shall not impart only according to the portion of his word which he doth grant unto the children of men, according to the heed and diligence which they give unto him. (Alma 12:9.)

I heard President Romney once counsel mission presidents and their wives in Geneva. "I do not tell all I know. I have never told my wife all I know, for I found out that if I talked too lightly of sacred things, thereafter the Lord would not trust me."

We are, I believe, to keep these things and ponder them in our hearts, as Luke said Mary did of the supernal events that surrounded the birth of Jesus. (See Luke 2:19.)

There is something else to learn. A testimony is not thrust upon you; a testimony grows. We become taller in testimony like we grow taller in physical stature, and hardly know it happens because it comes by growth.

It is not wise to wrestle with the revelations with such insistence as to demand immediate answers or blessings to your liking.

337

That All May Be Edified

You Cannot Force Spiritual Things

You cannot force spiritual things. Such words as *compel, coerce, constrain, pressure, demand* do not describe our privileges with the Spirit.

You can no more force the Spirit to respond than you can force a bean to sprout, or an egg to hatch before its time. You can create a climate to foster growth; you can nourish, and protect; but you cannot force or compel: You must await the growth.

Do not be impatient to gain great spiritual knowledge. Let it grow, help it grow; but do not force it, or you will open the way to be misled.

We are expected to use the light and knowledge we already possess to work out our lives. We should not need a revelation to instruct us to be up and about our duty, for we have been told that already in the scriptures; we should not expect revelation to replace the spiritual or temporal intelligence which we have already received—only to extend it. We must go about our life in an ordinary workaday way, following the routines and rules and regulations that govern life.

Rules and regulations and commandments are valuable protection. Should we stand in need of revealed instruction to alter our course, it will be waiting along the way as we arrive at the point of need. The counsel to be busily engaged is wise counsel indeed.

Philip and Nathanael

There is a wide difference in the spirituality of individuals. When Philip told Nathanael that he had found "him of whom Moses...and the prophets did write, Jesus of Nazareth, the son of Joseph," Nathanael's response was, "Can...any good thing come out of Nazareth?"

Philip said, "Come and see." Come he did, and he did see. What Nathanael must have felt! For with no further convincing, he exclaimed "Rabbi, thou art the Son of God!"

The Lord blessed him for his belief and said, "Verily, verily, I say unto you, Hereafter ye shall see heaven open, and the angels of God ascending and descending upon the Son of man." (John 1:45-51.)

Thomas is another story; the combined testimony of ten of the Apostles could not convince him that the Lord had risen. He required

338

The Candle of the Lord

tangible evidence. "Except I shall see in his hands the print of the nails, and put my finger into the print of the nails, and thrust my hand into his side, I will not believe."

Eight days later the Lord appeared. "Reach hither thy finger, and behold my hands, and reach hither thy hand and thrust it into my side: and be not faithless, but believing." *After* he had seen and felt for himself, Thomas responded, "My Lord and my God."

Then the Lord taught a profound lesson. "Thomas because thou has *seen* me, thou hast believed: blessed are they that have *not seen,* and yet have believed." (John 20:25-29; italics added.)

And so the title "Doubting Thomas," different indeed than the description of Nathanael, whom the Lord described as being "without guile."

With Thomas it was seeing is believing; with Nathanael it was the other way around, believing then seeing "heaven open, and the angels of God ascending and descending upon the Son of man." (John 1:51.)

Now, do not feel hesitant or ashamed if you do not know everything. Nephi said: "I know that he loveth his children; nevertheless, I do not know the meaning of all things." (1 Nephi 11:17.)

There may be more power in your testimony than even you realize. The Lord said to the Nephites:

> Whoso cometh unto me with a broken heart and a contrite spirit, him will I baptize with fire and with the Holy Ghost, even as the Lamanites, because of their faith in me at the time of their conversion, were baptized with fire and with the Holy Ghost, *and they knew it not.* (3 Nephi 9:20; italics added.)

Several years ago I met one of our sons in the mission field in a distant part of the world. He had been there for a year. His first question was this: "Dad, what can I do to grow spiritually? I have tried so hard to grow spiritually, and I just haven't made any progress."

That was his perception: to me it was otherwise. I could hardly believe the maturity, the spiritual growth that he had gained in just one year. He "knew it not," for it had come as growth, not as a startling spiritual experience.

It is not unusual to have a missionary say, "How can I bear testimony until I get one? How can I testify that God lives, that Jesus is the Christ and that the gospel is true? If I do not have such a testimony would that not be dishonest?"

339

That All May Be Edified

Testimony Is Found in Bearing It

Oh, if I could teach you this one principle! A testimony is to be *found* in the *bearing* of it. Somewhere in your quest for spiritual knowledge, there is that "leap of faith," as the philosophers call it. It is the moment when you have gone to the edge of the light and step into the darkness to discover that the way is lighted ahead for just a footstep or two. The spirit of man, as the scripture says, indeed is the candle of the Lord.

It is one thing to receive a witness from what you have read or what another has said; and that is a necessary beginning. It is quite another to have the Spirit confirm to you in your bosom that what *you* have testified is true. Can you not see that it will be supplied as you share it? As you give that which you have, there is a replacement, with increase!

The prophet Ether "did prophesy great and marvelous things unto the people, and they did not believe, because they saw them not. And now, I, Moroni, . . . would show unto the world that faith is things which are hoped for and not seen; wherefore, dispute not because ye see not, for ye receive no witness until after the trial of your faith." (Ether 12:5-6.) To speak out is the test of your faith.

If you will speak with humility and honest intent, the Lord will not leave you. The scriptures promise that. Consider this one:

> Therefore, verily I say unto you, lift up your voices unto this people; speak the thoughts that I *shall* [note that is future tense] put into your hearts, and you shall not be confounded before men;
>
> For it *shall* [again, note the future tense] be given you in the very hour, yea, in the very moment, what ye shall say.
>
> But a commandment I give unto you, that ye shall declare whatsoever thing ye declare in my name, in solemnity of heart, in the spirit of meekness, in all things.
>
> And I give unto you this promise, that inasmuch as ye do this the Holy Ghost shall be shed forth in bearing record unto all things whatsoever ye shall say. (D&C 100:5-8; italics added.)

Testimony Hidden from the Skeptic

The skeptic will say that to bear testimony when you may not know you possess one is to condition yourself—that the response is manufactured. One thing is for sure; the skeptic will never know, for he will not meet the requirement of faith, humility, and obedience to qualify him for the visitation of the Spirit.

340

The Candle of the Lord

Can you not see that that is where testimony is hidden, protected perfectly from the insincere, from the intellectual, from the mere experimenter, the arrogant, the faithless, the proud. It will not come to them.

Bear testimony of the things that you hope are true, as an act of faith. It is something of an experiment akin to the experiment that the prophet Alma proposed to his followers. We begin with faith. Not with a perfect knowledge of things. That sermon in the thirty-second chapter of Alma is one of the greatest messages in holy writ, for it is addressed to the beginner, to the novice, to the humble seeker. And it holds a key to a witness of the truth.

The Spirit and testimony of Christ will come to you for the most part *when,* and remain with you only *if,* you share it.

In that process is the *very essence* of the gospel.

Be Obedient to Promptings

Is not this a perfect demonstration of Christianity? You cannot find it, nor keep it, nor enlarge it unless and until you are willing to share it. It is by giving it away freely that it becomes yours.

Now, once you receive it, be obedient to the promptings you receive.

I learned a sobering lesson as a mission president. I was also a General Authority. I had been prompted several times, for the good of the work, to release one of my counselors. Besides praying about it, I had reasoned that it was the right thing to do. But I did not do it. I feared that it would injure a man who had given long service to the Church.

The Spirit withdrew from me. I could get no promptings on who should be called as a counselor should I release him. It lasted for several weeks. My prayers seemed to be contained within the room where I offered them. I tried a number of alternate ways to arrange the work, but to no avail. Finally I did as I was bidden to do by the Spirit. Immediately the gift returned. Oh, the exquisite sweetness to have that gift again! You know it, for you have it—the gift of the Holy Ghost. And the brother was not injured, indeed he was greatly blessed and immediately thereafter the work prospered.

Be ever on guard lest you be deceived by inspiration from an unworthy source. You can be given false spiritual messages. There are counterfeit spirits just as there are counterfeit angels (see Moroni 7:17). Be careful lest you be deceived, for the devil may come disguised as an angel of light.

The spiritual part of us and the emotional part of us are so closely linked that it is possible to mistake an emotional impulse for something spiritual. We occasionally find people who receive what they assume to be spiritual promptings from God when they are either centered in the emotions or they are from the adversary.

Avoid like the plague those who claim that some great spiritual experience authorizes them to challenge the constituted priesthood authority in the Church.

Do not be unsettled if you cannot explain every insinuation of the apostate or every challenge from the enemies who attack the Lord's Church. And we now face a tidal wave of that. In due time you will be able to confound the wicked and inspire the honest in heart.

As a missionary you will mature, develop a confidence, learn to speak up, to organize, to set goals, you learn about people and places, you learn to learn, and you learn many other things. These are lasting benefits that come as something of a reward for your dedicated service.

The Choicest Pearl

But these things do not compare with the most lasting reward. The choicest pearl, the one of great price, is to learn at an early age how one is guided by the Spirit of the Lord, a supernal gift. Indeed it is a guide and a protection. "The Spirit shall be given unto you by the prayer of faith; and if ye receive not the Spirit ye shall not teach." (D&C 42:14.)

There is great power in this work, great spiritual power. The ordinary member of the Church, like you, having received the gift of the Holy Ghost by confirmation, can do the work of the Lord.

Years ago a friend, who long since is gone, told this experience. He was seventeen-years-old and with his companion stopped at a cottage in the southern states. It was his first day in the mission field and was his first door. A gray-haired woman stood inside the screen and asked what they wanted. His companion nudged him to proceed. Frightened and somewhat tongue-tied he finally blurted out, "As man is God once was, and as God is man may become."

Strangely enough, she was interested and asked where he got that. He answered, "It's in the Bible." She left the door for a moment, returned with her Bible. Commenting that she was a minister of a congregation, she handed it to him and said, "Here, show me."

He took the Bible and nervously thumbed back and forth through it. Finally he handed it back saying, "Here, I can't find it. I'm not even sure that it's in there, and even if it is, I couldn't find it. I'm just a poor farm boy from out in Cache Valley in Utah. I haven't had much training. But I come from a family where we live the gospel of Jesus Christ. And it's done so much for our family that I've accepted a call to come on a mission for two years, at my own expense, to tell people how I feel about it."

After half a century, he could not hold back the tears as he told me how she pushed open the door and said, "Come in, my boy, I'd like to hear what you have to say."

There Is Great Power

There is great power in this work and the ordinary member of the Church, sustained by the Spirit, can do the work of the Lord.

There is so much more to say, but there is no time today to speak of prayer, of fasting, of priesthood and authority, of worthiness, all essential to revelation. When they are understood, it all fits together—perfectly.

Some things one must learn individually, alone, taught by the Spirit.

Nephi interrupted that great sermon on the Holy Ghost and on angels saying, "I...cannot say more, the Spirit stoppeth mine utterance." (2 Nephi 32:7.)

I have done the best I could with the words I have. Perchance the Spirit has opened the veil a little or confirmed to you a sacred principle of revelation, of spiritual communication.

I know by experience too sacred to touch upon in even this setting that God lives, that Jesus is the Christ, the gift of the Holy Ghost that is conferred upon us at confirmation is a supernal gift. The Book of Mormon is true. Jesus is the Christ! This is His Church. There presides over us a prophet of God. The day of miracles has not ceased, neither have angels ceased to appear and minister unto man. The spiritual gifts are with the Church. Choice among them is the gift of the Holy Ghost.

Of this I bear witness, in the name of Jesus Christ, amen.

Words

Over the years I have learned that there are reasons why we cannot read or listen to the words of the servants of the Lord in a passive way and gain the full power from the messages they give us. Whether it is to the written or the spoken word, it requires spiritual effort of the most exacting kind. The poetess, Mabel Jones Gabbott, expresses the idea of effort as it applies to reading the word.

The Words

The words were merely letters,
    spaced and formed
Into such meanings as the author chose.
Until I read them,
    Understood them, warmed
My faith against their truths.
    Then they arose
As luminous beacons for my every day
Waiting to bless, to enlighten,
    to be heard.
Here is wisdom, I thought
    this is the way;
And I recalled,
    "In the beginning was the Word."
(*Ensign,* May 1973, inside front cover.)

The history of the Lord's ancient covenant people chronicles events which are often disappointing and tragic. They were seldom willing to hear and be edified by the words of their prophets. Their problem is clearly stated by Ezekiel:

Come, I pray you, and hear what is the word that cometh forth from the Lord.
    And they come unto thee as the people cometh, and they sit before thee as my people, and they hear thy words.
    And, lo, thou art unto them as a very lovely song of one that hath a pleasant voice, and can play well on an instrument: for they hear thy words, but they do them not. (Ezekiel 33:30-32.)

President Marion G. Romney said, "It has been the rule of my life to find out if I could by listening closely to what they [the leaders] said and by asking the Lord to help me interpret what they had in mind for the Latter-day Saints and then to do it." (*Conference Report,* April 1941, p. 123.)

The building of the kingdom moves ahead. The Lord's servants seek to edify the Saints. There is need for every member of His Church to listen, to be converted, and to assist in the building.

Index

"Weasel words," 259
Weight control, 102
Welfare assistance, 87-89, 91
Wesleyan Society, 168
Whitney, Orson F., on literature, 276
   poems, 282-84
Wickedness, 203, 221, 222
Widows, 77
   "Church", 233
Widowers, 293
Widtsoe, John A., 44
   on teaching, 297
Wilford Ward, Idaho, Teton dam
   disaster, 220
Wilkinson, Ernest L., 47
Willard Peak, 312
Wilson, Woodrow, 259
Witness, 307-8
   of Savior, 311-15
Wives, to encourage husbands, 70-80,
   103, 232-33
   working, 230-32
Women, 103, 104, 230-32, 323-24
Woodruff, Wilford, missionary
   experiences, 23-24
   on priesthood, 30, 174
   on sealing families together, 173-74

present at organization of Genealogical
   Society, 175
remembered by LeGrand Richards, 145
revelation received by, 173-75, 178
Word of Wisdom, 30, 221
   spiritual value, 11, 337
Words, 345
   inadequate to describe the Spirit,
   333-36
Worldliness, of gifted people, 281, 284-85
Worry, 63, 64, 66
Writing, inspiration through, 274
Wrongdoing, not condoned by Church,
   156-57
Wyoming, 29-30

—Y—

Year's supply, 89
Young, Brigham, 147
   on Brigham Young University, 42
Youth, 142
   counsel to, 9-15, 209-12
   freedom of, 254
   steady leaders needed by, 264
Youth leaders, 129